CHOOSING A CAREER IN BUSINESS

by

Stephen A. Stumpf, Ph.D.

WITH

Celeste Kennon Rodgers

Illustrations by Wendy Stone

A FIRESIDE BOOK
Published by Simon & Schuster, Inc.
NEW YORK

Copyright ©1984 by Stephen A. Stumpf
All rights reserved
including the right of reproduction
in whole or in part in any form
Published by Simon & Schuster, Inc.
Simon & Schuster Building
Rockefeller Center
1230 Avenue of the Americas
New York, New York 10020
FIRESIDE and colophon are registered trademarks of Simon & Schuster, Inc.
Designed by Stanley S. Drate/Folio Graphics Co. Inc.
Manufactured in the United States of America
10 9 8 7 6 5 4
Library of Congress Cataloging in Publication Data
Stumpf, Stephen A.
    Choosing a career in business.
    "A Fireside book."
    Bibliography: p.
    Includes index.
    1. Business—Vocational guidance. I. Rodgers,
Celeste Kennon. II. Title.
HF5381.S897   1984   650'.023'73   84-10660
ISBN: 0-671-53063-1

ACKNOWLEDGMENTS

Although we are responsible for the content of this book, we are indebted to many people for their efforts on specific chapters, including Basia Altman, Pamela Brown, Thomas Foerster, William G. Greenbaum, Virginia Lee, Maura C. Lockhart, Heidi L. Osroff, Thomas C. Reynolds, Ellie Schwartz, and Amy Williams. Many colleagues influenced our thinking during the past three years: Special thanks are due to Manuel London, Karen Hartman, and Kathleen Kennedy. We are also thankful to the administration and staff of New York University's College of Business and Public Administration and the Graduate School of Business Administration for their support in this book's preparation, and to many NYU students for their cooperation in the research. The efforts of our editor, Deborah Chiel; the artist, Wendy Stone; and the support staff are greatly appreciated.

Special thanks also go to "Mary Johnson" for sharing her self assessment, and to "Steve Wilson" for sharing his career plans and actions with us.

Choosing a Career in Business is dedicated to those individuals who are trying to selectively manage their way through the maze of career possibilities.

S.A.S.
C.K.R.

New York, N.Y.

CONTENTS

1

Laying the Groundwork for Your Career*

Choosing a career in business that's right for you is a complicated and often difficult activity. We would like to provide you with some guidance to the job search process to improve your ability to manage your career. Your very first task should be self-assessment and the development of realistic career objectives and plans. Once you know what career areas are right for you, you can begin to look into specific positions and uncover the most direct routes to them. In this way, you will be most effective in your *job search process and career.*

How to Manage Your Career

To accomplish the first step in career management—discovering what position is right for you—two things are required. You must have an accurate view of where you are now—specifically, a knowledge of your skills, interests, and preferred lifestyle. Additionally, you must have a personal definition of career success—that is, an understanding of the work roles and activities that help you feel successful and the future positions that will satisfy your career, social, and family needs. Having settled upon a career choice—one for which you are qualified *and* which will satisfy your needs—you need a realistic plan to progress from where you are now to where you want to be, both in the short and long term. If your plans and actions are flexible, and if they enable you to

*This chapter is based on Manuel London and Stephen A. Stumpf, *Managing Careers*. (Reading, Mass.: Addison-Wesley, 1982), pp. 31–51.

capitalize on opportunities and make the best of constraints, they are more likely to result in the career success you desire.

These three elements—self-assessment, establishment of career objectives, and career planning and actions—are the essence of individual career management. Figure 1.1 shows the dynamic interaction between these three elements and illustrates that you cannot establish personally meaningful and feasible career objectives without an accurate self-assessment and review of both the opportunities and difficulties related to your career objectives.

The following case history of Steve Wilson (fictitious name), who is about to graduate with an MBA degree, shows the amount of time, effort, and thoughtfulness an effective self-assessment and career development plan require—as well as the impressive results they can deliver. Later in this chapter, we shall explain how you too can assess your skills and plan your career.

STEVE WILSON'S SELF-ASSESSMENT AND CAREER DEVELOPMENT PLAN

During the past six months I have thought about who I am, what I like and dislike, what makes me happy and unhappy, when I am comfortable or uncomfortable, and what I want to do with my life. I do not believe that I will ever come to firm conclusions on these matters because I am constantly changing. But some things are relatively static, and I do have some definite preferences.

I want to work in a people-oriented environment in which I can assume responsibility and avoid technically oriented procedures. This partially limits my career options, and excludes careers which are numbers-oriented or highly analytical. I am not inclined to pursue a

FIGURE 1.1

The Groundwork for Career Progression

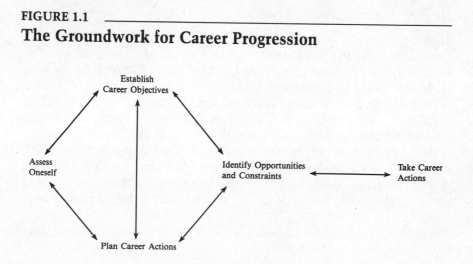

career in accounting, finance, or computer science. Instead I consider line management, consulting, or personnel as viable alternatives.

I have never considered marketing. My educational training in that field is limited. Furthermore, when I think of marketing I picture the highly ambitious manager who is actively monitoring the activities of both colleagues and competitors to make sure that he or she is a step ahead at all times. I envision a successful marketer as having deceived the public, something which is contrary to my values.

I enjoy interacting with people in a helping mode. I am concerned with getting along with others, and am influenced by them in my decision making. Although I realize that my characterization of a marketing professional is a stereotype, I believe that those qualities were instrumental in my disassociation from that area of business.

Line management is a viable career alternative for me, but I am eliminating it from consideration at this time. On the positive side, I evaluate a career in line management as providing the interactive environment I desire. It would give me a chance to assume responsibility as well as the opportunity to motivate others. On the other hand, line management also means maintaining an operation in a line environment. This would require such activities as developing budgets, maintaining equipment, and forecasting future needs. Therefore, while the "people side" of the job is consistent with my self-assessment, the equally important operations side of the job deviates somewhat from my interests.

Business consulting is another option I am currently eliminating. As a business consultant I would be analyzing management and business problems. This would allow me to be actively involved in critical decision making and planning, which is consistent with my enjoyment of responsibility and setting and achieving high work standards. These factors seem to indicate a good individual career fit, but there is more to the consultant's job: A good consultant is a confident decision maker and is able to confront others easily and sell ideas. I am not that self-assured. Although a consultant interacts with people in a helping fashion, much of the work is individual and project-oriented. Interaction with clients is limited during the first few years. Thus, affiliation with other people would play a subordinate role in my job responsibilities in this type of work. Also, extensive travel is typical. While travel is consistent with my preference for an active schedule, it would also create some inner tension, since it would disturb my close ties with family and friends. Another characteristic of the job that is inconsistent with my self-assessment is that a consultant functions in a relatively unstructured environment and usually works on several projects simultaneously. I prefer structured and organized activities.

I have decided to pursue a career in human-resource management.

Specifically, I am looking for a position with a large company, where I will be able to gain experience in each of the functional areas that compose the human-resource department. I would like to be part of an on-the-job training program that will allow me to work on three or four separate assignments in a variety of task areas during my first two years. Initially I hope to gain a generalist background in the areas of labor relations, equal employment opportunity, compensation and benefits, wage and salary administration, training and development, and recruitment and selection. This short-term career objective will provide me with an optimal type of experience, for after this generalist training I will be better equipped to make an educated decision to either remain a generalist (and supervise a personnel department) or specialize in a specific functional area.

Personnel administrators must be able to communicate effectively and work with people at all levels of education and experience. They also must be able to see both the employee's and employer's points of view. In addition, they should be able to work as part of a team. I enjoy affiliation with people and am concerned about getting along with them. Also, a personnel administrator must be a good business person and manager. He or she must have the ability to supervise and accept responsibility. I like responsibility and the chance to assume a leadership role. In addition, my MBA degree has given me a general understanding of business. The informational interview I had with an employment specialist at General Foods indicated that human-resource management positions generally require flexibility and the ability to handle a dynamic, fast-moving, challenging work environment. I enjoy a busy schedule. Although I sometimes resist change, once a change is accepted, I adjust rapidly. This past summer, for example, involved lots of activity and changes. I was usually on the go, interviewing different corporate executives and placement directors."

STEVE WILSON'S CAREER MANAGEMENT

The above excerpt from Steve Wilson's career development plan shows that through self-assessment and analysis of career objectives, Steve has arrived at a reasonable idea of what he is looking for. He also tested some of his assumptions and stereotypes regarding human-resource management by interviewing an employment specialist at General Foods and working as a summer intern in personnel.

Steve put his career plan into motion by tailoring his resume and cover letters to the human-resource management area. Many of his past activities, projects, and work roles were reanalyzed to emphasize accomplishments in human-resource management. His career objective was clearly stated on his resume, and the experience and qualifications he listed highlighted human-resource functions. (Targeting your resume and cover letters is discussed in detail in chapter 14.)

Since relatively few organizations recruit for human-resource management positions at Steve Wilson's graduate school, Steve decided to augment his five on-campus interviews with a letter campaign. Steve mailed out thirty-five letters to Fortune 500 companies headquartered in the New York metropolitan area. His cover letter indicated his career preference for on-the-job experience in a variety of human-resource functions over the first two years.

His thirty-five letters generated ten interview offers. Of these Steve accepted eight. He also went to five interviews set up by the college placement office. From these thirteen first interviews, he received eleven call-back interviews. He accepted six of these, and obtained four competitive job offers from which he selected the one he felt best fit his career plan.

The success of Steve Wilson's job search was partially due to his efforts in self-assessment, establishing career objectives, developing a workable career plan, and taking targeted career actions. He succeeded also because he focused his efforts on those organizations that offered him the career opportunities he wanted. As a result, he did not waste time and energy generating career opportunities that were inappropriate for him.

Performing the self-assessment and developing a career plan do not guarantee your landing the ideal job. Some individuals who form accurate self-assessments do not receive as many or as favorable job offers as Steve did, either because their search is poorly focused, the opportunities in their preferred area are few, or their records and job-related abilities are not favorable. Others lack the necessary job search skills. Nevertheless, career planning gives you a definite headstart. Recruiters report that individuals who have specific career goals receive far more favorable reactions than those who have vague or ambiguous goals. Any successful career management program must begin with self-assessment.

Conducting a Self-Assessment

Self-assessment involves systematically generating data about yourself, and analyzing that data to provide guidance for career and life decisions. Self-assessment typically leads to greater personal awareness and understanding. It can be used to define possible career roles, identify training and development needs, and guide your career progression. An accurate self-assessment can help you decide—

1. which jobs and positions to seek or avoid.
2. what strategy to employ for getting a particular job.
3. which job to select from among alternative job offers.
4. whether to accept assignments, transfers, and location changes.
5. what sequence of job moves will help you attain your preferred position.

Self-assessment can help create a better match between you and a job. Given its benefits, it is not surprising that there are dozens of books that advocate self-assessment as part of career planning. You can conduct your own self-assessment or obtain an accurate and meaningful assessment without doing the entire analysis yourself.

You can consult career and vocational counselors, who provide assessments based on valid, reliable instruments and years of clinical experience. You might also speak with your supervisors and peers, who might have insights about your job-related skills and abilities, or family members, who may help you define your career interests and goals. The most accurate assessment would involve a combination of different sources of information and multiple analyses.

GUIDELINES FOR EFFECTIVE SELF-ASSESSMENT

Developing an accurate self-assessment is difficult because you are so intimately familiar and involved with the data. Your perception of your performance may not agree with how others perceive it. There-fore, certain methods need to be followed in performing a self-assess-ment to increase its accuracy. We offer the following guidelines:

1. *Generate information without evaluating it.* The most common problem individuals have in self-assessment is that in their rush to analyze the data, they fail to gather all available and relevant information. For example, if your self-assessment indicates that you have many personal contacts each day, you may conclude based on this evidence alone that you are highly social. However, you may be overlooking the real meaning behind this behavior: "Many personal contacts" may actually be more supportive of the assessment that you enjoy many activities or have a people-centered leadership style. Very often, unless you gather further data, you may draw inaccurate conclusions. Remember—you should first generate information fully and completely, and only then analyze it for meaning.
2. *Generate useful information from multiple methods and sources.* Don't worry about redundancy here. The more data you have on yourself, the more likely it is that you will have tapped most aspects of your identity. Every method used to collect data and

TABLE 1.1

Self-Assessment Exercises and Instruments

1. Write an autobiographical summary, including a general scenario of your life, the people in your life, your feelings about the future, major changes which have occurred, turning points, and pros and cons of various career-related decisions.
2. Complete the Allport-Vernon-Lindsey (AVL) Study of Values. The values indexed are theoretical, economic, aesthetic, social, political, and religious.
3. Maintain a diary of what you do over one or more 24-hour periods.
4. Complete the Strong-Campbell Interest Inventory.
5. Develop a representation of your lifestyle (i.e., a pictorial, graphic, or written representation of your current lifestyle).
6. Document your feelings immediately after completing other instruments and exercises.
7. Review your college application.
8. Summarize your biographical data.

every source of information has its limitations. By using several, you may partially compensate for the weaknesses of each method.

Table 1.1 lists several useful self-assessment exercises and instruments. Writing an autobiographical sketch (suggested in *Self-Assessment and Career Development,* by Kotter, Faux, and McArthur*) is an excellent place to begin the self-assessment process. Your autobiography should focus on past activities, acquaintances, and work roles. Then, you can augment or support aspects of it using several methods. Completing a values instrument (for example, the Allport-Vernon-Lindsey Study of Values) helps you determine your set of values. An interest inventory (for example, the Strong-Campbell Interest Inventory) provides information regarding your personal interests. (See the bibliography for sources for obtaining these instruments.) Several authors have suggested some additional methods: Keep a diary of the activities you engage in; display graphically your visions of the future; review past goal statements (for example, the essays on your college applications); generate a list of goals; document your major accomplishments and analyze them in terms of skill dimensions; and so forth. Again, in performing a self-assessment you should use as many methods and sources of information as possible.

*Kotter, J., Faux, V., and McArthur, C. *Self-Assessment and Career Development.* (Englewood Cliff, N.J.: Prentice-Hall, 1978.)

3. *Interpret information in the form and context in which it is generated.* While prematurely evaluating your data is the foremost problem in developing an accurate self-assessment, misinterpreting the data is another common problem. Misinterpretation often occurs when the context in which information is generated is ignored. For example, a frequently used self-assessment instrument is the Strong-Campbell Interest Inventory (SCII). This inventory provides an analysis of a person's interests; it provides *no* information on the user's skills, abilities, or values. SCII results only reflect a person's interests and compare them to the interests of people in various occupations. Interpreting SCII results as an indication of which jobs you would do well or which occupations you should pursue would be erroneous.

4. *Organize information into identity statements.* The most difficult and rewarding process in self-assessment is analyzing the data. The analysis starts with specific bits of information and moves to generalizations, which are called identity statements. It is important to stay close to the data, making as few inferences and assumptions as possible, until a tentative identity statement is defined and substantially supported. Table 1.2 provides information supportive of a "need for diversity" identity statement that characterizes Mary Johnson (fictitious name). Mary generated her self-assessment data during her senior year of college by the procedures outlined in Table 1.1. This included writing a twenty-eight-page autobiographical paper, generating a twenty-four-hour diary, completing the SCII, drawing a lifestyle representation, maintaining a record of how she felt when completing other instruments in her self-assessment, and reviewing her college application. In analyzing the information, she uncovered twenty-one identity statements, of which "need for diversity" was one.

The analysis process used by Mary was as follows: First she clustered her data into tentative identity groups; then she labeled each group completely, descriptively, and non-evaluatively with an identity statement. By postponing the labeling process until all the data was reviewed several times, it was easier to avoid premature evaluation of data. Patterns were searched for rather than imposed because of preconceptions. Inferences and assumptions could be checked by reviewing the grouped data to see whether the information converged. Contradictory bits of information could be identified and used to challenge the integrity of an identity statement.

The development of identity statements is a time-consuming, emotionally demanding process that requires substantial analytical skill. Unfortunately, not all people are good at self-analysis; some

TABLE 1.2

Support for Mary Johnson's "Need for Diversity" Identity Statement

Quotes from Her Written Autobiographical Interview:

My career position was too stagnant (after one year).
I wanted to make a move.
Became involved in all activities from softball to Spanish club to drama; was class president.
Lifeguard during summers; would have preferred a variety of experiences.
I was anxious to leave Jonesville.
Always wanted to study abroad.
Denver opened up new opportunities.
I became more inclined to try new things.
My existence revolved around myself, which I found very depressing.
I split with boyfriend, who never liked to do anything different.
Learned how important "mixing" is to me.
Went to Paris and Madrid alone to pursue activities and friends of my own choosing.
Attracted to Denver and college by new and interesting people and experiences.
My second job at NBC represented an exciting world.

Twenty-four-hour Diary:

I didn't finish class assignment—too boring.
Noted over fifteen different activities within twenty-four hours.
Changed activities quickly once closure was obtained.

College Application:

My application listed many diverse activities.

Feelings Record:

Written autobiography: I got bored with writing about myself.
Lifestyle representation: I feel relief at present lifestyle—more time for friends and other activities.

need assistance in the process. Books on self-assessment and career planning can provide exercises to guide your analytical thinking, encourage you to work with others (classmates, work associates, supervisors, friends, family), and identify sources of career counseling.

5. *Assess the accuracy and importance of identity statements.* Once you have generated and organized your self-assessment information into tentative identity groups, you need to review the data within each group and apply descriptive, nonevaluative labels. The labels provide a way of concisely communicating your identity. The accuracy of a label can be estimated by examining the similarities among the data supporting it. If many bits of information from many sources tell a consistent story with few contradictions, then the identity statement is likely to be both accurate and important. In contrast, if there are relatively few bits of information from few sources, and they give a mixed or contradictory message, the identity statement is likely to be less accurate and less important. Reviewing identity statements for accuracy and importance makes it possible to refine your self-assessment.

6. *Cluster identity statements to facilitate drawing implications for career decision making.* Just as several consistent bits of information provide greater support for an identity statement, clusters of identity statements provide greater support for the work role and life implications to be drawn from those statements. Mary Johnson's identity statements are presented in five clusters in Table 1.3. These were developed by her without counseling, as the output of her self-assessment.

Mary developed a set of twenty-one identity statements, grouped into five categories. It should be noted that other self-assessments will identify different identity statements and categories. In reviewing several hundred self-assessments, we have discovered scores of possible themes. Twenty to thirty identity statements usually suffice to characterize each individual.

7. *Draw implications for career decision making.* The self-assessment process will be of little value to you unless you draw reasonable career implications from your identity statements. Identity statements should be used to analyze the feasibility of various career possibilities.

Table 1.4 presents some of Mary Johnson's career implications. Here she has begun to focus her attention on industries that involve creativity, medium-size organizations, and positions with many different activities and interaction with people. She also wants the position to enable her to maintain control over her hours, activities, and affiliations, and thereby balance work and family roles.

TABLE 1.3

Mary Johnson's Twenty-One Identity Statements as Developed and Grouped by Her

Artistic Interests and Inclinations

1. attraction to aesthetically pleasing elements in life
2. desire for attractive surroundings
3. importance of money as a vehicle for obtaining aesthetic satisfaction
4. fascination with and desire for exposure to foreign cultures

Need to Maintain Control over Life's Many Facets

5. balance of work, social life, and family
6. control over time and activity
7. need to be focused to accomplish tasks
8. need for diversity to enrich life's activities [See Table 1.2 for support of this identity statement.]

Strong Internal Pressure to Accomplish Things

9. high need to achieve
10. expected high performance in all tasks
11. priority given to challenging activities
12. taking initiative to get things done
13. need to be recognized for performance
14. attraction to symbols of prestige

Need to Operate from a Secure Position

15. strong affiliation with family as source of support
16. resistance to unfamiliar situations that seem to have high risk
17. avoidance of conflict in favor of compromise

Need for Social Interaction and Influence

18. relationships with colleagues affecting career decisions
19. fulfillment from influencing others through social interaction
20. frequent expression of opinions and feelings to influence others
21. preference for performing alone when attempts to influence are ineffective

TABLE 1.4 _____

Excerpts from Mary Johnson's Career Implications Based on Her Identity Statements

On the basis of my self-assessment, I believe that my career is the logical focus of my life. It has the potential to satisfy my need to accomplish things and my need for security as well as my aesthetic interests, if managed effectively.

I plan to seek a position in a creative industry such as cosmetics or advertising. While the industry should be creative, the *position* needs to be creative only to the extent that I can engage in many different types of activity and interact with different people.

While my career should be demanding in order to fulfill my need to achieve and be recognized, it should not run me. I must be in control and able to establish a balanced life. I would probably not be satisfied with a 9:00-5:00 job, and I must feel free enough to help my spouse in his career, manage our home, and devote attention to our marriage. I would not mind working late, but not for show. Time wasted is time I could spend achieving a balance.

I would probably be more satisfied with a medium-size rather than large institution. I need a place to shine, to seek out challenges and demonstrate my abilities. A medium-size, though still prestigious organization might be more impressesd with my credentials and give me the opportunity to influence others and form relationships.

I have a strong need for "people contact," and, in fact, dynamic interaction with people has often served as a prime source of satisfaction. However, I don't prefer to work on a team. Therefore, I should engage in work which I can accomplish alone, but which requires a large degree of interaction with people.

In order to satisfy my desire to influence people, I should be in a position to provide input to my boss, who presumably would be effective with his or her boss. I must be able to function as an individual and express my opinions so that they will be heard.

I would prefer to have friendly, although not close, relationships with people at work. I fulfill my need for closeness through my family, and am not inclined to devote the time to becoming close to many people outside that sphere. However, I find friendly relationships gratifying, and I prefer to work in a warm atmosphere where conflicts can be easily resolved.

Self-assessment has several benefits:

1. It helps identify your strengths and weaknesses, so that you can establish realistic career objectives.
2. It provides an information base for you to tap when presenting yourself in a resume or at a job interview.
3. It provides a framework for generating questions to be answered in the career exploration process.
4. It suggests which work roles are incompatible with your identity.

How Career Objectives Help You Plan Your Career

As the Cheshire Cat said to Alice, it doesn't matter which way you go if you don't know where you want to end up. But of course we all know where we want to end up—or do we? When asked what their career goals are, most people respond in socially acceptable generalities. Responses we have heard from students and young managers include: "a high-level position in either marketing or finance," "accountant and general partner at a big-eight public accounting firm," "president of my own firm," "a high-level manager in a Fortune 500 company." While these are career objectives, they are generally sought with relatively little knowledge of the work roles and activities associated with these positions.

Few people systematically investigate target jobs and the career paths that will lead to the attainment of these jobs. Establishing career objectives requires more than merely stating a possible target job. It is knowing (1) the target job's work-related activities, (2) its social and political aspects, (3) its demands on your personal time and family, and (4) the series of possible positions that would prepare you to perform effectively in the target job. The process of assessing organizations and positions discussed below provides methods of learning about them that enable you to understand fully these four aspects of a target position.

Evaluating Organizations and Positions

Just as individuals have varied identities, so do organizations and positions. The attributes of an organization are often defined by the organization's work and social climate; by its authority, task, reward, and power structures; and by its policies and decision-making methods. Positions can be characterized by the functions they fulfill, various dimensions of the work, and who reports to whom. Part of managing your career involves investigating these organizational and position-related attributes so that your goals, job assignments, and developmental activities reflect organizational reality. Through investigation you can discover whether particular organizations and positions do or do not fit your goals, skills, or interests.

Essentially, you assess organizations and positions in much the same way as you assess yourself. However, there is one notable addition: You must also analyze the fit between you and the organization or position. (See Table 1.5). Once again, you should collect information from many sources, with little evaluation during the collection phase. Once a substantial amount of information is available, then examine it and compare it with your self-assessment.

TABLE 1.5 _____

Guidelines for Assessing Organizations and Positions

1. Generate information about organizations or positions that may fit your career identity. Do not evaluate the information.
2. Generate information from multiple methods and sources.
3. Interpret information in the form and context in which it is generated.
4. Analyze information; identify organizational or positional attributes.
5. Assess the accuracy and pervasiveness of these attributes relative to your self-assessment.
6. Analyze the fit between your identity and the organization's attributes.

In order to learn about organizations and positions, sift through material available in libraries, annual reports, and so forth, and then focus on specific organizations and positions of interest. One of the more effective methods of investigation is to conduct informational interviews—in the case of organizations, with current employees; in the case of positions, with the incumbent in that particular job or other knowledgeable individuals. Informational interviews differ from job interviews in that you seek information, not a position—yet! When you do not personally know any members of the organization or job incumbents, referrals from someone who knows someone in the particular organization or position generally result in the desired informational interview.

Possible sources of information about organizations and positions are shown in Table 1.6. Written material and information from non-employees can help define the general dimensions of an industry or company. Interviews with potential supervisors and peers, as well as direct observation, provide the richest information on career possibilities and will meaningfully augment other information you obtain on job activities.

Having gathered information from a variety of sources, you must analyze the fit between you and the organization or position. Your self-assessment defines the areas for exploration through your identity statements, which indicate your areas of strength, weakness, and interest. Does the target job utilize your strengths, minimize your weaknesses, and conform to your interests? Information-seeking questions that are tailored to your needs can be asked in interviews with friends, associates, and incumbents in target jobs. By exploring a target job, it is possible to refine your career objectives, evolve a career development plan, and take positive career development action.

TABLE 1.6

Sources of Information and Referrals About Organizations and Positions

Friends and Family

> who work in industry or company of interest
> who know people in industry or company of interest
> who know people with contacts

Written Sources

> career libraries
> placement offices
> Department of Labor's *Occupational Outlook Handbook*
> corporate annual reports
> investment analyst reports
> trade publications and directories
> periodicals running articles about companies (e.g., *Forbes*)
> recruiting brochures
> advertisements
> newspaper articles
> industry or company case studies

People in Industry or Profession

> alumni
> trade associations
> professional societies
> visiting speakers
> chambers of commerce

Social, Religious, and Political Organizations

> Kiwanis, etc.
> Rotary Club
> church groups
> political parties

People with Contacts

> bankers
> doctors, dentists
> lawyers
> accountants
> insurance agents
> investment analysts

2

Commercial Banking*

Commercial banking is the oldest element in today's financial services industry. The word "bank" is evocative of the contemporary industry's origins with the founders of modern-day commerce, the Renaissance Italians. (The root of bank is the Italian *banca* which means bench, the place where early Italian bankers conducted their business.)

The primary function of commercial banking is the transfer of funds from those parts of the economy with cash surplus to those parts with cash needs. Acting as the intermediary between these parties, banks expect to make a profit. The business of commercial banking, however, has become extremely intricate, due to the inherent complexity of collection and disbursement of money, the enormity of today's world economy, and the social, governmental, and legal restrictions imposed on the industry.

In addition to being complex, commercial banking has become an industry of continual change brought about by external and internal pressures. The external pressures are the result of changes in the legal, legislative, and regulatory environments surrounding the financial services industry in general and commercial banking in particular. The entrance of many large, non-bank entities, such as securities investment firms, into what was once regarded as the domain of commercial banking, with such quasi-demand-deposit services as cash management accounts, has put new pressures on banks. However, commercial banks have been constrained in their response to this encroachment by laws that limit their activity. For instance, the Glass-Steagall Act forbids commercial banks from undertaking securities activities, except for the buying or selling of securities on instruction for customer accounts. The

*This chapter is based on a paper written by Basia Altman.

Bank Holding Company Act of 1956, as amended in 1970, also prohibits banks from engaging in activities "not closely related to banking." Commercial banks have responded to these legal restrictions by trying to expand and improve the types of services they may legally provide. Banks are also emphasizing strategic planning, so they will be ready to act offensively in the face of further regulatory changes, rather than having to react defensively.

The commercial banking industry has also been changing rapidly in response to internal financial pressures. Recent periods of high inflation, both domestic and foreign, have made it necessary for banks to consider the increased time value of money. Fast and reliable transfer of funds has become critical. These and other factors have led commercial banking into the high technology areas of communications, computers, and information services.

In light of the increased competition commercial banks face, future emphasis will probably be placed on managerial aggressiveness and innovation. Continued change in the regulatory environment will create new job opportunities, as will the increased utilization of sophisticated new banking technologies. The old view of bankers as staid traditionalists averse to change or innovation is an anachronism in today's banking industry. Therefore, today's banks are seeking people with a wide range of skills.

Commercial Banking Industry Composition

At the end of 1983 there were nearly fifteen thousand commercial banks in the United States. Within this group, there is tremendous variation in size and composition. Approximately 75 percent of them have less than $25 million in deposits; less than 2 percent have deposits of more than $500 million. Banks of the latter size control vast resources of capital, and it is estimated that the top eighty commercial banks hold more than 40 percent of all bank deposits in the United States. The largest commercial bank, for example, had deposits of more than $100 billion in 1983.

Banks not only vary in size; they also differ in structure, using either unit or branch banking. In unit banking, a single office provides all banking services. In branch banking, a lead office controls corporate policy and regulations, while branch offices serve the banking needs of customers on a local basis. Banks involved in retail consumer banking are more likely to engage in branch banking. Branch banking, although limited in some states, has been growing in recent years and will continue to do so as laws and regulations prohibiting interstate banking are eased or repealed.

The activities of most regional banks would be limited by their relatively small size if they had to rely on their own resources alone. Therefore a system of "correspondent banking" has developed. In this system, large banks, called money center banks, offer services to the smaller regional banks in return for the smaller bank leaving funds at the money center bank (called compensatory balances) and various fees. Money center banks also participate in loans arranged by regional banks when the regional bank is too small to carry the entire sum alone. In this way regional and local banks across the nation are connected with large money center banks. Many of the largest commercial banks have correspondent banking relationships with regional banks.

CLASSICAL BANKING ACTIVITIES

Historically, an important source of money for commercial banks to lend has been savings. Though savings continues to be an important source of funds, banks have had to rely more heavily on other sources for money in recent years, such as purchasing money from other corporations and the federal government. Loans are the main money-producing activity of banking and take many forms, including small consumer loans, home mortgages, corporate loans, real estate loans, institutional loans, and government loans.

Most commercial banks divide their activity into retail consumer banking and wholesale banking. This division recognizes the inherent difference in types of loans made: A car loan or home mortgage is treated differently from a multimillion-dollar loan to a large corporation or to a government. Because of the sophistication of the modern financial industry, however, retail consumer banking is involved in much more than savings and small loan administration, and wholesale banking is involved in more than the securing and administration of large loans. A possible organizational chart of a large bank is shown in Figure 2.1.

Retail Consumer Banking

Retail consumer banking concentrates on serving the various banking needs of the individual, family, or small business, providing such services as consumer or small-business loans, home mortgages, savings accounts, demand accounts, credit cards, traveler's checks, and financial management advice. This part of commercial banking is changing rapidly in response to further developments in electronic, automated, and home banking, as well as changes in the regulatory environment surrounding branch and interstate banking.

You will find employment opportunities in retail consumer banking to be diverse. Important positions in branch consumer banking include consumer loan officer, mortgage officer, community small-business loan

FIGURE 2.1

Organization of a Large Commercial Bank

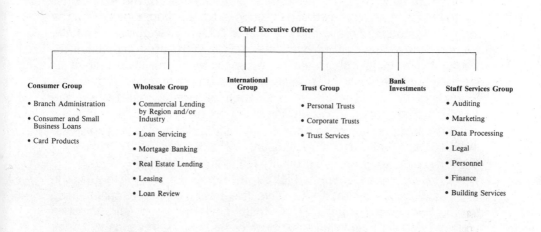

officer, and branch manager. Opportunities in indirect consumer financial services exist in both branch and home offices; many involve working with traveler's checks, bank credit cards, and other fee-based services.

BRANCH CONSUMER BANKING

Consumer loan officer. The consumer loan officer administrates small loans taken out by consumers to pay for a car, home improvements, recreational equipment, and so forth. The work is generally straightforward, since eligibility requirements and interest rates are set by bank corporate policy.

Mortgage officer. This position, like that of the consumer loan officer, is not complicated, and usually involves the administration of mortgage loans for family homes. Eligibility standards and interest rates in this field are also set by central policy.

Community small-business loan officer. In this position, you would be involved in activities similar to those of corporate lending officers in the wholesale banking division, but on a smaller scale. You would deal with community businesses with modest capital needs. For instance, a local firm might need financing to cover the costs of a seasonal inventory, or a farmer might need financing to cover the cost of seed. Typically, community small-business loans require more detailed credit analyses than consumer loans. The loan officer generally works closely with the branch manager in deciding whether or not a loan will be made.

Branch manager. The branch manager is involved in three main areas of activity: branch–home office relations, branch management, and community relations.

A branch bank office is, in essence, a retail outlet of the main bank. As a branch manager, you would report to the home office on the status, position, and profitability of your branch. You would be responsible for seeing that central bank policy is implemented and followed. Within the branch, you would be responsible for management of all systems and personnel. This can involve—among other activities— hiring and firing, supervising installation of new administrative and technical systems, periodically checking to make sure checking and savings accounts adhere to bank policy, and determining work assignments. You would also work closely with loan officers in reviewing business loans to ensure that quality loans are being made.

As branch manager, you would be the representative of the bank in the community, and therefore have the responsibility of maintaining good community relations. You would have to foster and maintain relationships with individuals and businesses, and be responsive to the needs of the community. Participation in community affairs is commonly done to promote the bank's good-neighbor image.

Managers of small branches usually have had three or more years of bank experience. From this position one can advance to management of a larger branch and eventually into the home office as manager of a number of branches or a region.

INDIRECT CONSUMER FINANCIAL SERVICES

Activities in this sector of retail consumer banking focus on financial services ancillary to traditional savings and demand deposits and loans, such as bank credit cards and traveler's checks. Employees working in the bank credit card sector are involved with the credit analysis of customers, marketing card products to potential customers, and working with local merchants in the distribution and proper maintenance of credit systems. Work in traveler's checks can involve the marketing of checks to other banks for in-branch purchase by their customers, as well as marketing traveler's checks directly to your bank's customers.

Wholesale Banking

The wholesale banking division in a commercial bank is responsible for providing financial services to large corporate, institutional, and government clients. In order to fully serve the financial requirements of these clients, the bank offers a variety of services that extend beyond the traditional deposit and loan functions.

A wholesale bank offers services to a variety of organizations, ranging from manufacturing corporations to retail department stores, from pharmaceuticals manufacturers to utility companies, from city to foreign governments. To promote efficiency, the wholesale banking area is often divided according to industry type, industry size, and geographical lines, often with complex interconnecting relationships. A possible banking division structure is shown in Table 2.1.

Services offered by wholesale divisions of commercial banks include loans, depository services, cash management assistance, investment advice, advisory treasury services, and systems analysis, to name a few. Some large banks offer hundreds of fee-based, non-loan services to clients on the principle that in a successful bank-client relationship the client comes to the bank for most if not all of its financial service needs, not just to deposit or withdraw money or request loan funds. Banks try to actively involve themselves in all financial aspects of the client's business, not only fulfilling requests but anticipating them.

Central to the bank-client relationship is the loan officer. The term *loan officer* is somewhat outdated, as today's officer is involved in much

TABLE 2.1

Domestic Wholesale Banking Divisions

Institutional Banking

> Correspondent banks
> Brokerage firms
> Investment banks
> Insurance firms

Geographical

> Southwest
> Pacific Northwest
> Midwest
> Northeast
> South Central
> Southeast

Corporate Banking

> Energy
> Transport
> Utilities
> Special industries
> Real estate
> Middle-market corporations ($5 to $100 million in sales)

more than lending. Other titles used for this position are relationship manager, account officer, and calling officer.

THE LOAN OFFICER

The loan officer is the bank's primary representative to a customer or client. In this position, you would foster, maintain, and if possible extend the bank-client relationship. This involves administering present accounts and loans the client company has with the bank and showing it the need for additional financial services.

To be able to fulfill your responsibilities as a loan officer you must be knowledgeable about the other financial services the bank offers. If you cannot fulfill a client's financial request with the resources at hand, you must be able to direct the request to someone in a different area at the bank who can. Many times loan officers, recognizing areas within a client's financial organization that could be helped by services the bank offers, work with a specialty-area staff to make a selling presentation to the client.

In order to administer a client company's banking business and anticipate further financial needs, you must be informed about its business situation. This involves understanding its balance sheet and income statements as well as being knowledgeable about its business as a whole: what it does, how it does it, problems and opportunities it experiences, and where it is going or trying to go. When clients have ideas about what they want to accomplish but are not sure how to go about it, you should be in a position to provide creative financial solutions to these questions.

The basic responsibilities of loan officers are similar throughout the banking industry. But the tasks they do and the problems and issues they face vary according to the types of client they serve. For instance, in deciding whether or not to extend a loan, if the client is a well-established blue-chip corporation, there are different issues involved from those if it is an entrepreneurial venture. Similarly, the financial services required by a corporation are different from those required by a government. Therefore, loan officers often specialize early in their career in the type of client they serve. The following sections examine the work of loan officers in some typical banking divisions, discussing types of clients they serve and their main activities.

Corporate banking. The corporate-banking sector of a commercial bank is often subdivided into industry categories, and its loan officers will tend to specialize in certain industries. As a loan officer in corporate banking, you would spend much time analyzing companies to decide whether they are acceptable risks. If they are deemed acceptable, you would then prepare and administer the loans. When a large, well-established company is being considered, the job involves less analysis of risk and more salesmanship. For example, if IBM wants to take out a loan, the question is not whether to lend them the money, but rather who *gets to* lend them the money. You must show that your bank can provide the required capital at the best terms with the best service.

However, most firms requesting capital are considerably smaller and of lower standing than IBM. Many banks have lending sectors that specialize in medium-size firms having sales of approximately $5–$100 million. These businesses are often entrepreneurial concerns, possibly in new industries; here, risk analysis is an important part of the lending officer's activity. The lending officer must weigh correctly how much risk the bank is willing to assume against the potential return—not only in terms of the loan being considered, but also the future business that a successful, growing corporation could give the bank over ten or twenty years.

As a lending officer, you would also be a financial consultant to large or small corporations. With large corporations, you would identify the capital needs of a client, and try to sell it additional loans to meet these needs. With medium-size corporations, you would provide help on a variety of financial matters in addition to loans, by tapping the large resources the bank has that the client lacks. You must maintain profitable relationships with clients and help them grow.

Lending officers also try to generate new clients. This involves researching a potential client company by studying financial statements and other material, and trying to establish whether a company needs a loan or other bank service. After financial needs are established, a sales call on the corporation's executives is arranged by the bank. If the call is successful, the lending officer will proceed to service the client's financial needs, on an ongoing basis. Even if the call is unsuccessful, it will have left an impression with the company of assertiveness, initiative, and creative thinking.

Real estate lending. Real estate lending, a specialized area of corporate banking, is complex and generally entails higher risk than other areas of corporate lending. Two main types of real estate loans are land development and construction. Land development loans are considered more desirable because they may result in a long-term relationship with the client, while construction loans tend to be one-time arrangements.

As a lending officer working with real estate business deals, you would have to have specialized skills: knowledge of construction methods and materials, perceptivity about construction and development trends nationwide, familiarity with local zoning and legal issues, and familiarity with real estate appraisal techniques.

Institutional banking. Institutional clients include correspondent commercial banks, insurance companies, savings and loan associations, thrift societies, and other financial service companies. A fundamental difference between a commercial bank's relationship with an institutional client and that with a corporate client is that institutional clients do not need capital to buy goods. They need funds for liquidity or to lend themselves. Therefore, the bank often participates in financial deals with the client rather than simply lending money. For example, when a bank provides money to a security-firm client for the purchase of stocks or bonds, it may receive part of the proceeds from the resale, or securities themselves, as payment.

As a loan officer in this area, you would spend a lot of time marketing non-loan services to institutional clients—for example, trust management services to insurance companies. Many fee-based services are extended to client correspondent banks, such as advisory services on bankroll and credit analysis and employee training programs. These are in addition to the check clearing commonly performed for the client bank in exchange for a compensatory balance held by that bank at the large money center bank.

International banking. Clients handled in the international banking division include foreign corporations, banks and other financial institutions, governments, and subsidiaries of multinational corporations. International banking, like domestic banking, is usually divided along geographical lines and according to type of client (corporate or institutional) and industry. As a loan officer in international banking, your assignment might be in Far Eastern institutional lending, or perhaps Argentinian medium-size corporations. International banking activities are conducted both at commercial banks' corporate headquarters in the United States and in branch or representative offices abroad. Alternatively, an international banking position may be working for a foreign financial institution in the U.S. In this situation you become the "foreigner" within the corporation.

The main differences between banking activity that involves domestic parties only and activity that involves foreign parties are foreign exchange rates and their fluctuation and greater financial risk or uncertainty. An American bank lending money to a foreign corporation must take into consideration not only the risk associated with that corporation but also "country risk" due to potential political problems in the particular country, inflation, and also the risk associated with currency fluctuation. In complicated loans involving several institutions or corporations in several countries, two, three, or even more currencies can be involved, each with a different fluctuation possibility. The loan officer must determine what currency provides the least amount of risk, and in what currency the loan should be made. He or she must also know when to determine when risks associated with the corporation's external environment—such as political instability—outweigh financial gains from the loan.

In international banking, your knowledge of the foreign culture and market are as important as your financial analysis skills. You must actively promote fee-based services to institutional and corporate clients, such as international money transferring, international check clearing, and letters of credit. In addition, you must be knowledgeable about a broad scope of international business issues and trends in import-export industries. This knowledge is essential for extending further services to existing clients and for developing new clients.

You must have good language skills; knowledge of at least one foreign language is generally a prerequisite. A loan officer interested in international banking must also feel comfortable in, and be adaptable to, foreign cultures. Foreign relocation may be part of an assignment.

Other Banking Areas

You will find opportunities in many other areas within commercial banking. Banks, like other corporations, need people to work in human-resource management, marketing, and other nonfinancial areas. These areas are discussed at length in their respective chapters which follow. We limit discussion here to areas in commercial banks where financial skills are used.

CREDIT MANAGEMENT

Personnel in credit management analyze the credit risk of potential loan clients, working in support of and in conjunction with the loan officers. In some banks, this department is also responsible for reviewing the bank's entire loan portfolio to assess quality and inherent risk. Many bank trainees start in this department, where they get experience in fundamental financial analysis as well as exposure to many other facets of the bank's business.

TREASURY

This department is involved in many activities commonly associated with corporate finance, including managing the bank's own asset portfolio, which is comprised of the major assets of outstanding loans, security investments, reserve position, and related money market assets. Traders, often placed in the treasury department, are responsible for managing the bank's liquidity needs. As commercial banks rely less on deposited savings for liquidity, traders must buy liquidity in various money markets, including the Federal Reserve.

PORTFOLIO AND TRUST

The portfolio and trust department manages asset portfolios for such clients as corporate employee-benefits funds, pension plans, profit-sharing plans, foundations, charitable organizations, endowments, and very wealthy individuals. The job of the portfolio and trust area is to recommend, select, and manage the assets (such as stocks, bonds, etc.) so that they will continue to produce expected returns. Since the portfolio may be protecting, for instance, the retirement fund of thousands of people, the portfolio manager usually chooses safe rather than high-risk–high-return investments.

As a manager in the trust department, you would need marketing ability as well as financial analysis ability. Portfolio management is a highly competitive field—banks face competition not only from other banks but from investment counselors in other financial-service sectors. You would make frequent sales calls to potential clients not only to stress the security and maximum returns which the bank provides, but also to present other services which the bank offers, such as cash management assistance and detailed tax and financial management reporting.

INVESTMENT BANKING

As an extension of the bank's role as financial consultant, the investment banking segment of a commercial bank provides assistance with private securities placements for its clients, as well as advice on mergers and acquisitions. It is also involved in the underwriting of municipal securities, a process similar to investment banking activities described in chapter 4.

OPERATIONS

Bank operations is the area which involves the actual delivery and accounting procedures necessary to provide the services offered by the bank. It has been rapidly expanding in recent years, and will continue to do so, due partly to the commercial bank's need to compete with other financial services by expanding its own service offerings, and partly in response to technological developments. Operations employees can work in support of the bank itself and on a consulting basis to large corporate or institutional clients. The operating services a bank is able to provide often keep clients loyal or help attract new ones. Cash management, a substantial area of operations, is one important service banks offer to their clients. People who work in operations must work closely with those in systems analysis (see chapter 12), and often need to combine their financial skills with other areas of expertise, such as accounting and computer systems analysis.

Required Skills and Educational Background

We have already touched on some of the specific skills and abilities necessary to succeed in various areas of commercial banking. Here we mention some general abilities, and expand on the specific background and skill requirements of loan officers.

An MBA can help you enter a professional banking career. Large banks do hire people with bachelor's degrees (who often have quantitative or finance backgrounds or receive such backgrounds in training programs offered by the banks), but generally not at the same level as MBAs (who may have undergraduate backgrounds in almost any area).

A loan officer must have a general background in finance, including accounting, principles of economics, corporate finance, and credit analysis. These quantitative abilities must be combined with many other qualities, especially marketing ability, good written and oral communication skills, and analytical ability. Analytical ability is perhaps the most important, for no successful decision can be reached if numerical analysis is not combined with good judgment.

Loan officers must be able to work effectively with others. Banking is a team effort, and those who cannot interact effectively cannot be effective bankers. In addition, officers must work well within the highly structured world that banking is.

A conservativeness that shows caution and seriousness but not an aversion to change is an important attribute for a loan officer. This quality must be combined with an entrepreneurial spirit. Many profitable relationships for a bank appear unprofitable at first—loan officers must be willing to take intelligent chances. Conservativeness, common sense, and good judgment must be combined with creativity and confidence.

Ambition is also a virtue in loan officers. As banking has become more competitive, many of the so-called gentlemanly qualities of banking have given way to assertiveness and competitiveness. As a result, loan officers anticipate the financial requirements of their clients, rather than wait for opportunities to present themselves. Personal advancement only comes to those who can consistently produce for the bank.

3

Securities Analysis*

Securities brokerage firms occupy an important position in the financial services industry at the center of capital market activity, linking deficit units of the economy—corporations and governments—with surplus units—corporate, institutional, and individual investors. Brokerage firms are also active in the secondary capital market—the trading of securities after first issuance.

Securities are traded in both the organized and over-the-counter markets. Organized markets consist of stock exchanges, each with a specific location for trading, a formal administrative structure, prescribed rules of procedure, a defined membership body, and facilities for providing various related services, such as stock quotations, to members. The United States has fourteen exchanges registered with the Securities and Exchange Commission (SEC), the chief regulatory body of U.S. financial markets. The two dominant exchanges are national—the New York Stock Exchange (NYSE) and American Stock Exchange (ASE). The remainder are regional, the largest being the Midwest and Pacific Coast exchanges.

All purchases and sales outside the stock exchanges take place in the over-the-counter (OTC) market, which is not defined by any geographical barriers or central marketplace. The OTC market is a telecommunications network which links a large number of brokers and dealers, who may or may not be members of an exchange. Since these securities transactions occur in many different places and are not reported to one central agency, it is difficult to determine the exact size of this market. However, in dollar volume substantially more securities are traded over the counter than on all national exchanges combined. Tens of thousands of corporations have issued publicly held securities; all these securities, except for approximately six thousand issues listed on the exchanges, are traded over the counter.

*This chapter is based on a paper written by Virginia Lee.

Regulation of Capital Markets

The Securities and Exchange Commission (SEC) was created by an act of Congress entitled the Securities Exchange Act of 1934. The SEC is an independent, bipartisan, quasi-judicial, federal agency which administers the financial markets through statutes designed to protect the interests of investors and the public. Its enactment followed the stock market crash of 1929 and sought to remedy many abuses that had led to the event. Most of these abuses emanated either from inadequate disclosure of information necessary for appraisal of the investment worthiness of a stock, or excessive manipulation of stock prices through interference in the supply-and-demand balance of a security. The laws administered by the commission, along with controls to minimize the creation of artificial forces of supply and demand, contribute to orderly financial markets.

RECENT CHANGES IN STRUCTURE OF SECURITIES MARKETS

The last two decades have witnessed more fundamental changes in the organization of the securities market for corporate equities than any comparable period since the 1930s. Some of the most significant developments have been:

1. In February 1971, the National Association of Securities Dealers (NASD) made an automated system available to brokers and dealers. This fundamentally altered the structure of the over-the-counter market by accelerating the disclosure of price information through high-speed telecommunications and electronic data-processing systems.
2. In the early 1970s, responding to widespread concern over the progressive fragmentation of the equities markets (i.e., stock markets) during the 1960s and early 1970s, Congress and the SEC initiated a period of rule-making and legislative activity that culminated in 1975 in the abolition of fixed minimum commission rates (May 1, 1975) and the enactment of the Securities Act Amendments of 1975, which mandated development of a National Market System (NMS).
3. The SEC departed from its historical position of favoring competing but separate marketplaces by advocating development of a Central Market System (CMS) to (a) centralize all buying and selling interests in order to maximize the opportunity for them to meet without recourse to a dealer, and (b) maximize market-making capacity in order to provide the greatest possible liquidity for large transactions.

All these changes—the automation of the OTC market, advent of negotiated commission rates, and proposed development of a National Market System—coupled with economic conditions of the early 1980s—high and volatile interest rates, rising inflation, depressed automotive and housing industries, erratic economic activity, and increased volume in the stock market—have had a profound effect on financial institutions and the markets they serve.

Negotiated commission rates mean reduced commissions for financial service institutions; rising trading volume and the resulting need for fast execution necessitate economies of scale; and heightened volatility demands larger financial cushions as risk insurance. Securities firms have had to become larger to meet these demands and survive. This has led to an acceleration of the interbrokerage mergers that began in the early 1970s, and has resulted in fewer, larger securities firms.

In the past few years, a number of financial hybrids have been created by mergers of different types of financial and non-financial service firms (e.g., Sears Roebuck with Dean Witter Reynolds; American Express with Shearson Loeb Rhoades; Prudential Insurance with Bache Halsey Stuart; Phibro with Salomon Brothers). The result has been the growth of complex organizations that offer several new financial services and instruments. Such changes are creating more employment opportunities in the financial services industry, and in securities brokerage firms in particular. What follows is an overview of career possibilities available to you—and the skills they require.

Brokerage Firm Activities

The amount and types of services performed vary by firm. Some limit their activities to securities brokerage, the basic service of buying and selling stocks or bonds for customers. Others, called full-service brokerage firms, offer clients a myriad of financial services, including brokerage, trading, investment banking, financial research analysis, real estate management, and specialized investment planning.

The types of client served vary both by firm and within individual firms. The largest group served, by number of clients, is made up of individual investors. Firms develop what is referred to as a retail-trade business to handle these individual accounts. Another group of customers is institutional clients. Typical institutional clients are insurance companies, pension plan funds, corporations, and common trust funds. These clients are usually handled by large, full-service brokerage firms, as only they can provide the sophisticated, comprehensive services demanded. A third group of clients handled by full-service firms is composed of other firms in the financial service industry. For instance, brokerage firms often trade securities for commercial banks. They may

FIGURE 3.1

The Full-Service Brokerage Firm Departments and Interrelationships

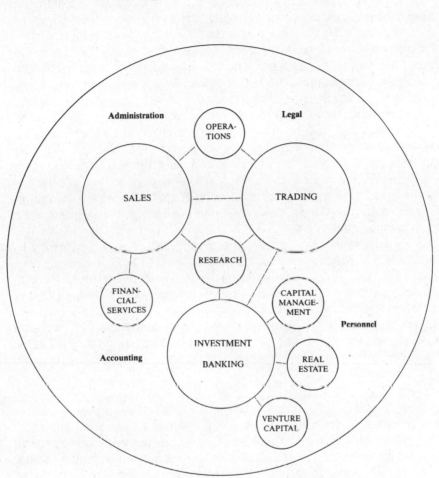

also have other brokerage firms as clients—perhaps trading or purchasing securities the client firm controls—or as participants in large financial transactions.

Security brokerage firms earn money in a variety of ways. One source of income is the commission charged on securities bought or sold on a client's behalf; this fee is determined by the monetary value of the transaction. Fees from corporate clients for investment banking services constitute another source of revenue. Here, too, the fee varies according to the size of the transaction or deal. Firms also generate revenue when their traders buy securities at one price and sell them at a higher price, the firm keeping the difference (called the spread) as profit.

In full-service security brokerage firms, specialized departments often handle the various activities and services offered. Structure varies by firm, but typically there are the following departments: sales, trading, investment banking, services, and research. There are elements of both independence and interdependence in departmental relations. For example, both the sales department and investment banking department turn to the research department for information, but interaction between the first two is restricted by law, to avoid possible conflicts of interest. The relative roles and interrelations of departments are shown in Figure 3.1. The size of each circle in Figure 3.1 reflects the typical emphasis placed on a department. The lines suggest primary work relationships across departments. The largest circle, encompassing all departments and containing the words *administration, accounting, legal,* and *personnel,* implies that those areas affect all department activities.

What follows is a description of the general activities performed by the main departments of a full-service brokerage firm, beginning with sales. We have saved discussion of the research department for last, because its role in the securities industry requires knowledge of other parts of the business, and because people with advanced business degrees, such as an MBA, often work in this department. The security analyst position is discussed at length in that section, as it is the most common position in most research departments.

SALES

In many firms the sales force represents the largest group of professionals. Salespeople work under various titles, such as stockbroker, broker, or account executive. Brokers, as we shall call them, are the firm's primary representatives to existing and potential clients. They serve as disseminators of information on the financial services the company offers, services that encompass security transactions, portfolio management, and specialized services. Brokers are crucial to a firm's profitability, as the bulk of its revenue is linked to the brokers' ability to arrange and execute trades of securities.

The broker's job is predominately a sales position, and the ability to sell is important to anyone in this position. (The broker's role as a salesperson is discussed in chapter 10.) In order to sell effectively as a broker you would have to coordinate clients' needs with the personnel in your firm able to fulfill them. You would do this by first talking with clients and determining their objectives and then working with appropriate people within the firm to devise strategies to meet these objectives.

You would then arrange the transaction, be it buying or selling. Because interaction between brokers and personnel in other departments is so important, you must be well informed about each department in the firm. You must also develop and maintain good working relationships with specialists, especially in the research department, to facilitate good business relationships with clients.

TRADING

People who work in the trading department execute the transactions arranged by brokers: They buy and sell securities. Only a small percentage of all the securities bought and sold are listed on the large stock exchanges (New York, American, Chicago, etc.). Others, traded over-the-counter, include traditional corporate stocks, banker's acceptances, certificates of deposit, convertible bonds, corporate bonds, Eurobonds, municipal bonds and notes, municipal-bond tax swaps, U.S. Treasury and agency securities, Yankee and Canadian bonds, commodity futures, and options. In other words, many securities transactions are not listed or published on a formal exchange; it is up to the traders to know what trading is taking place, when, between whom, and at what price. To be effective, traders generally specialize in particular products and markets, thus becoming familiar with large buyers and sellers, market behavior, and standard and aberrant pricing.

Traders working for a brokerage firm are in constant touch with the specialty markets in order to execute trades at the best price. Large firms also retain traders on the floors of the large exchanges to trade large blocks of stock on their behalf. The objective of these traders is to buy blocks of stock either at the price specified by the firm (for the firm's clients), or at a low price for resale to another trader at a higher price, making a profit for the firm and him- or herself. Obviously, the second objective is not always met.

Traders also assist in "private placement" of securities—when a corporation wants to issue a block of stock and not have it published on any exchange board or OTC list. This is done by corporations, generally with the advice of their investment bankers, either at the brokerage firm, at a commercial bank, or at another investment banking firm. In such a transaction, the trader is responsible for locating suitable trading partners and assisting the buyer and seller in negotiating the terms of the sale.

INVESTMENT BANKING

Most large securities brokerage firms supplement traditional brokerage operations with investment banking activities for emerging and established companies, municipalities, and foreign governments. The investment banking department helps clients determine whether they need long-term capital for investment, expansion, or other purposes, and, if so, what is the best means of obtaining it. The investment banker may decide that capital should be obtained by the issuance of stocks or bonds, or perhaps that expansion should be achieved through merger with or acquisition of another company. (A more detailed discussion of these activities is found in chapter 4.)

A firm's investment banking department is kept separate from its brokerage sales area to avoid conflicts of interest within the firm and between clients. The reason for separate and confidential operation by the investment banking department is that if brokers know that a merger between two companies is being considered, they are tempted to inform their clients, hoping to make commissions on the flurry of trading that ensues. The resulting rise in stock prices could adversely affect the proposed merger. Use of such "insider information" is illegal, punishable by imprisonment and fines. This is an ethical problem for securities firms as well; the leakage of indirect information regarding mergers and acquisitions is hard to eliminate, because both the sales and investment banking departments use services provided by the research department. Information can inadvertently slip out.

SUPPORT SERVICES

The service department encompasses all support systems of brokerage firms, such as operations and data processing, human-resource management, accounting, marketing and advertising, and systems analysis. Opportunities in each of these areas are extensive in large firms.

One area which deserves discussion here is operations and data processing. Timely and efficient flow of information is especially crucial in this fast-paced industry where "time is money." The back office of brokerage firms—where records of customer accounts are maintained and the securities certificates representing transactions are physically transferred—is important to the firm's profitability. The failure of back-office operations and data processing to keep up with the hectic pace of the "go-go" years of the late sixties highlighted the importance of this previously neglected area, and identified the need for more extensive managerial skills and sophisticated equipment. Automation has replaced much of the clerical labor that traditionally staffed the back office, although even today operations may still falter during periods of extremely high volume on the exchange. Operations and data processing experts—equipped with computer, work-flow management, and data processing skills—are in high demand to ensure efficiency and efficacy in this vulnerable area.

RESEARCH

The research department is the informational core of a securities brokerage firm and, as information is so crucial to the investment community, an important center of activity. The organization of departments varies by firm. Table 3.1 shows some of the possible positions in a large research department. A typical hierarchical structure is shown in Figure 3.2.

Director of research. The director of research manages and administers the department and represents it to the rest of the firm. It is a powerful position within the corporate structure; the director may sit on the company's investment policy or steering committee to help develop and implement coordinated policy to guide the activities of research, sales, trading, capital management, and investment banking.

As manager of the research department, the director develops and oversees investment policy and research effort. As administrator he or she hires, fires, and grants salary increases or promotions. In large research departments there may be a support staff, including an office manager and assistant director, to help run administrative details, leaving the director free to manage research activities.

FIGURE 3.2

A Typical Research Department of a Full-Service Brokerage Firm

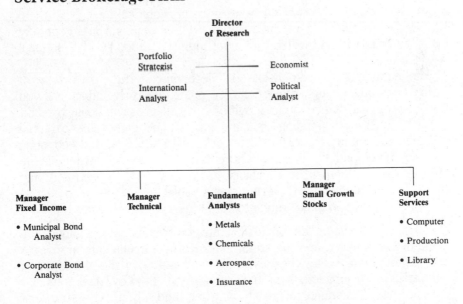

TABLE 3.1

Roster of a Research Department

Director of research
Economist
Portfolio strategist
Manager, fixed income research
Manager, technical research
Manager, small growth stocks
Political analyst
International analyst
Fundamental securities analysts:
   aerospace, chemicals, consumer durables, metals, etc.
Technical analysts
Fixed income analysts
Support services:
   Computer
   Production
   Library

Economist. The economist occupies a key position in the research department and in the firm as a whole. Generally, economists hold advanced degrees (either M.A. or Ph.D.) and have been involved in academic research, thus bringing a rigorous analytical background and knowledge of the field to the position. Their opinions are generally taken as prescriptions within the firm, and sometimes receive national media attention.

The economist is responsible for determining the firm's view of future economic events; projections are made quarterly and annually on key dimensions of economic activity, such as gross national product (GNP), consumer spending, housing starts, and disposable personal income. Frequently the economist works with sophisticated economic models developed by independent economic research firms having state-of-the-art computer capability. The research department and other firm personnel use the economist's projections to develop investment strategies and make estimates of industry and company activity.

Portfolio strategist. The portfolio strategist translates ideas about the economy as a whole and the stock market in particular into an overall investment plan, using the advice of analysts who monitor specific industries and subsectors of the economy. The key questions addressed are how much to invest, in what, and when. The strategist imagines a cash sum of money which a hypothetical investor with certain financial requirements can allocate among financial instruments. He or she then determines what portions of that sum the investor should leave as cash, invest in equity and fixed income securities, and put in other types of investments. Furthermore, the strategist determines which industries are most attractive for investment, and may even identify a subset of firms within an industry for further consideration.

International and political analysts. The international analyst addresses the effect international economic activity has on the firm's and its clients' investments. The political analyst focuses on the current political climate and its possible effect on economic activity. These two positions augment the advisory functions of the director of research, economist, and portfolio strategist.

THE SECURITIES ANALYST

Securities analysts make up the bulk of a research department's professional staff, conducting most of the actual research. As this position is a key position in brokerage firms, and is a common professional starting point in the industry, we shall look at the activities and responsibilities of securities analysts in some depth, followed by an analysis of the skills required for the position.

Securities analysts usually are assigned to cover one industry, such as chemicals, consumer durables, foods, insurance, transportation, telecommunications, or banking, to name a few. Their primary function is to monitor companies in that industry in order to discover companies that are attractive investment opportunities. Specialization allows analysts to become expert in a particular industry and alert to movement and possible investment opportunities.

Uncovering new investment opportunities is an analyst's most challenging and rewarding activity. It centers on the identification of a corporate stock's "real worth." As an analyst, your aim would be to discover stocks with a current market price below this real-worth figure. These stocks represent buying opportunities. In determining a stock's real worth you would apply investigative, analytical, and intuitive skills. This activity also comprises your three primary functions as researcher, writer, and marketer.

Researcher. Analysts new to an industry must collect and read all the secondary material they can find on the industry—its products, services, and markets in order to obtain an overview. This includes books, trade publications, newspaper and magazine articles, and reference services such as *Standard and Poor's Outlook*. Analysts may also contact trade associations and attend their conferences to keep abreast of industry developments.

The next step is to make a roster of publicly traded companies in the industry. This list is then edited considerably, as you tailor it to the investment needs of your firm's clients. For instance, if the firm's client orientation is primarily institutional, the companies you consider must have adequate market capitalization (number of shares outstanding) and daily trading volume in order to qualify as a possible investment opportunity. Other criteria may also be considered; it all depends upon your firm's investment policy.

Once a "short list" has been developed, you would gather and review publicly available information on the companies. This includes annual reports, financial documents such as 10K's and 10Q's, proxy statements, prospectuses, and secondary material. In reading through the material some firms' achievements may catch your eye: a good product mix, savvy acquisition, or efficient distribution mechanism. Sometimes analysts do "computer screen analysis" along key operating and stock performance dimensions—such as growth of earnings per share, operating margins, price to earnings ratio, or book value to market value ratio—to pick out promising companies.

If you decide that a company deserves further consideration, you may arrange a visit to speak with its personnel in order to assess their operation first-hand and evolve an understanding of its corporate or business strategy. In preparation for the visit, you would study the company thoroughly. This might include reading the past ten years of annual reports for key events (acquisitions, divestments, management changes, geographical expansion), performing a computerized time-series financial statement analysis, and assessing absolute and relative stock price performance. You would then prepare a comprehensive list of questions to ask the company's controller, financial relations representative, or president.

Your direct assessment of management and company operations may or may not confirm your initial impression of the company. If the visit is disappointing, information gathered thus far may be shelved for possible use in the future, and your present inquiry stopped. On the other hand, if the visit confirms your hopes, you would probably recommend the stock for purchase if it is currently undervalued.

Writer. In recommending purchase of a stock, writing skills become important to the analyst. Recommendations for purchase include a summary of the financial data analyzed, in which the accompanying prose is as important as, if not more important than, the figures themselves. The rationale for purchasing a stock must be clearly and persuasively stated. These reports normally contain extensive investment arguments.

Typically, as an analyst's company coverage grows, he or she spends more time on "maintenance research" and less time making new discoveries. Maintenance research often requires prodigious output of written materials; this is expected by both the firm and client. These reports cover company quarterly results, investment implications of key developments, stock price performance and trading behavior, and general industry conditions. An annual publication list of the work done by a typical security analyst might include the studies and reports listed in Table 3.2.

The importance of timeliness with these reports varies. Quick reaction to quarterly company results and major special events, such as a merger or acquisition, is essential. Other reports, such as special ones issued on an "as desired" basis, may have more flexible publication schedules. However, analysts generally work according to stock market time, which is fast paced.

Marketer. Brokerage firms receive revenues when they trade securities: The more they trade, the more fees they collect. Therefore,

TABLE 3.2
Publication List of Typical Securities Analyst

A. **Industry Studies**

Quarterly review of industry trends: normally statistical with abbreviated commentary. The analyst may review the industry in a single product or product line or a series of related products.

Quarterly review of stock price performance: absolute and relative stock price performance of key sectors of the industry and individual stocks—dividend, yield, price-earnings ratio

Special reports: issued on an "as desired" basis. Examples are in-depth product report, special consumer survey, legislative activity with investment implications

B. **Company Reports** (average coverage of approximately fifteen companies)

initial basic report introducing new investment idea; quarterly reports on an individual company's operating results; special events, such as an acquisition, new president, change in strategy, etc.

C. **Miscellaneous**

dividend notices, earnings estimates prior to company quarterly announcements, calendar of company appearances before professional associations

NOTE: Each analyst would write all of these reports in the course of a year.

analysts must conduct research that is likely to result in the trading of securities. The increased competition among brokerage firms in the past decade has resulted in analysts having to spend more time marketing their "products" to both brokers and institutional clients. The sales department is primarily responsible for selling the firms' services to clients, and analysts must sell their services to the brokers.

Although some securities trades are client initiated, many occur because brokers or analysts alert their clients to trading opportunities. Keeping clients aware of these opportunities can expand the firm's business by encouraging them to buy or sell. Therefore, it behooves the analyst to keep the research product before brokers and clients as much as possible. For small accounts he or she may retain a client on a mailing list and respond to calls. With large clients, however, successful analysts are usually more visible. They may support trading activity by contacting clients regularly to keep them up to date. With corporate or institutional clients, analysts often cultivate a close working relationship with their counterpart analyst in the client's finance department (the "buy-side" analyst).

Most firms keep records of analysts' written and oral communication with clients: to whom they speak, for how long, and about what. Firms may subject analysts to call quotas, circulate monthly summaries of "client contacts," and report page counts by analysts in order to stimulate competition and productivity.

Both intrafirm and interfirm competition exists, which underscores the importance of marketing to the analyst's job. Greenwich Research Associates of Connecticut furnishes a comparative rating of rival brokerage firms' research products, based on buy-side analysts' rating of sell-side analysts' work. *Institutional Investor* sponsors an annual contest that assembles an "All-American Research Team" of "number one" analysts, with second-place, third-place, and runner-up teams. These contests are taken very seriously.

Your success as an analyst will be measured to a great extent by your marketing ability. You will succeed if your firm's clients find your research useful in making investment decisions, and execute transactions based on your recommendations through the firm's sales force. Generally, your compensation will reflect your degree of success with clients. Therefore, you must couple thorough, well-written research with aggressive, persuasive marketing.

Required Skills and Educational Background

In many ways, being a securities analyst requires that you act as a corporate entrepreneur and empire builder: You must always look for expansion and growth. Although it varies by position and firm, many analysts enjoy a great deal of license in determining their own style of work and how best to cover their assigned industry. Approaches vary, but the research and writing are characteristically solitary pursuits involving little interaction with other analysts and firm personnel. Generally analysts are not team players.

Many of the skills and abilities you need to succeed as a securities analyst already have been covered, but the following list outlines the most important:

facility with numbers
analytical orientation: an inclination to figure out how and
    why things work
thoroughness
organizational ability
good memory
ability to communicate effectively, both orally and in writing
powers of persuasion
diligence and tenacity

Many different types of people succeed as securities analysts, but it is possible to isolate some personal characteristics common to successful ones: a strong ego and sense of self, individualism, the ability to exude confidence, and being outgoing and competitive.

The educational background of securities analysts varies, but it is commonly a prerequisite to have a degree in business, usually an MBA. Those hired without MBAs are encouraged to pursue one on a part-time basis. Some analysts have had prior business experience in the financial service industry, perhaps including time as a buy-side analyst. Some have moved from a background in statistical research, either at the same firm or another research group, to their present securities analysis position. Still others have had work experience in an industry which they subsequently cover as an analyst. While working as analysts, some continue studies in the field by participating in programs conducted by the Institute of Chartered Financial Analysts. These programs prepare applicants for three rigorous examinations, which upon completion entitle them to carry the assignation Certified Financial Analyst.

4

Investment Banking*

Many corporations within our economy encounter attractive business opportunities which they would like to pursue. An electronics firm may wish to build a new factory to produce a recently invented product. A chemical company may want to expand its plant to meet increased demand. Investments of this nature require significant amounts of money, often greatly exceeding the funds the company has on hand. Therefore, in order to expand, the company must seek a source of funds outside the corporation.

A common source of money for corporations is the commercial bank loans. Commercial banks, however, prefer to lend for short periods of time, usually a few years. When a large investment, such as construction of a factory, is anticipated, a bank loan is generally not appropriate. The factory usually will not generate enough profit during the first few years of operation to repay a loan for the total construction cost. Therefore, a long-term method of financing is needed, and for this the corporation will often turn to an investment bank.

An investment bank is a financial intermediary; it functions as a liaison between those with excess funds to invest and those wishing to use the funds. The role of an investment banker is that of advisor to the corporation wishing to raise money. To perform this service, the investment banker analyzes the client's financial situation, recommends the preferred method of raising the required funds, and implements the agreed-upon course of action.

*This chapter is based on a paper written by Thomas Foerster.

Industry Structure

Many companies that engage in investment banking are partnerships or internally held corporations. Under this form of organization, senior members of the firm are part owners of the company and therefore entitled to a share of its profits. Other investment banks are wholly owned subsidiaries of larger corporations. In these organizations, employees do not necessarily hold an ownership interest in the company.

In addition to traditional investment banks, some of the larger commercial banks and full-service brokerage houses offer investment banking services. They provide the same basic services available at the major investment banks, with the exception that commercial banks cannot perform the function of underwriting most securities.

Organizational Structure

Most investment banks consist of two main departments: corporate finance and public finance. Although the structure of companies may vary, a typical departmental breakdown is shown in Table 4.1. This division into two departments is based upon the types of securities issued: The corporate finance department handles taxable bonds and stocks, while the public finance department handles tax-exempt bonds.

In many firms, the corporate finance department is divided into industry and specialty groups, shown in Table 4.1. The personnel in industry groups are financial generalists responsible for servicing a particular industry sector. For example, the energy group is responsible for business relating to the oil, gas, and coal industries. They are generalists in that they are familiar with all of the various financing techniques appropriate for their clients.

TABLE 4.1

Departmental Structure

Corporate Finance Department	Public Finance Department
Industry Groups:	Industry Groups:
Energy group	Transportation group
Communications group	Health care and housing group
Financial service group	Public power group
Specialty Groups:	Utility group
Private placement group	
Mergers and acquisitions group	

The specialty groups are responsible for specific types of financial arrangement regardless of industry served. The personnel in these groups are specialists in a particular area, such as mergers and acquisitions, and work with personnel in the industry groups when their special skills are required.

The public finance department typically consists of industry groups, such as the public power group which handles the accounts of electric companies. The personnel in these groups are generalists dealing with a variety of financing techniques.

In order to carry out their tasks effectively, investment bankers must maintain a thorough familiarity with the investment needs of those with funds to invest as well as of those who require funds. These suppliers of funds include insurance companies, pension funds, investment companies, corporations, and individuals. Accordingly, investment bankers must look at securities issuances from the perspective of both buyer and seller and be able to structure marketable deals for their clients (sellers).

Although position titles in investment banking vary, the hierarchy of a typical firm may be represented as follows:

managing director
vice president
assistant vice president
associate

The managing directors are responsible for administration of the departments and groups within the organization and maintain contact with the firm's largest clients. The vice presidents and assistant vice presidents are responsible for carrying out the investment banking activities of a particular industry or specialty group. In this capacity, they assume total responsibility for providing the required services for a particular client's account or individual deal.

Most investment banks do not have formal training programs. Instead, training of entry-level associates is accomplished on the job. A new associate joining the corporate or public finance department becomes a member of an associate pool. This pool of personnel is assigned to one particular industry or specialty group, but individuals will work with a variety of groups in the department.

When a client requires financial assistance, the managing director or the vice president responsible for the deal assembles a team consisting of one or more associates and senior personnel. For example, a team may comprise a managing director, vice president, and two associates. Within certain limits, the associates are given a significant amount of flexibility and autonomy in structuring their work load. For example, an associate who prefers working on mergers and acquisitions generally will be permitted to concentrate more heavily in that area if the workload demands it and he or she has proved effective in this area. However, the client's needs always come first, and the basis for the associate pool is to permit training as generalists. In most firms the associate is expected to complete assignments in all areas of the department in order to develop a broad background and a thorough understanding of the various services the department provides. (For similar training and organizational structures see the section in chapter 6 on accounting and chapter 13 on business consulting).

The associate pool is an unstructured environment wherein you, as an associate, would not have one particular boss. Instead, you would work with various superiors on a variety of deals, often discussing your work with a vice president or assistant vice president before becoming involved in a deal. After joining a team, you would be committed to meeting any deadlines required to provide effective service to the client, regardless of additional responsibilities from your participation in other deals. You therefore must be capable of managing your time and work load. A typical work load can involve an average 60–70 hours per week, and include weekend work.

Performance evaluations are conducted with input from the various senior members of the firm with whom the associate has worked. An associate who is promoted to assistant vice president joins a particular industry or specialty group within the department. Which group the new assistant vice president joins depends upon the company's staffing requirements and the individual's preferences and capabilities.

The rate at which an associate progresses through the company depends upon his or her contribution, but a typical career path can be considered to be three or four years as an associate and five years as assistant vice president. The amount of time it takes to move from vice president to managing director is highly variable. Compensation in investment banks is usually salary plus bonus, the latter determined by the employee's accomplishments as well as the firm's overall profitability.

Investment Banking Services

Most investment banks offer a wide range of financial services to meet the needs of clients; the most important are discussed below.

UNDERWRITING

As mentioned previously, a corporation's issuance of equity and debt securities (stocks and bonds, respectively) provides it with a means of raising large amounts of capital. Investment banks perform the role of "underwriter" in this process by purchasing the securities (stocks or bonds) from the client and then reselling them to institutions (i.e., insurance companies, pension funds) and individual investors. The investment banking firm realizes a profit by reselling the securities at a higher price than paid for them.

Private placements provide clients with a means of raising funds by entering into a private securities transaction with an institution such as an insurance company or pension fund without having the transaction published by a major stock exchange. These transactions are usually in the form of a long-term debt agreement committing the client to repay funds to the institution at a negotiated interest rate.

MERGERS AND ACQUISITIONS

Mergers and acquisitions provide clients with a means of expanding their company through the purchase of another firm. Conversely, this service also provides clients with a means of resisting the unwanted sale of their company to another firm. The process of arranging a merger or acquisition is often a lengthy one handled primarily by senior management. The associates' role here is generally one of financial analysis—similar to that of the securities analyst described in chapter 3.

PROJECT FINANCE

Project finance provides clients with a method of raising funds by issuing bonds for a specific venture or project. The revenues realized from the project will be used to retire (buy back) the bonds. For example, an electric utility company may use project finance to secure funds for construction of a hydroelectric plant. The revenue realized from the sale of electricity generated by this plant would be used to repay the funds. Again, as with the two following services, the associate's role is likely to be that of a financial analyst focusing on a particular firm and project.

FINANCIAL ADVISORY SERVICES

Financial advisory services provided by investment banks offer clients recommendations for planning the financial structure of their organizations. Areas of investigation may include long-term financial planning, stock re-purchase decisions, dividend policy, and working capital management.

LEASE FINANCING

Lease financing provides clients with a means of acquiring equipment or facilities without purchasing them outright. Investment bankers analyze individual situations for their clients to determine whether leasing or buying assets will prove the most profitable, taking into consideration the client's present financing and tax factors and current opportunities. Exchange of investment tax credits between corporations through a leasing agreement may be involved.

The Investment Banker

Three primary functions constitute the role of an investment banker: developing new business, structuring transactions, and making client presentations. A new associate usually spends the first year of employment structuring transactions, which is the basis of on-the-job training. These tasks utilize the analytical abilities developed in business school and provide experience in processing a variety of deals. The experience gained in this way forms the foundation for expanding the associate's role to include developing new business and making presentations to clients. The latter tasks involve client interaction, which eventually will account for over 50 percent of an investment banker's job.

DEVELOPING NEW BUSINESS

Traditionally, large corporations have maintained a close, ongoing relationship with a particular investment bank. In recent years, this type of exclusive client relationship has been threatened by increased competition from other investment banks. This situation has greatly affected the role of the investment banker: When dealing with established clients, sitting by the phone waiting for the client to call for assistance is likely to lead to a loss of business. Instead, bankers now must aggressively maintain ongoing familiarity with a client's financial situation, and have a thorough understanding of new and innovative means of financing, which now are being developed with ever-increasing frequency. The most effective means of maintaining understanding of a client's needs is routine interaction, which is a main function of a managing director and vice president.

Proper execution of this aspect of an investment banker's job will, at best, maintain existing clientele. However, few companies are content with a no-growth policy. Therefore an essential aspect of your job as an investment banker would be establishing new business. Potential clients must be actively approached in your effort to sell the investment bank's services. Usually a managing director or vice president will contact the treasurer or controller of the potential client corporation and arrange a meeting. During this meeting, your team would discuss your firm's capabilities and expertise, and may also explore the financial situation of the prospective client. Sales calls of this nature often require a lot of travel by the investment banker.

As an associate, you would assist the senior member of your firm in preparing for these sales presentations by analyzing the prospective client company. During this analysis, you might use your firm's library to locate information, such as annual reports and 10K's, in order to determine the potential client's historical financial performance, current financial position, and general business description.

Eventually you will be expected to develop effective sales capabilities. Salesmanship is essential in all aspects of investment banking, from establishing client relationships to completing a deal. When a managing director or vice president feels you have developed sufficient capability to be an asset in a sales presentation, you will be asked to accompany him or her. This arrangement will augment your analytical experience with exposure to effective sales techniques.

STRUCTURING TRANSACTIONS AND CLIENT PRESENTATIONS

The structure of a transaction and the subsequent client presentation depend upon what services the investment bank is supplying. The main services—underwriting, private placement, and mergers and acquisitions—each involves different structures and presentations, as shown below.

Underwriting. As mentioned previously, the underwriting process involves the purchase of a corporation's stocks or bonds by one or more investment banking units at a given price, and the subsequent resale of these securities to the public at a higher price. For example, several investment banks and investment banking units within brokerage firms may purchase an issue of five hundred thousand shares of stock from a company for $97 a share, for a total of $48.5 million. Then the investment banks collectively resell this stock to the public for $98 a share, or $49 million, realizing a profit of $500,000. Table 4.2 outlines the major aspects of the underwriting process.

As an associate, your role in this process would vary depending upon your experience and capabilities. It generally will include company analysis and preparation of written documents. Under the direction of the managing director or vice president who is heading the team, you would compile and analyze relevant information regarding the company, industry, and proposed security to be issued. This information is analyzed to determine the financial strength of the company, including such factors as the debt-to-equity ratio, interest and dividend coverage, and earnings growth and stability. This analysis is often performed with a handheld calculator, though personal computers are now commonly used.

You will also have to develop a clear understanding of the general business of the client company. Such factors as products produced, inventory, raw materials, competition, quality of management, corpo-

TABLE 4.2

Underwriting Process

1. investigation and analysis of a corporate client, its industry, and the type of security appropriate for financing
2. preparation and filing of the registration statement and prospectus with the Securities and Exchange Commission
3. formation of underwriting group
4. meeting with the underwriters and officials of the client corporation, their respective counsel, and other experts—engineers, accountants, etc.—to discuss the registration statement and prospectus
5. qualifying, or "blue skying," the issue under the securities law as to the various states in which it will be offered
6. underwriting or signing agreements setting forth terms of financing
7. marketing or distributing the securities through a public offering

rate and business-level strategies, and use of the proceeds from the proposed financing must be assessed. In addition, similar information regarding the client's industry as a whole must be assembled.

You would compile this information from a number of sources, including material found in your firm's library, and from securities analysts who follow the industry and company in question. Finally, you might discuss these issues with personnel of the client's company, either over the phone or by traveling to the client's headquarters. The personnel approached would include the treasurer and relevant production managers, accountants, engineers, and lawyers.

You would then communicate the information obtained from this investigation and analysis to the managing director and vice president, along with recommendations on the structure of the financing (stocks or bonds). These recommendations are the result of your analysis, knowledge of financial markets, and conversations with traders and salespeople within the firm. (In some firms, associates now use computer programs to help determine the optimum structure of financing.) The managing director or vice president responsible for the deal then makes the final decision regarding the structure to be recommended to the client.

The managing director or vice president then travels to the client's headquarters to give a presentation based on your analysis. The investment banker is essentially an advisor to the client, and this presentation details the recommended course of action and the rationale for this recommendation. If you have developed sufficient experience in underwriting and have secured the confidence of your superiors, you may be asked to assist in the client presentation. This requires good interpersonal ability, effective communication skills, and a strong personal presence.

After the client approves the investment banker's recommendation, you prepare a registration statement and prospectus to be filed with the Securities and Exchange Commission (SEC). The registration statement formalizes the client company's intention to issue securities; the prospectus is a document which will ultimately be distributed to interested investors during the sale of the issue. These documents include descriptions of the company and the issue offered for sale, as well as the names of company officers, major stockholders, underwriters, and lawyers. Under federal law, all persons involved in the preparation of these documents are liable for damages—such as losses to investors resulting from material misrepresentations of fact in these documents. For this reason, as well as for the sake of the reputation of the firms involved, associates must be exceedingly thorough in their tasks. Mistakes are not tolerated; documents are systematically checked by other associates and superiors before becoming publicly available.

Because input is required from your superiors, other associates, security analysts, traders, and salespeople within the firm, as well as client personnel and outside lawyers, you must schedule your time carefully. Conversations with these people usually take place in the 9:00-5:00 period; therefore the research, number analysis, and writing of the registration statement and prospectus usually take place after 5:00 P.M. Associates often work from ten to fourteen hours a day, including some weekends, to meet the deadlines of underwriting.

While you, as an associate, are compiling information and preparing documents, the senior member of the team begins to form an underwriting group or syndicate. This stage of the underwriting process involves contacting other investment banks and asking them to participate in the deal. There are a number of reasons why investment bankers find it desirable to form underwriting groups. Often a client is issuing equity securities with a face value exceeding the amount of funds the investment bank has available. In this event other investment banks may be willing to join the deal and supply needed additional funds. More important, however, formation of an underwriting group reduces the risk the investment bank faces, the major risk being the inability to sell the securities at a profit after purchasing them from the client. Diversification of ownership reduces this risk, while introduction of additional investment banks to the deal expands the sales force which will offer the securities to the investment community. Therefore, while competition for new business does exist in the industry, a close cooperative relationship is also maintained among investment banks. The associate's role in the formation of the syndicate varies, depending on experience, from distribution of information to participating firms to active involvement in developing potential participants.

In similar fashion, a selling group at an investment bank may also be assembled to sell the securities to the public. Unlike the underwriting group, however, the selling group does not have capital at stake. Instead, they receive a predetermined commission for securities sold.

Prior to the sale of the securities, a "due diligence" meeting is held among the underwriters, client officers, and lawyers, to confirm that the underwriters are exercising proper diligence in offering the securities for sale to the public. The selling price of the issue is then determined by the investment bank's lead manager, a decision which requires experience and expertise. Based on this price, members of the underwriting group decide on their actual degree of participation. Shortly thereafter, public sale begins. Generally, the associate aids the sales force by supplying information about the client company.

Private placement. As explained previously, this is the sale of securities by a corporation directly to a small group of sophisticated investors with the investment bank acting as liaison. Most companies utilizing private placement are smaller than those active in the public market. If, for example, a corporation wants to raise $10 million, interest among the public may be limited, because the small size of the issue will not create an active secondary trading market. As a result of these limited future trading possibilities, the corporation may have to pay a higher yield than its credit rating warrants in order to stimulate sufficient market interest.

The existence of the private placement market offers the corporation a lower-cost alternative source of funds. The main purchasers of private placements, life insurance companies, have large amounts of funds to invest each year. In addition, they have fairly predictable cash flow and are willing to purchase a security with a thin secondary market if they can receive a higher yield.

The investment banker's role in a private placement is that of advisor to the issuing corporation. Unlike underwriting, the investment banker does not assume ownership of the security, and therefore does not bear the market risk. The fee for this advisory service is negotiated, and is generally a function of the size and complexity of the issue and the credit rating of the client company.

Table 4.3 presents the steps in the private placement process.

As an associate, you begin work on a private placement when your investment bank is hired by a corporation. You then begin to compile and analyze information on the company. This is similar to the analysis stage of underwriting. However, because the firms utilizing the private placement market are generally smaller and less known than firms in the public market, less written material may be available and securities

TABLE 4.3

Private Placement Process

1. investigation and analysis of the client corporation and its industry
2. structuring financing and preparing offering memorandum
3. presentation of recommendations to client
4. developing marketing plan
5. contacting potential investors
6. documentation and transfer of funds

---

analysts may be unfamiliar with the company. As a result, more information may have to be obtained from the client's personnel. As in underwriting, analysis in private placement is a time-consuming task requiring long hours.

The information obtained from this analysis is utilized to determine the structure of the financing and to develop an offering memorandum. The offering memorandum is a comprehensive document which provides a picture of the client company's past, present, and anticipated future performance. This document is the heart of the sales presentation when potential investors are approached; it should present the client's company as favorably as possible. As with underwriting's SEC registration statement and prospectus, full disclosure is essential in an offering memorandum. Similar civil liabilities apply for material misrepresentation or lack of due diligence. In addition, investment bankers maintain continuing relationships with portfolio managers of major insurance companies, since they may be involved in future private placements. Therefore, accuracy and thoroughness are essential in an offering memorandum.

The final portion of the package to be offered to potential investors is the structure of the financing. Unlike offerings in the public market, in private placements, a small group of professional investors are approached. As a result of this one-to-one contact, complex financial structures can be developed and explained to them. Using your analysis of the client company's future cash flow, you as an associate would determine a means of financing tailored to the client's needs. (Associates in some firms use computers to assist them in developing these structures, which are typically long-term debt.) Many private placement structures also include "equity kickers," which allow the investor to share in a portion of the company's future profits. A private placement structure also includes covenants, usually restrictions on the future financial activity of the company.

The offering memorandum, including recommended financing structure, is then presented to the client by the managing director or vice president. You may also assist in this presentation if you possess sufficient experience and capability.

If the client approves the investment banker's recommendations, a marketing plan is then developed. Usually only a few potential investors will be contacted, and proper selection is necessary to optimize the chances of successful placement. You as associate would review in-house research data on possible investors and likely discuss the situation with industry analysts, salespeople, and traders. The goal of this investigation is to determine which investors would be most interested in the client and its industry. You must determine just how many companies to contact.

Under the guidance of the senior member of the team, the list of selected investors to be contacted is determined and presented to the client for approval. Once approved, the deal progresses quickly. The associate usually writes a brief memo describing the deal, which is used for telephone contact with potential investors. During telephone conversations you would disclose the client's name and industry, briefly discuss the nature of their business and explain the rate and structure of the proposed financing. If the institution is interested in the deal, the offering memorandum is delivered—usually in a matter of hours. Once these initial contacts are made, time is of the essence, because any significant change in the market will affect the financing rate. Generally, the institution will respond to the deal within one day, with all questions being answered by the vice president or you. The timely nature of this situation reinforces the need for accuracy and thoroughness in the offering memorandum; ideally you have answered most of the investor's questions in this document.

If the institutions' response is favorable, they will discuss with the investment banker the amount of participation in which they are interested. Since more than one investor is usually contacted, participation is on a first-come, first-served basis. Again, due to possible market movement, a favorable response is only valid for a few days. Unlike a public offering, a private placement has a structure open to negotiation, during which phase the investment banker continues in the role of advisor to the client.

The managing director or vice president usually conducts any negotiations with the client at the investment bank's offices. When the negotiations are complete, the investment bankers and the investors will often visit the client's facilities. Once an agreement has been reached, the investors draft a commitment letter stating their agreement to lend. Then the documentation phase occurs; legal documents are prepared and signed. This is followed by the transfer of funds.

Mergers and acquisitions (M&A). Generally, an investment bank's involvement in M&A activities does not involve raising funds for a corporation. Instead, this aspect of investment banking deals with corporations wishing to expand by merging with or purchasing another company. Due to the variety and custom nature of investment banking activities in this area, it is difficult to describe a representative scenario like those presented above for underwriting and private placement.

As an associate, your main function in many M&A activities would be to locate a suitable candidate for merger or acquisition by the client company. Considering the thousands of active companies in the economy, this task can be extensive and time-consuming. You would be seeking a "good fit" between buyer and seller, and your task would be to develop an understanding of the client company's business and financial situation by analyzing it.

You might begin the search for a possible acquisition candidate by confining your efforts to a particular industry of interest to the client. Review of the client's requirements and financial situation may further narrow the list. This process of elimination is continued based upon the constraints imposed by the client.

The remaining companies are analyzed to determine if acquisition is appropriate. Information on these companies—such as annual reports, 10K's, and analysts' reports—might be available in the investment bank's library. Each company is then reviewed to determine if a favorable integration of business activities with the client company is possible. Consolidated financial reports are prepared and analyzed to determine the strength of the company if such a merger or acquisition were to occur. Additional factors such as possible antitrust violation and major holders of the target company's stock are also investigated. A report on possible acquisition candidates would then be prepared by you and reviewed with the managing director or vice president responsible for the deal.

The managing director or vice president then presents the firm's recommendations to the client. If the client wishes to pursue the matter, the senior members of the team develop a plan for approaching the target company. This plan is implemented by the managing director and vice president after approval by the client. Due to the unpredictable nature of M&A attempts, you as an associate are rarely involved in client interaction or company negotiations.

Required Skills and Educational Background

Having an MBA is almost always a prerequisite for employment as an investment banker. Major investment banks usually hire MBA graduates only from prestigious business schools. Those in the industry who do not have an MBA usually have significant and applicable work experience or a law degree.

To be an investment banker you must have strong quantitative and financial skills, as do most people in the financial service industry. You must also have mature, developed analytical skills and the ability to think creatively. Unlike someone, such as a loan officer, who works in a specialized segment of the financial service industry, an investment banker must synthesize all aspects of the industry, which requires imaginative, innovative thinking. He or she needs good oral and written communication skills, for even the best ideas must be well communicated in order to be sold.

Investment banking work is typically very demanding, and you must be willing and able to spend long hours in the office and traveling. You must be able to work well under pressure—from bosses, clients, and the clock. In addition, it is important to remember that investment banking is a highly competitive field, and the most successful investment bankers are those who combine superior intelligence and skills with strong, powerful internal motivation and desire for achievement. In summary, most successful investment bankers exhibit the following personal characteristics:

very strong interpersonal skills
superior analytical skills
oral and written communication skills
willingness to travel and work long hours
strong desire for success and achievement
internal motivation
high intelligence

5

Corporate Finance*

Corporate finance is broadly defined as the financial matters concerning a corporation. The finance department of a corporation is not directly involved in the production of the firm's product, but rather in the managing of capital associated with that product. This activity ranges from securing loans to cash management to reinvesting profits.

The corporate finance function varies depending on the industry and organization size. Since a position in a smaller firm usually combines the functions of several positions held by separate individuals in larger firms, an analysis of the various positions at larger corporations will provide the background for understanding the responsibilities that exist in corporations of any size.

Organizational Structure

A typical corporate finance department structure is shown in Figure 5.1. The vice president of finance is the chief financial officer; this is often one of the most powerful positions in a corporation. His or her responsibilities are centered on managing and coordinating the activities of the two main groups in the finance department: the treasury and controller groups. Financial policy making and corporate financial planning may be directly controlled by the vice president or delegated to either the treasurer or controller.

The treasurer is directly responsible for obtaining financing, managing the firm's cash account, and maintaining relationships with banks and other financial institutions. In small firms the treasurer may be the only financial executive. Generally, larger corporations have a controller whose functions are to see that money is used efficiently and to manage budgeting, accounting, auditing, and tax activities. Entry-level positions exist in both the treasury and controller areas of corporate finance. There is movement both within and between the two groups, so it is

*This chapter is based on a paper written by Thomas C. Reynolds.

FIGURE 5.1
Typical Financial Structure

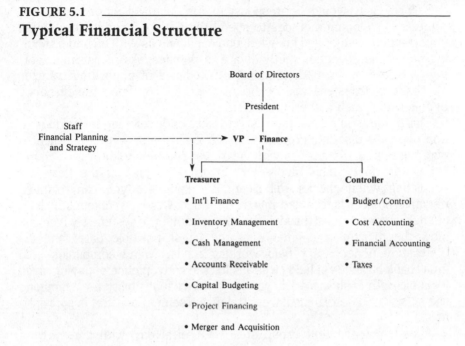

worthwhile to consider them both. Discussed below are the main functions performed within each group and the types of activity common to most positions in corporate finance.

Treasury Functions

WORKING-CAPITAL MANAGEMENT

Working-capital management includes management of the firm's cash, accounts receivable, and inventory assets, each of which is described below in some detail.

Cash management. This function is also known as collections and disbursements. Given current high interest rates, many companies have been motivated to reduce cash balances and examine the amount of time required to collect receivables (i.e., money owed them by others). Successful cash management personnel usually work closely with the company's banks, and daily interaction takes three forms. First, as a cash management officer, you would be responsible for producing funds on short notice at or close to the prime rate offered by commercial banks. Your performance evaluation will partially depend on your ability to obtain funds quickly.

Second, you would be responsible for cash collection from customers. Developing methods to speed the flow of incoming cash is an important challenge, and knowledgeable individuals with an understanding of various collection methods are in demand. As a cash manager, you should have an understanding of the uses of depositing transfer checks, wire transfers, and lockboxes in order to optimize the efficiency of an existing cash gathering system.

Third, you would have the responsibility of developing techniques to improve cash disbursing procedures. A typical function is to synchronize the timing of transfers with clearings, commonly known as "monitoring the float." This involves estimating the size of the float and predicting when checks will clear. By doing so, you can maintain negative book balances and invest the float. Other techniques include (1) delaying payments through the use of computer systems, which can slow the mailing of payments to the latest possible date, and (2) eliminating unnecessary field working funds. Many companies hold small bank balances in field locations for the convenience of paying small local bills. As cash manager, you have the responsibility for examining the situation to determine if a central disbursement account is appropriate.

A cash management group starts a typical day with a review of outstanding loans, receivables, and payables maturing that day. Based on the previous day's operation, the office forecasts total gatherings and disbursements. Once all transaction forecasts are reviewed, an estimate is made of the cash needed during the day.

At this point, you as cash manager would have to make a decision. If the availability of funds is more than ample for the day's needs, you must decide how to invest the extra funds. Depending on the size of the corporation, you might solicit outside help from a securities analyst or investment banker. If, on the other hand, money is in short supply, funds must be obtained. Now decisions must be made relating to sources and their terms for obtaining funds. If by noon the money has not been raised, you might elect to withdraw some of the firm's compensating balances at its bank, or to rely on the commercial paper market, if it provides a less expensive source of funds.

Most of the cash management department's functions are carried out in the morning. Occasionally, there will be an afternoon crisis of unexpected uninvested cash surplus or shortage. However, most cash managers will find the day fairly structured, making for a secure environment with normal working hours ranging from forty to fifty per week.

While cash management sounds routine, it usually takes about two years before a newly hired employee is given responsibility for handling interactions that commit large cash sums. Training usually involves on-the-job coaching and frequent assignment rotations.

Accounts receivable management. An area related to cash management is accounts receivable management. In small corporations the two functions may be combined. Large corporations separate them, with accounts receivable concentrating on credit policy (which involves determining the optimal credit period), collection policy, discount policy, and credit standards for customers.

As an accounts receivable manager, you will need to be comfortable with computer systems, as daily computer use is the norm. You would use computers to determine the optimal credit period, based on the premise that lengthening the credit period will stimulate sales to customers while shortening it will most likely depress sales. Increased sales volume from the extension of the credit period results in an increase of working capital to fund the increase in receivables. Although credit period determination is not a weekly activity, the question is readdressed whenever there is a substantial fluctuation in interest rates, major change in variable costs, or a decrease or increase in sales resulting in a serious problem of over- or underproduction.

A second function you would perform as accounts receivable manager is determination of collection policy, which refers to the procedures the firm uses to collect past-due accounts. The collection policy may be either to turn over past-due accounts to an outside collection agency for a fee, or to have staff make collections. The latter typically consists of making phone calls, sending warning notices, or involving legal counsel.

You will also be responsible for determining cash discounts for early payments. The trade-offs among the level of discount taken, how discount affects customers, and reduction of average collection period are critical in determining the optimal level of discount. Once again, computer programs are often used to determine the optimal discount.

Lastly, you would be responsible for determining credit standards for customers. The credit screening process is often carried out by means of a statistical technique called discriminant analysis, through which various characteristics of a customer are analyzed to determine credit worthiness. If the applicant falls above a cutoff value, credit will be granted. A value below the cutoff will be deemed a bad risk, and no credit will be issued.

To set up a credit scoring and screening system as described above, you need to be familiar with statistical analysis and computer applications. If you cannot write the programs yourself, a programmer would be assigned to the project. Whether you are the architect or not, developing a credit evaluation system can be very rewarding.

Much of an accounts receivable manager's activities involve keeping systems up to date and monitoring the customer-information data base. After one or two years as an accounts receivable manager, you will probably move to other areas of working-capital management. An assignment in accounts receivable is generally a starting point for a career in corporate finance; it is seldom considered permanent.

Inventory and operations management. The task of inventory management is to assess the costs and benefits of holding different amounts of inventory for each product. In manufacturing companies a production or operations manager may be responsible for this decision. However, in some manufacturing companies and most financial institutions with sizable consumer businesses (e.g., consumer banks and brokerage firms), financial managers are involved with operations and inventory control.

Inventories, which may be classified as raw materials, work-in-process, and finished goods, are essential to business operations. While accounts receivable accumulate after sales, inventories are established before sales and are dependent on production-run efficiencies. It would be one of your functions as an inventory manager to forecast sales and coordinate with production and operations managers so that target inventory levels can be determined. If these forecasts are made by the marketing department, you would need to work closely with both marketing and production personnel. If, however, the inventory manager makes the forecasts—which is typical of small corporations—an understanding of forecasting techniques is necessary. Some corporations use a commercially available automated system which requires few redesign efforts. However, forecasts from such systems still need to be incorporated into the inventory management system.

To this end, corporations use various techniques, from educated "guesstimation" to such operations management concepts as economic order quantity (EOQ). If a system is not already designed and in operation, the inventory manager may spend several days per month (how many depends upon the number of products) calculating optimum order quantities and timing. Consideration must be given to the amount of investment capital tied up in inventory and to the needs of the production department for raw materials.

An inventory manager is often labeled operations manager. Operations personnel are primarily a support function for the financial staff. In addition to the inventory control function, operations is concerned with evaluation of management controls, which may involve assessing the efficiency and effectiveness of operations and operating procedures and recommending a course of action when necessary. It is the operation person's responsibility to determine the reliability of the financial and management information provided to senior management for their use in decision making.

Finally, as operations manager you would be responsible for product distribution, which may be a separate job function depending on the size and nature of the business. Responsibilities in distribution involve determination of the most effective and efficient means of product distribution. Frequent interaction with both the marketing and production control departments is essential during this determination process. Organizations that hire financial managers for inventory or operations management generally require that he or she also have knowledge of production systems.

CAPITAL BUDGETING AND INVESTMENT ANALYSIS

Another important function in the treasury department is capital budgeting and investment analysis. The activities of a financial analyst working in this area can be divided into project evaluation and project financing.

Project evaluation. In large corporations senior management often receives requests from operating units or divisions for investment often called venture capital. Financial analysts in the capital budgeting and investment analysis area must analyze these proposals, determine their value, and provide recommendations to senior management about them. The proposals vary in format, but usually contain the information necessary for a complete financial analysis. Sometimes a completed financial analysis is included, and only an evaluation is needed.

A financial analysis usually involves the following: project classification, estimation of cash flow and sensitivity analysis, project evaluation and ranking, and post-completion audit. Project classification facilitates management's review. A project classified as an expansion usually involves more detailed analysis than one classified as a replacement project, and a high-cost project usually requires a detailed analysis regardless of category. Possible classifications are shown in Table 5.1.

Once you have classified a project, various paths may be taken to complete the analysis, depending on the project's category. Usually, for simple replacement or cost reduction projects, a cost/benefit analysis will suffice. Larger investments or expansion projects require a detailed cash-flow analysis that goes beyond most cost/benefit analyses. You may have to travel to operating units or installations to obtain the necessary information.

The most important and most difficult step in analyzing a project is calculating cash flow. Numerous factors are involved in forecasting project cash flow and many hours are spent developing spread sheets such as the one shown in Table 5.2. (A personal computer or calculator

TABLE 5.1
Project Classifications

1. *Replacement: maintenance of business.* Expenditures necessary to replace worn-out or damaged equipment are in this group.
2. *Replacement: cost reduction.* Expenditures to replace serviceable but obsolete equipment fall into this category. The purpose of these expenditures is to lower the cost of labor, materials, or other items such as energy input.
3. *Expansion of existing products or markets.* Expenditures to increase production of existing products or expand outlets and distribution facilities in markets now being served.
4. *Expansion into new products or markets.* Expenditures necessary to produce a new product or expand into a new geographic area or customer group.
5. *Safety and environmental projects.* Expenditures necessary to comply with government orders, labor agreements, or insurance policy terms. These expenditures are often called mandatory investments, or non-revenue-producing projects.
6. *Other.* Expenditures on office buildings, parking lots, and so on.

will assist in the numerous computations.) It is often necessary to repeat calculations with small changes to evaluate "what if" alternative outcomes. This is called a sensitivity analysis; it is done to determine the changes in expected cash flow given changes in forecasts.

Several projects are typically reviewed each quarter, and it would be your responsibility to rank them according to financial merit. There are several methods used to rank projects, including net present value, project payback, average return on book, internal rate of return, and profitability index. These methods are used frequently in business today. You should be familiar with them, aware of the limitations of each technique, and able to apply multiple methods of analysis to ensure accurate project evaluation. Once the projects have been evaluated, they are ranked according to both financial and operating criteria. Middle or senior management generally performs this ranking, while the financial analyst consults and recommends.

After projects have been approved and carried out, the analyst completes the final aspect in the capital budgeting procedure—the post-completion audit. This audit involves a comparison between actual project results with those predicted, and an explanation of the differences. This audit of new projects is often assigned to the controller (whose responsibilities are described below).

The capital budgeting function of a financial analyst is rarely routine, due to the various projects being considered and evaluated. This position also offers the opportunity for wide exposure to the company's operations. The entry-level analyst often spends a significant amount of time making calculations, developing spread sheets, doing sensitivity analyses, and gathering information for senior-level analyst decision making. Since it may take two or more years to become a senior analyst, the early years can be frustrating for those wanting to make decisions. However, senior analysts generally feel that the tasks performed initially form a necessary developmental process for the positions of authority attained later. Positions of higher authority, such as vice president of finance, treasurer, and assistant treasurer, usually decide the fate of projects as well as arrange financing for their implementation.

Project financing. Projects can be financed by cash and marketable securities reserves, long-term debt (bond) issues, equity issues, or long-term debt from commercial banks. The decision regarding which source to use is a difficult one, and corporate financial managers seldom have sufficiently broad knowledge of the existing financial market to choose the most effective method of project financing. A common practice is to consult with a corporate finance expert in a commercial or investment bank (as described in chapters 2 and 4). Such financial institutions have considerable expertise in corporate capital structure formulation.

FINANCIAL PLANNING STRATEGY

As we have noted, the capital budgeting and investment analysis group is involved in the evaluation of capital venture proposals and the securing of funds to support recommended projects. Another group in the treasury department, responsible for financial planning and strategy, links these activities to the corporation as a whole, taking into consideration the combined effect of investment and financing decisions. This includes financial planning and possible mergers and acquisitions.

Financial planning. The planning function is usually divided into the following four responsibilities:

1. analyzing the financing and investment choices open to the firm
2. projecting consequences of present decisions in order to avoid surprises and to understand the linkages between present and future decisions
3. deciding which alternatives to undertake
4. measuring subsequent performance against the goals of the financial plan

Analyzing the various combinations of financing and investment choices open to the firm often demands ingenuity if funds are to be

TABLE 5.2
Spread Sheet: Cash Flow Analysis for Product X

			Estimated Profits and Cash Flows		
	1985	1986	1987	...	1998
Quantity shipped (units)	75,000	90,000	100,000	...	100,000
Gross sales (dollars)	$5,564,000	$6,477,000	$7,085,000	...	$7,085,000
Less Freight	46,000	55,000	61,000	...	61,000
Cash discounts	+18,000	+22,000	+24,000	...	+24,000
Total deductions	64,000	77,000	85,000	...	85,000
Net sales (Gross sales – Total deductions)	$5,500,000	$6,400,000	$7,000,000	...	$7,000,000
Sales Costs					
Variable	$2,340,000	$2,880,000	$3,240,000	...	$3,240,000
Fixed, excluding depreciation and depletion	360,000	360,000	360,000	...	360,000
Break-in costs	351,000	144,000	—	...	—
Total	3,051,000	3,384,000	3,600,000	...	3,600,000
Depreciation	+437,550	+408,380	+379,210	...	+29,120
Total sales costs	$3,488,550	$3,792,380	$3,979,210	...	$3,629,120

Gross profit (Net sales – Total sales costs)	$2,011,450	$2,607,620	$3,020,790	$3,370,880
Selling expenses	$1,240,000	1,240,000	1,240,000	1,240,000
Advertising	130,000	105,000	90,000	90,000
Administrative	300,000	300,000	300,000	300,000
Provision for bad debts	26,825	31,325	34,325	34,325
Total selling etc. costs	$1,696,825	1,676,325	1,664,325	1,664,325
Net income before tax (Gross profit – Total selling etc. costs)	$ 314,625	$ 931,295	$1,356,465	$1,706,555
State and federal income tax @ 48%	– 151,020	– 447,022	– 651,103	– 819,146
Net income	163,605	484,273	705,362	887,409
Add back depreciation	+ 437,550	+ 408,380	+ 379,210	+ 29,120
Net cash flow	$ 601,155	$ 892,653	$1,084,572	$ 916,529
Salvage value: buildings and machines				$ 0
Recovery of working capital				$1,500,000
Net cash flow year 1997				$2,416,529

obtained for all desired projects. A typical entry-level position in financial planning would involve analyzing the alternatives suggested by senior management personnel. Although financial planning is similar to capital budgeting in this respect, it differs in that planners are concerned with an overall strategy for the company's operations.

This planning process usually begins with the financial planner obtaining from the operating units a business plan, often in the form of a five-year outlook. Each plan may be structured with several scenarios, one perhaps built around aggressive growth, another around normal growth, and another around retrenchment or divestiture. If not already done at the operating unit level, the calculation of cash flow for each alternative is computed by the financial planner. With the cash flow analysis at hand, the financial planner then examines the alternatives as mutually exclusive capital projects. They become the basis for a consolidated corporate financial and strategic plan.

The second major function of the financial planner is to project the consequences of decisions. This involves forecasting the effects of the economy and industry competition on the company's earnings. Since some companies do not have the information resources and technical expertise to do accurate forecasts, they may hire firms which specialize in preparing macroeconomic and industry forecasts.

Once a company has its "best" forecast, the financial planner has accumulated enough information for senior management to decide which of the alternatives to undertake. As in capital budgeting, your role as financial planner at this stage would be to gather information, perform calculations, and recommend possible alternatives—the third function in this process. Sometimes, however, recommending an alternative is reserved for middle management.

The final function of the financial planner is to compare actual financial performance to the stated goals in the financial plan. However, this may also be the responsibility of the controller's office and is therefore discussed below.

For a financial planner written communication skills are essential. It would be your responsibility as financial planner not only to develop pro forma financial statements consisting of "best estimates" of earnings, but to describe and explain planned capital expenditures. In addition, a clear description of the business strategies and financing planned to achieve these goals is necessary. Hence, the results of your numerical and analytic skills must be translated into concise, persuasive statements of desired courses of action.

Financial planning positions offer an opportunity to be exposed to all of a corporation's financial functions. They also involve two aspects which can be particularly advantageous for your career. First, you would interact regularly with higher level managers. Second, you would be exposed to the major financial functions and decisions of the firm. This facilitates mobility as a financial manager both within and between organizations.

Your hours as a financial planner tend to be longer than those for other entry-level financial positions, due to the necessity of meeting report deadlines. The manager of entry-level financial planning personnel is often the vice president of finance or the treasurer. When this is the case, entry-level people also serve as "assistants" to this senior staff member; this work may involve substantial "busy work." Performing both financial planning and assistant functions may increase your work load to as much as 50–55 hours per week. However, this will depend on the attitude of your superior toward you and the financial planning function.

Mergers and acquisitions. Mergers and acquisitions involve both investment and financing decisions and therefore are included under financial planning strategy. Mergers and acquisitions are not regular events; there is seldom a separate M&A department within the firm.

The basic principles of capital investment decision making are used in corporate merger and acquisition evaluations. However, this analysis is not as easy as that for capital project investment, owing to the complex tax, legal, political, personnel, and accounting issues which must be considered. Most corporations, without a merger and acquisition staff, rely on the expert advice of investment banks in dealing with these complex issues. Corporate merger and acquisition functions were described in chapter 4.

INTERNATIONAL FINANCIAL MANAGEMENT

The above discussion of financial functions has ignored the possibility of international corporate activities. Although basic objectives in international financial management are the same as domestic objectives, some specific problems typically addressed by an international financial management group are described below.

The unique feature of international financial management is that more than one currency is involved; hence, various exchange risks exist. One function of the international financial manager is to reduce these risks through various foreign-exchange market operations, commonly known as "hedging."

Another important aspect of an international financial manager's function is to concentrate the company's financial investments in countries with the least risk and most favorable interest rate. On the other hand, an expansion strategy often evolves to spread investments to various countries to reduce the total risk of the investment. As an international financial analyst you would be responsible for analyzing the factors involved in investing in various countries and recommending strategies accordingly.

In addition to currency management, international financial managers must consider the problems in the capital budgeting and project financing processes. Typical questions include: What discount rate should be used? Should the company finance the operation locally? How does the financing method affect the project choice?

Working in an international financial management unit may involve travel in order to analyze potential projects. Otherwise, your work role and responsibilities are similar to those of positions in capital budgeting.

Controller Functions

The other main group in a corporate finance structure is the controller's department. The main function of this group, as the name implies, is to control the corporation's money. It is concerned with inspection of corporate expenditures to ensure that the capital is being used efficiently and as planned. The functions usually performed under the controller are budgeting and control, accounting, auditing, and taxation planning. Only the area of budgeting and control is examined below as a corporate finance role. Accounting, auditing, and taxation are discussed in chapter 6.

The budgeting and control function generally exists at each divisional level of the corporation, with a central budgeting and control function at corporate headquarters. An entry-level position in this area is usually given the title of financial analyst. As a financial analyst you would review

1. divisional budgets,
2. strategic plans and product line strategies,
3. monthly, quarterly, and yearly operating results.

Reviewing divisional and corporate budgets means monitoring performance against the planned budget of the division or operating unit. In order to carry out this responsibility effectively, you will need to understand what is happening at the division or operating unit level. This involves soliciting financial performance reports and ensuring cooperation in the accurate preparation of reports. A budget review is usually divided into the following sections: current operating results, explanations of these results and any variance from projected levels, and expected future performance. Although concise reports are preferred, it is not uncommon to see performance reports of twenty pages; this depends on the problems in the operating unit and the amount of detail required by senior management.

A large amount of your time will be spent gathering information, which requires communication between you and operating unit personnel. Often it will be necessary for you to go to the operating unit to obtain an accurate picture of events. Only after you have discussed operating expenditures with operating unit management will you be able to write an accurate review of the unit's performance with respect to the corporate budget.

Reviewing strategic plans and product-line strategies is another area in which you may be involved. When strategic plans are made by the financial planning department, which is often positioned under the treasurer or vice president of finance, it becomes your job as financial analyst within the controller's unit to ascertain whether predicted results are occurring. You would need to prepare scheduled progress reports for senior management with thorough explanations of results.

Reviewing monthly, quarterly, and yearly performance is the final function of financial analyst under the controller. Like the budget review function, periodic review of performance would involve contact between you and personnel of the division being reviewed. As with the strategic-plan review function, detailed industry or division reviews must be prepared for senior managers. Usually, review of periodic performance of operations is done by comparing actual operating results to predicted results. In addition, comparison is made to industry-wide performance. This requires that you be aware of performance and innovations within the industry as a whole as well as within your company.

In this review function, operating results are compared with the predictions of the previous year. Unlike strategic or long-range planning, short-term planning is rarely concerned with time frames greater than twelve months. The one-year forecast and plan consists of pro forma financial statements, capital expenditure and business strategy, and financing plans.

The pro forma balance sheets and income statements reflect both the forecasts and the goals management hopes to achieve for the coming year or quarter. Unless the pro forma balance sheet and income sheet ratios are subject to drastic change, the balance sheet usually is expressed as a percentage of sales.

The second aspect of the short-term plan that you would be responsible for is the description of planned capital expenditures. You provide a narrative description of planned expenditures, explain why the specified amounts are necessary, and state the strategy to reach set goals. Other areas of discussion that may be included involve research and development efforts, steps to improve productivity, design and marketing of new products, and pricing.

Finally, there is often a section which summarizes planned financing for the following period. Financial need is based on the pro forma financial statements, or more commonly a cash flow budget. The latter is usually prepared by a financial analyst and is designed to determine the firm's short-term cash needs. Once this estimate of cash needs is completed, the financing plan can be developed. This portion of the plan may also be handled by members of the cash management department, who are familiar with methods of raising short-term capital.

As a financial analyst under the controller, you would write often and therefore need excellent written communication skills. There is a substantial amount of calculation to be performed in an analysis, although less than in capital budgeting.

While working under the controller, you often will have close contact with high-level executives, affording excellent opportunities for career growth. The exposure to various aspects of company operations will offer you the opportunity to develop an understanding of corporate operations. While you will seldom make the financial decisions at this stage, senior financial managers will in all likelihood frequently encourage you to participate in discussions at corporate strategy meetings.

You may travel up to one-third of the time, depending on the geographic location of operating units. The feeling of being worked hard and needing assistance for data analysis is sometimes reported by analysts in the controller's area, who may experience long work hours (from fifty to fifty-five hours per week) because of heavy work loads and deadlines set by senior management.

Required Skills and Educational Background

In today's increasingly complex world of corporate finance, it is important to have formal training in finance. Most individuals employed in the corporate finance function have an MBA or BA in business. In the latter case, an employee will often be encouraged by the company to get an MBA over a period of several years by attending classes at night.

In some cases, individuals received a BA in business prior to their MBA, although there is no clear advantage to this once an MBA is obtained. In some instances, companies in high technology industries prefer individuals with technical or engineering backgrounds who are already familiar with the products and their applications. Overall, individuals in corporate finance come from a wide variety of undergraduate programs.

There is no one career path within the corporation leading to a top position in corporate finance. If you desire an eventual executive position, it is essential to acquire a wide range of experience in both the controller and treasury areas. Often an individual will spend from two to five years in the treasury and then transfer to the controller function.

Later, he or she may move back to the treasury or into a staff position under the vice president of finance. There are varied paths up the corporate ranks. However, movement into the treasury or controller areas from other departments, such as marketing, sales, manufacturing, or R&D, is rare after two to four years of employment, due to lack of applicable experience.

The desire to succeed and assume responsibility are important characteristics for a financial manager. You must be tolerant of the structured environment and current company policies, which may conflict with more effective practices learned in business school or previous work. Without this tolerance you will feel frustrated, which perhaps will make it difficult to adapt to the company's environment. On the other hand, frustrated financial managers often improve the practices within their company. The most successful financial managers are those who can initiate changes subtly and at the same time endure present company policies.

Finally, financial managers tend to be devoted to, but not obsessed with, their jobs. Although positions in the corporate finance function normally consist of forty-to-fifty hour weeks, you will on occasion have to spend more time at work to meet deadlines. Since these occurrences are infrequent, you will be able to devote reasonable time to your personal life. Unlike an investment banker, who spends much more time on the job, a financial manager can typically balance work and personal life demands.

In addition to the specialized skills and abilities needed to be a successful financial manager discussed above, there are several common skills and abilities required in most financial positions. Oral and written communication skills are of prime importance; at any entry-level position, it may be your task to examine various proposals and make a written analysis or oral presentation to senior management.

Another needed skill is the ability to interpret financial statements and anticipate the effects various strategy changes can have on future financial performance. Most financial managers agree that an understanding of accounting is needed here, and that courses in financial management and accounting principles, while necessary, are not sufficient background.

As with many positions in business, administrative skills are important in financial management. Usually several projects are going on concurrently, and much paperwork is involved. Good administrative skills allow you to spend more time on relevant matters rather than waste time relocating information.

You should also have leadership ability. As your career progresses, you will have to delegate more responsibility—meaning more need for coordination and less for actual financial analysis.

6

Accounting*

The accounting profession is divided into two sectors: public accounting and private accounting. The primary concern of both sectors is the collection, organization, and reporting of financial data. The motivation behind these activities is *control:* in private accounting, control of an organization's scarce resources; in public accounting, control to effect reliable financial information made available to the public or financial institutions. This separation of public and private accounting recognizes the necessity for these two types of control, and the difference between information needed by internal corporate managers on the one hand, and external investors, potential investors, government agencies, and financial institutions on the other.

There are many types of employment opportunities within the accounting profession. We outline the major ones below. Because different functional areas in accounting firms or departments perform different activities and require different educational backgrounds and attributes, we have subdivided these categories by functional area.

Public Accounting

Public accounting is performed by accountants, in most cases Certified Public Accountants (CPAs). Public accounting firms are typically organized as partnerships, and vary in size from large, international firms employing thousands of people to small firms or even individual practitioners serving the needs of a local area. These firms offer varied services to the general public, their clients. The types of services rendered vary according to firm size and orientation. The most common service is the review and issuance of professional opinions on client financial statements, known as auditing. Management advisory services (a public accounting firm's consulting unit) and tax consultation constitute the two most common services offered in addition to auditing.

*This chapter is based on a paper written by Amy Williams.

Firm size is a major factor determining what services a firm offers its clients. Small firms or solo practitioners usually work as generalists. (Their activities are described later in this chapter under "Private Accounting.") These firms service individual clients or small businesses that lack their own internal accountants or accounting department. Construction of client financial statements, known as write-up services, is another major service offered by smaller firms. Other services include creating and maintaining bookkeeping systems, performing monthly reviews or closings, and filing tax returns.

Large firms without small-business departments will not perform these write-up services and typically do not seek out small businesses or individuals as clients—at least as audit clients. These firms generally handle large organizations and corporations, offering expertise and experience in numerous specialized areas within each service classification. Billing rates are higher than in small practices. The "Big Eight," a term coined for the eight largest and most influential American public accounting firms operating nationally and internationally, possess large pools of talent, and serve 98 percent of New York Stock Exchange companies.

Regardless of size, most CPA firms are similarly structured, with nearly identical requirements for attainment of higher job levels. Figure 6.1 depicts the typical organizational structure of a public accounting firm. At the highest level of management are the firm's partners— individuals who generally have made a capital contribution. Partners head regional offices, practice sections within these offices, and serve on the firm's managing committees. While they do perform some accounting duties, their role focuses primarily on generating new business, maintaining existing client relationships, and guiding the firm's future progress.

Accountants with four to six years experience are generally promoted to the position of manager. Here, they act as liaison between the partners and the lower ranks. Managers perform substantial amounts of accounting work and are responsible for supervising and directing projects within their service groups.

One step further down the ladder is the senior level generally reached after two to four years experience. At this point, as an accountant, you must possess a substantial amount of technical knowledge and supervisory skill; if you are in auditing or tax divisions, you should have successfully completed the CPA exam.

Entry-level accountants act as staff accountants, and perform much of the "nuts-and-bolts" work of the firm.

Below we discuss the three main departments of the public accounting firm: auditing, tax, and management advisory services.

FIGURE 6.1

Organizational Structure of Public Accounting Firm

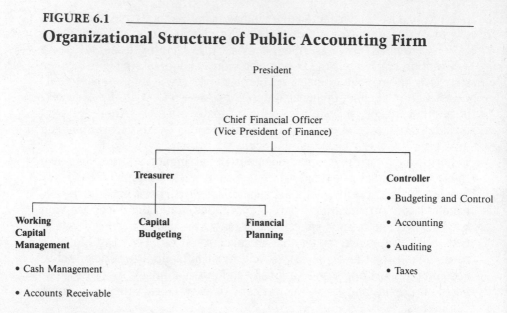

AUDITING

The audit department is typically the largest department within a firm in terms of both number of employees and amount of business generated. It is also the career starting point for most entry-level public accountants.

Activities and responsibilities. The audit department's primary responsibility is to review and issue professional opinions on clients' financial statements, typically the year-end financial statements required by the Securities and Exchange Commission. However, since not all organizations come under the SEC's jurisdiction, other types of audits, such as compliance audits, audits for specific government agencies, or audits for privately held companies, are sometimes performed instead. Professional opinions are also rendered on annual reports given to shareholders and potential investors.

Perfomance of audits is controlled to a large degree by specific professional and industry guidelines. Professional standards—specifically, Generally Accepted Accounting Principles (GAAP) and Generally Accepted Auditing Standards (GAAS)—determine for the public accounting industry and auditors how to account for various transactions. Professional boards update the body of accounting theory and establish standards of ethics for the profession. These pronouncements are very much in use in audit practice, and signed audit reports attest to the fact that the audit has been performed in accordance with both GAAP and GAAS.

Before the audit begins, the auditor-client relationship must be formally established. Many client relationships are long-standing ones, but generating of new business is an ongoing process that is vital to a firm's success. Firms constantly vie with each other for large audit accounts. However, direct client solicitation is prohibited in public accounting. Upon invitation by clients, competing auditing firms prepare and submit extensive proposals outlining the services their firm can offer and the fees involved. As mentioned previously, responsibility for generating new business rests with the firm's partners. A good deal of business is brought in through contacts with industry executives.

Once the client relationship has been established, the audit planning process begins. Audit planning is extensive with new clients. It begins with reviewing available documentation, such as the previous years' financial statements, to familiarize the auditors with the client's operations and financial position. The orientation process might also include physical inspection of the client's facilities, interviews with key personnel, and conferences with predecessor auditors (upon client's approval). While auditing to a large extent confines itself to client accounting records and financial statements, anything having a material or significant effect on the financial statements is taken into consideration. Thus, auditing includes a comprehensive review of a firm's operations and procedures, in addition to review of its accounting records.

For already established client relationships, audit planning involves reviewing financial statements and audit work papers of prior years, plus listing any developments since last year's audit that have had an effect on this year's financial statements. Typically, interim audits or auditor reviews are performed mid-year to keep auditors in touch with client operations.

Audits begin before the client fiscal year ends, sometimes months in advance. Planning the audit involves specifying the type and amount of work to be performed, its timing, and the size and composition of the audit team. Typically, managers plan audit engagements with the assistance of senior auditors, although large audit engagements may require the efforts of a large planning team composed of partners, managers, and senior staff.

Based on pre-audit investigation, the manager delineates the amount and type of work to be done. Not every accounting item or transaction is audited. Which items will be audited is decided by sophisticated quantitative methods, taking into consideration budget constraints and the need to ascertain the fairness of the financial statements. Audit planning cannot be haphazard; not only must sampling techniques be rigorously followed, but planning must be realistic and efficient so that the engagement is completed at or under budget, as fees are based on billable hours.

After the planning process is completed, the manager composes and sends an "engagement" letter to the client, outlining fees and what financial statements will be audited. This serves as the contract formalizing the audit relationship. Prior to the audit's commencement, the partner or the manager discusses the plan with the client to find out if there are any special considerations of which the auditors should be aware. Procedural information, such as the location of the various records and documents to be audited, is also covered.

Once the groundwork has been established, field work or actual auditing begins at the client's location. For large accounts, the partner in charge closely supervises progress, keeps in contact with client personnel, and reviews daily findings with the audit manager. For small accounts partners generally communicate less with the client, reviewing results only at the end.

Audit responsibilities vary according to staff classification. Junior auditors, often after having completed an audit training program, perform the bulk of the stereotypical auditing duties: footing or adding columns of numbers, counting inventory, and constructing bank reconciliation statements. Thus, as a junior auditor you would work with the less complicated accounts and procedures. Other duties include counting cash, verifying receivables, and photocopying work papers and documents. Junior staff have no supervisory responsibilities and perform their duties under the authority of senior supervisors.

The senior audit position also performs a great deal of audit work, in addition to supervising junior auditors. Depending on the amount of experience, the position carries a substantial amount of responsibility for actually conducting the audit. The senior auditor reviews junior work papers, deals with audit and personnel problems as they arise, and confers with client management on any problems affecting the progress of the audit. When an engagement is small or generates relatively low fees, the senior auditor may supervise the entire audit, and have only completed work reviewed by audit managers or partners.

A senior auditor is commonly promoted to the position of audit manager after four to six years experience. This position is responsible for the overall functioning of the audit, for performing the more complex auditing duties such as the stockholders' equity section of the balance sheet, and for assisting client management in writing notes to the financial statements. Assuring the forward progression of the work by skillful coordination of subordinate tasks is perhaps the manager's most crucial role, as he or she is responsible for finishing engagements at or under budget. This role naturally becomes more difficult when managers supervise several audit engagements at once. The manager must review in detail the findings of junior staff, solve any major problems, and adjust the audit's scope to deal with unexpected occurrences. The manager communicates with the client throughout—specifically, with the client's audit committee or controller—and must resolve any differences tactfully without expending large amounts of time.

When an audit is completed the manager reviews the findings with a partner. Partners are the ones eventually responsible for the audit, as they sign their names to the financial statement. The partner also provides input to the manager on the "management letter," which serves as a summary of the engagement and outlines the auditor's comments and recommendations to the client.

Depending on size and type of firm, an auditing position may infringe on your lifestyle because of overtime. Typically, the heavy auditing season begins in December and runs through March, with overtime and weekend work common regardless of position level. In most firms, overtime is either compensated or accumulated as vacation time. Smaller firms may be more suitable for those who are unwilling to handle great amounts of overtime or pressure. Travel is also a consideration: out-of-town auditing engagements may require trips lasting anywhere from a week to a month.

Educational background and training. The typical educational requirement for entry into the auditing field is a bachelor of science degree in an accredited program of accounting. Master's degrees are not the norm, and are not required in the auditing area of the firm, although those with undergraduate degrees in areas other than accounting might have MBAs.

On-the-job training usually plays the most important part in the auditor's success. However, an accounting degree is perhaps one of the more immediately applicable college degrees; courses taken in an accredited accounting program have direct application from the first day auditors begin their career. The accounting principles and auditing standards that must be applied to auditing constitute a major part of undergraduate accounting study. Courses that include study of recent accounting pronouncements and auditing standards are most important, as these will be put to use early in the auditor's first year and are also essential for successful completion of the CPA exam.

Any prior experience, acquired perhaps through part-time or summer work, is an asset to the beginning auditor, both in terms of finding a position and giving him or her an edge over less experienced peers. Also, starting salaries are based somewhat on prior experience. Depending on firm size, training may be a highly formalized and continuing process in the auditor's career or simply a matter of on-the-job learning. Small firms without the resources or need for training departments typically train the junior auditor on actual work assignments. Large firms—specifically, the "Big Eight"—place great emphasis on in-house training, and have developed training programs and courses for all position levels within each division.

As an entry-level auditor in a large firm, you would probably start your career with full-time audit training courses lasting from one to four weeks. Beginning courses attempt to bridge the gap between the accounting and auditing theory taught in college courses and actual practice, with special emphasis on the firm's individual approach to auditing practice. A typical training exercise would run you through a simulated audit complete with documentation, work-paper examples, audit reports, and letters. You may also receive—depending again on the particular firm—self-guided training courses for study toward the CPA examination. You would be encouraged to begin immediate study for this exam, as the amount of study required is extensive. For those auditors without access to formalized instruction, CPA review can be done through private instruction and is recommended in addition to self-study.

Since most states require varying amounts of "continuing professional education" (CPE) in order for an accountant to maintain the CPA license, training is necessarily an ongoing process, whether it is acquired in-house or from external sources such as seminars or college courses. In addition to technical courses specifically concerned with accounting or auditing, large firms may offer non-accounting training courses, recognizing the need for skills such as written and oral communication and group leadership. The training offered by large accounting firms is an advantage to be considered when searching for a position, as smaller firms generally do not have the resources necessary for training.

Attributes of successful auditors. Technical accounting and auditing knowledge and the corresponding analytical skills necessary to put the technical knowledge to work are important attributes you need to develop to be a successful auditor. You must be intimately familiar with all aspects of the accounting process and with the technical industry standards and pronouncements guiding those processes. As accounting theory and practice are constantly in transition, you must keep your technical know-how updated and ready to be applied in practice.

As accounting is not an exact science, analytical skill and good judgment are crucial. Although there are guidelines that spell out how most transactions are to be accounted for, situations always arise for which there are no specific answers. You must use your judgment in making decisions in an environment where there is little time for decision making. Supervisors working under pressure to complete engagements do not have the time necessary to answer constant questions or otherwise guide junior staff throughout the tenure of the engagement. While this does not mean questions are never answered, you must set priorities in terms of questions' importance and relevance, using your own judgment on less important matters.

Supervisory skill is a perhaps overlooked, yet crucial, attribute of successful auditors. Promotion to higher levels depends to a large extent on highly developed supervisory skills.

Interpersonal skills also come into play on a daily basis, in terms of both communicating with fellow auditors and establishing good rapport with the client's personnel. The auditor must keep in mind the effect his or her presence can have on personnel. Auditing disrupts the client's regular work routine and is sometimes viewed as "policing"; auditors are seen as searching for employees' accounting errors. This can evoke a defensive attitude from these personnel. At the same time, auditors must often request assistance in locating documents and require explanations of various client records. Thus, auditors must attempt to acquire all the audit information they require, while simultaneously dealing tactfully with the client so as to ensure cooperation.

Supervisors generally evaluate subordinates after each audit engagement, eventually compiling these individual evaluations into an annual review upon which salary increases and promotions are based. Auditors will find that supervisory and interpersonal skills are on an equal basis with technical excellence when promotion decisions are made.

The two-year mark in the auditor's career is generally the juncture where career options are most numerous. Having completed the two-year experience requirement mandated by most states for the CPA license, many auditors either seek positions in the private accounting sector as highly sought-after CPAs, or look for transfers to other divisions. A typical internal transfer would be a move to the tax, management advisory, or small business department—or perhaps a move to a smaller CPA firm where higher position visibility is possible and competition for manager and partner positions is not as intense as in large firms. Those remaining within auditing often choose to specialize within specific industry groups, such as utility companies or hospitals.

TAX SERVICES

Activities and responsibilities. The scope of a public accounting firm's tax department depends on firm size. Smaller firms may confine tax practice to tax-return planning and preparation, while large firms offer the full range of tax services, including tax planning and tax compliance. Tax planning can be defined as directing clients in structuring business transactions and operations in order to reduce tax liabilities. It includes such activities as selecting the proper tax-accounting method and the most advantageous time for a business transaction. Tax compliance involves the preparation of federal, state, and local tax returns, representing clients at IRS and administrative hearings, and reviewing private-sector tax departments to improve their efficiency. Specialization opportunities within the tax field are numerous, including merger and acquisition taxation, taxation for expatriates, and estate and trust taxation.

Tax and auditing departments are similarly structured, with partners heading the various specialties within the division. Tax clients—both individuals and organizations— are served either by individual accountants or by teams of accountants for major or complex problems requiring a coordinated effort by tax accountants in different specialties.

Junior or first-year tax staff begin their career with extensive tax-return preparation under senior staff supervision, including local, state, and individual tax returns for individuals, partnerships, and, in some cases, corporations. This establishes the groundwork for more extensive tax work in the future. As junior accountants begin to assimilate tax law and master basic return preparation, they are given increasingly complex tax returns to complete. Although tax-return preparation may be tedious, it is necessary for an accountant's development; without such experience tax planning and research is impossible.

Senior tax accountants, who generally have had at least two years experience at the junior level, continue to prepare tax returns, although they handle the more difficult ones, such as consolidated corporate returns. The coordination and review of junior staff work is a major role of the senior tax accountant. He or she also begins to be exposed to tax research and planning by assisting managers in business client or individual tax work. At this point senior staff may begin to focus on specialized areas within taxation, such as corporate distribution and liquidations, either through on-the-job training or formalized training courses.

Tax managers function either as tax specialists or generalists, depending on preference. Generalists serve the needs of several business clients, organizations, or individuals, and handle the complete range of tax work for them, assisting in tax planning and return preparation. Tax managers who have chosen specialized work spend most of their time dealing with one specific area of taxation. Whether a generalist or a specialist, managers spend a great deal of time on tax research, shifting through tax law, regulations, and cases, and creatively devising solutions to their client's tax problems.

Educational background and training. The educational and work-experience backgrounds of entry-level tax accountants vary, depending to a large extent on firm policy. Entry-level college graduates with no prior experience generally must indicate a strong interest in taxation or have a concentration in undergraduate tax courses to be hired into tax departments. Typically, audit personnel with one or two years of experience and a career interest in taxes may transfer into the tax area. Many tax departments recruit law-school graduates with a major in tax law, although tax departments do not practice law as such. The law student's exposure to tax law is a valuable asset in understanding and working with the Internal Revenue Code. A person with an MBA or Master's in taxation makes another attractive tax department recruit. Prior work experience is also taken into account, as is evidenced by the number of former IRS staffers hired by public accounting firms for the tax department.

Regardless of educational background, those without prior experience will begin their career with tax-return preparation. Those with tax or general accounting experience might begin with more advanced duties. Any exposure to tax-return preparation, whether through college courses or actual job experience, will permit more rapid advancement within the department.

Tax accountants working for firms with training programs will probably take a formal tax or audit training program before beginning a career. Auditing experience is especially valuable. Knowledge of how businesses operate and are organized financially has direct application to tax practice. An understanding of accounting concepts, such as depreciation or inventory pricing, is also required when dealing with their tax implications. Since some states require audit experience for their CPA candidates, occasional work assignments to the auditing department to perform a general audit or audit of tax accounts might occur.

Attributes of successful tax accountants. Having a thorough knowledge of the tax law (Internal Revenue Code) and keeping abreast of current tax developments are major attributes of successful tax accountants. As new tax laws emerge and accounting methods and procedures change, the tax accountant must not only understand the changes but have the ability to apply them to varying tax situations. In addition to new tax law, rulings by IRS and various administrative bodies must be included in the tax accountant's body of knowledge, along with emerging business and economic trends.

Research, writing, and analytical skills must be applied to tax problems; quite often problem structuring requires more analysis than does devising the actual tax solution. As a tax accountant, you would have to break down the problem into its components and then decide on the needed type of research and research sources, such as internal revenue statutes and related tax cases and rulings. Once you have devised solutions, you would prepare summary reports detailing findings and explaining how clients are to put them into practice.

Similarly, oral communication plays a part in tax practice. Many cases require substantial work with other tax accountants to create successful solutions. Since client work is an ongoing process, you will be called on continually to deal with client problems and developments requiring tax expertise. This requires communicating with clients on short notice and responding quickly and concisely to their requests.

Finally, levelheadedness and the ability to work well under pressure are crucial in busy tax departments. The heavy tax season lasts from January to April, and fourteen-hour days, seven days per week, are common. Travel may be required, but is not as common as overtime. Working well under this type of pressure and producing work of quality is important; those unable or unwilling to deal with time pressure will find the going rough.

Promotion within tax departments is based on factors such as technical knowledge, research expertise, and supervisory skills. As in auditing, supervisory skills are crucial. Individuals possessing solid technical knowledge but poor or nonexistent supervisory skills will find career progress hampered.

Tax personnel are sometimes called in on audits to review tax accounts whose complexity prevents audit personnel from performing the work themselves. However, transfers of staff from the tax department to auditing are not common. Tax personnel also do occasional work assignments with other divisions, such as management advisory services (MAS) or small business, on projects requiring tax expertise. Transfers from the tax department to MAS or small-business divisions sometimes occur. Tax personnel with anywhere from two to five years experience will find their services actively sought by firms in the private sector. Those with CPA licenses will be in special demand, and can enter into a business corporation's tax department or smaller CPA firm as a tax manager.

Enjoyment of tax work requires that you enjoy sifting through large amounts of information, both legal and quantitative, creatively molding that information to devise solutions to tax problems. Although tax work requires communication with fellow tax accountants and clients, it also involves hours of individual research, thought, and report writing. People desiring a constant level of human interaction will probably not find tax work stimulating. Perhaps the most common characteristic tax accountants share is the knowledge that they understand and can put to use a body of technical and complex knowledge not readily understood by most people.

MANAGEMENT ADVISORY SERVICES

Management advisory services (MAS) is the arm of a public accounting firm that acts as a consulting department. MAS departments are growing in size and importance and are firmly established within most large public accounting firms.

Activities and responsibilities. Typical services offered by management advisory services departments include development of accounting, reporting, and budgeting systems; design and installation of computerized information systems; and operations research and management science services. Regardless of the type of service offered, the MAS objective is to improve the client's operations by recommending changes in management policy or practice. The type of work performed by MAS consultants is often similar to that of a systems analyst (see chapter 12) or business consultant (see chapter 13).

Most MAS projects result in the design and installation of computerized accounting and financial information systems. All projects are customized to one degree or another to meet the client's needs, and many involve designing entire electronic-data-processing (EDP) systems for clients making the transition from a manual to a computerized accounting system. Another common project involves designing specialized systems such as inventory tracking systems. These projects may involve not only consultation with clients on the design and implementation of systems, but also planning training sessions for client personnel to familiarize them with the new system.

Responding either to vague or specific requests, a consulting team decides upon and designs programs to suit the client's needs. Project teams are selected by MAS managers to include the various talents needed to carry out the project. Teams generally include staff consultants with specific areas of technical expertise. The average MAS project lasts several months, although larger projects can take a year or more.

Clients are typically acquired through a bidding process, where one MAS department bids against another from a competing accounting or business consulting firm. Consultants take information about clients' needs and prepare proposals outlining project work, the required time, and fees. With large projects for prestigious clients the competition between firms becomes fierce, and bids often are modified to show lower billable hours to improve competitive position. In consequence, many MAS projects have tight schedules, putting pressure on staff consultants to perform within limited time parameters.

Partners or principals (non-CPAs equal in stature to partners) are responsible for generating new MAS business, and also for directly supervising large, prestigious accounts. Managers in MAS have administrative responsibilities similar in scope to those in auditing or tax services. Generally, they supervise several small engagements or one major project, and are responsible for planning project work, assigning and supervising staff consultants, collecting fees, and seeing that projects are completed within budget.

Managers spend much time visiting client locations to review staff consultants' work and confer with client personnel about project progress. Managers also spend considerable time documenting project progress and editing reports prepared by senior consultants for review by the partner or principal in charge of the project.

Early in their careers, consultants often work in a "staff consultant pool" arrangement, and are assigned to projects as they occur. They spend the majority of their time at client facilities working on the design, programming, and testing of systems. They too must continually document project results and progress. As staff consultants revolve to various projects they generally veer in direction according to personal interest, preparing to take a specialized position as promotions occur. After two to four years of experience a staff consultant becomes a senior consultant, and is then given increasing responsibility for structuring and carrying out projects.

Educational background and training. Entry-level MAS consultants generally possess either an MBA, an undergraduate background in engineering, management, or computer science, or several years work experience in general business or a technical area. Most firms do not hire people as consultants who do not have either an MBA or significant work experience. The nature of consulting work requires a well-educated, mature individual: Someone with two to four years business experience, including work with computers and an MBA, would be an ideal MAS candidate.

Most formalized MAS training programs include work in computer applications and programming courses, as well as, depending on whether there are specific divisions within the MAS department, a variety of courses in areas such as operations research, budgeting, and forecasting. A training program might also include industry-related courses such as study of the hospital industry. Consultants in large firms receive exposure to a wide variety of projects in their first two years, while consultants in small MAS departments may find exposure limited.

Transfers from MAS into other departments within accounting firms are not the norm, although MAS consultants may work in conjunction with auditors or tax personnel in computer applications. Unlike other sections such as auditing, where accountants transfer to private-sector practice after acquiring the CPA license, MAS career movement generally works in reverse. Many MAS consultants have already worked in private-sector practice and are hired into MAS after several years of business experience. The CPA license is not a requirement for attaining manager status, as is evidenced by the number of principals (non-CPA partners) working in MAS.

Attributes of successful MAS consultants. To be a successful MAS consultant, you need to be a project-oriented individual who enjoys the challenge of devising solutions to complex problems. You would not be as stringently guided by law or professional guidelines as auditing and tax accountants. Therefore, you will have more freedom in planning your work. However, to work effectively in such an environment, you must be self-motivated and able to manage your time well.

The atmosphere in an MAS department is generally more relaxed than in tax or auditing departments. Seasonal overtime is not a way of life. However, there may well be overtime for a project bid down to a small number of billable hours. Extensive travel is common. Consultants often travel to out-of-town clients returning home each weekend until project work is completed.

Technical knowledge within areas of specialization is extremely important for your success. Since most MAS projects involve some work with computers, computer aptitude, training, and facility are also important. In addition to technical expertise, written and oral communication skills are important. From the start of your career you will be constantly writing to both clients and superiors. As you progress up the management hierarchy, this skill will continue to be exercised daily. Oral communication skills are also needed much of the time at all levels of MAS: Principals talk to prospective clients; managers talk to clients to ascertain needs and information and to subordinates to assign work; staff consultants talk to superiors and client personnel. Along with these communication abilities must go well-developed supervisory skills, since you will spend more time supervising work as you advance.

Consultant evaluations take place after most engagements, reviewing technical knowledge, supervisory skills, client communication, and other attributes. Promotion and salary increases typically occur on a yearly basis, taking into account the attainment of the above skills and individual performance.

Private Accounting

The private accounting field, also known as industrial or management accounting, encompasses all accountants who, in varying capacities, handle the accounting needs of a single employer. The field is composed of both profit-making and non-profit organizations (e.g., hospitals, colleges, and charities). The public accountant's independent status does not exist for the private accountant, who must acquire an intimate knowledge of his or her company's operations, including both internal and external forces affecting its welfare.

Distinct from the firm-to-firm consistent activities and nearly identical hierarchical structures of public accounting firms, the organizational structure and job functions within private accounting departments vary widely, covering the spectrum from the highly functionalized accounting system of a Fortune 500 firm to a small firm where a single accountant performs all duties. While company size and complexity determine to a large extent the accounting system's structure and scope, most systems apply identical accounting principles and share a common goal: organizing and processing financial data in a form usable by company management and external parties as a basis for decision making.

As described in chapter 5, "Corporate Finance," the vice president of finance is the chief financial officer, and reports directly to the company president. This position oversees both the finance and accounting departments, with direct subordinates being the treasurer and controller. The treasurer's and treasury department's responsibilities are discussed at length in chapter 5.

As the controller (or comptroller) is the chief accounting executive, we shall discuss briefly this position's responsibilities (already touched on in chapter 5). The controller is responsible for all company accounting functions and departments, including general accounting, taxes, budgets and forecasting, cost accounting, and in some organizations internal auditing. The controller's role, while requiring technical accounting excellence, is best described as a managerial role involving the coordination of all accounting departments. Consequently, the controller must maintain good lateral relationships (for example, with the sales, marketing, and production departments), and must necessarily keep abreast of external factors affecting the company in general and the various accounting departments in particular. New government agency regulations, legal issues, and the general state of the economy are examples of the latter; they are important factors to consider in the context of an accounting department and its procedures.

The controller's responsibilities include reporting and interpreting the results of operations to all levels of management, administering the organization's tax program, supervising the preparation of government agency reports, protecting company assets (by establishing proper internal control procedures and, in some cases, supervising internal audit functions), and maintaining relationships with outside parties, including the organization's outside auditors. This position's requirements include, in addition to technical competence, a solid managerial background and overall knowledge of the business environment.

Required background and years of experience to assume controllership vary with company size. Fortune 500 controllers are typically veteran accountants with anywhere from ten to twenty years experience. A small organization's controller position may be filled by a public accountant with five to six years experience who has made the transition to private-sector practice.

Chief accountant, accounting manager, or supervisor are examples of job titles for positions either equal to or lower than an assistant controller position but higher than senior staff. These positions supervise and coordinate the activities of accounting department areas and report directly to an assistant controller or controller.

As private accounting departments vary widely in organizational structure and size, job positions below the controller ranks are hard to generalize about. However, it is common that senior staff accountants who have two to five years experience perform either as a functional area head, such as supervisor of an accounts receivable department, or as an accounting analyst within another department, such as budget or forecasting. Entry-level accountants and those with up to two years experience are considered junior staff and work in all accounting areas. A possible accounting department structure is shown in Figure 6.2.

FIGURE 6.2
Organizational Structure of Private Accounting Department

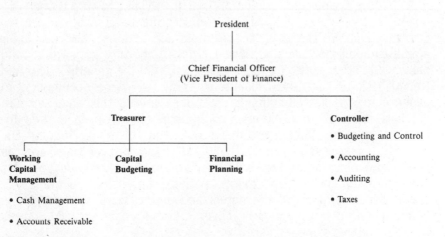

GENERAL ACCOUNTING DEPARTMENT

The general accounting department collects, records, and summarizes all accounting data used in preparing financial statements and internal managerial reports. The divisions within the general accounting department in most companies include accounts receivable, accounts payable, general ledger, payroll, and, if the accounting system is computerized, electronic data processing (EDP). If the company is large, other areas such as taxes, budgeting, and forecasting may also exist as separate entities. In small companies accountants may perform in all functional areas, while in large organizations, where accounting departments are highly functionalized, accountants may perform in one area only and never receive broad exposure to operations as a whole. Below we shall discuss the general activities found in all accounting departments, large or small.

Activities and responsibilities. The following is a generalized scenario of accounting department operation. Within the accounting department work operates cyclically, revolving around monthy and quarterly book closings and financial statement preparation at the fiscal year's end. Accounting clerks (typically with a two-year college degree) are chiefly responsible for the entry of all source documents (invoices, purchase orders, etc.) into the accounting system. In organizations with computerized systems, all accounting information is entered directly into the computer system; at the end of each month the various monthly accounting activity data are given out by the EDP department.

At month's end the accountant must assign, by a rational and objective procedure, the various transactions to general ledger accounts, which are the financial statement accounts. At this time junior staff commonly performs account analyses, whereby transactions and particularly irregular accounts are selected from the general ledger and traced back through the accounting "trail" to source documents. In essence, this is a "self-auditing" exercise. Also at this time, account accruals, deferrals, corrections, and adjustments to journal entries are entered into the computerized system, and the final product—the monthly financial statements—is put out. Quarterly closings are the compilation of three months of financial statements, and annual reports summarize the entire year's financial activity. As a staff accountant, you would perform much of the actual accounting work that results in financial statement preparation. This involves account analysis, journal entries, and performing bank reconciliations.

As you become more senior, your duties will involve more use of technical and accounting judgment, both in your own work and the decisions you make regarding staff accountants' work. Senior staff handles the preparation of more complex financial statement accounts, such as complex consolidations or foreign-currency translation.

Accountants are responsible for significant amounts of written work as well as numerical analysis. In accordance with legal requirements, financial and qualitative reports must be filed by qualified companies with various government agencies; these are prepared by staff accountants. Also, qualified organizations must file an official annual report and a 10K Form with the SEC, a report which includes, along with audited financial statements, detailed descriptions of the company's operations and policies. The staff accountant, in addition to assisting in the preparation of financial statements, may write a section of the 10K, explaining, for example, properties and leases or transactions with foreign affiliates. Similarly, senior staff assists in preparing the management notes to the financial statements, which are included in the annual report. Depending on the company's business, certain other government agencies, such as the Federal Trade Commission, or creditors and suppliers may require financial statements and detailed management reports.

At times, financial accounting functions overlap and staff accountants may perform special projects of a financial-analysis nature, such as creating specialized financial forecasts or investigating alternative investment methods. In the absence of a treasury or finance department, the controller and subordinates perform treasury-finance functions. Similarly, if a separate tax department does not exist, staff accountants may assist in tax-return preparation or tax planning, although due to the complexity of this area, a separate tax department or outside tax professional generally performs these functions.

When deciding whether to work for a small company or a large one, you must weigh the advantages and disadvantages involved. For instance, working in a small company may offer you higher visibility and exposure to top management, yet opportunities for advancement may be limited. On the other hand, large companies can offer you formalized training programs and diverse opportunities for advancement or transfer, yet the climb to higher positions may be a long one. Furthermore, you must weigh such considerations as what type of work will be most rewarding: general accountng work, where you would perform duties in all areas, or more focused work, where you would specialize in specific functional areas.

Educational background and training. The basic requirement for entry into the private accounting field is a Bachelor of Science degree in accounting. Some entry-level positions do exist for those without experience or educational background in accounting, especially in large corporations with training programs. In this case you would typically be assigned to temporary, rotating positions to facilitate immediate exposure to various accounting areas. But overall, prior accounting experience is a major factor when you are being considered for a private accounting position.

An accountant with public accounting experience, particularly with a Big Eight firm, is viewed as having excellent experience. Many college graduates join the Big Eight firms, work long enough to satisfy state CPA experience requirements, and then transfer into the private accounting sector, where they are enthusiastically welcomed. Public accounting firms do not object to this practice, as staffing present and potential clients with former staffers may ensure future client relations.

Former Big Eight accountants with advanced experience (at the managerial level and above) are often recruited directly into controller positions. In fact, some companies have a policy of hiring only accountants with public accounting experience. Thus, for college graduates desiring to begin their career in the private sector, some sort of accounting experience preferably in a public accounting firm—if only summer accounting experience—can be crucial in finding a position. Similarly, for MBAs wishing to follow the accounting career path to controller, experience is equally important. Although it is unusual, MBAs without accounting experience are sometimes hired into equivalent positions as BS graduates with experience but at larger salaries.

Attributes of successful private accountants. The most important attribute a successful private accountant needs is a high degree of skill in working with numbers. This involves the ability not only to gather and organize accounting data, but the ability to analyze and develop the data into a form useful to company management in decision making. Thus, you must be comfortable with and enjoy working with numbers; this requires an organized and detail-oriented attitude.

In addition to adeptness at working with numbers, you must possess highly developed writing skills. As you attain higher job positions you will need to be able to translate accounting data into comprehensible written material.

Interpersonal skills are also necessary attributes, especially in higher management positions. Controllers, assistant controllers, and functional department heads spend a good deal of time communicating with subordinates, peers, and superiors as well as with external auditors, government agency representatives, and legal counsel. To communicate effectively with outside parties, you must keep abreast of current professional accounting standards, pronouncements, and issues, as well as with government regulations or laws affecting the industry as a whole, your company, and specifically the accounting department and its operations. Thus, the private accountant's interests and knowledge must expand outside the scope of the accounting profession to include the entire business environment.

CPA certification. A Certified Public Account license is not a legal or professional requirement for working in private accounting, but it is advantageous. Generally, CPAs command higher salaries than non-CPAs, and in some cases receive first consideration for promotion. Although uncommon, certain state boards of accountancy will consider private accounting experience toward satisfaction of the CPA experience requirement, but only if that experience closely resembles public accounting experience. The candidate must first pass the CPA exam before petitioning the state board of accountancy for acceptance of the experience toward the license.

The National Association of Accountants (NAA) offers a "Certificate in Management Accounting," administered by an NAA-established institute, the Institute of Management Accounting. Candidates for the CMA must pass a four-part exam, and satisfy a two-year management-accounting experience requirement. To sit for the exam, applicants must either hold a baccalaureate degree (in any area) from an accredited college or university and achieve a satisfactory score on either the Graduate Record Exam (GRE) or Graduate Management Admission Test (GMAT), or be a CPA, or hold a comparable professional qualification. CMA's must also, upon receiving the license, satisfy a continuing education requirement.

While licenses in many cases are not a legal or employer requirement, they are generally advantageous in achieving a higher salary, promotion, or positive professional reputation.

INTERNAL AUDITING

The internal auditing department fulfills a company's need for self-regulation and control. It is responsible for overseeing the accounting department and other nonfinancial departments in the company. The department's major goals include protecting company assets, timely and proper recording of transactions, exposing inefficient and faulty operations, and protecting the business from waste, fraud, and loss.

Activities and responsibilities. Internal auditing is of three types: operational audits, financial audits, and regulation audits. Large internal auditing departments typically separate these three functions. All three are conducted through adherence to prepared audit plans, generally designed by senior internal auditors familiar with the audit-targeted operations within the corporation. Comprehensive written reports detailing the audit's findings and recommendations are prepared and submitted to senior auditors or the audit manager before submission to higher corporate management. The heads or managers of the audited departments receive the findings, discuss and negotiate them with the audit manager, and instigate agreed-upon recommendations. Follow-up audits determine compliance with previous audit's recommendations.

Auditing department organizational structure varies with company size. In most cases it is an independent department reporting to high-level management. Junior auditors, either entry-level or with two or three years' experience, perform the bulk of the work under supervision of senior auditors. They may also participate in audit planning or report writing.

Senior auditors, who have three years' experience and up, perform less auditing and participate more in audit planning, report writing, supervising auditing staff, and meeting with heads of audited departments.

Operational audits—the broadest in scope—determine how closely the company's prescribed policies and procedures are being adhered to in various functional areas. Dependent upon the nature of the business, the operational audit seeks to improve operations, through either stricter employee compliance to company policy, elimination of inefficient operations, or altering company policies and procedures. For example, an operational audit of a retail clothing outlet would answer the following questions: Is merchandise properly recorded in inventory records? Are customer check and credit-card transactions being authorized according to company policy? Are personnel properly trained and supervised? Are security regulations correctly followed?

The operational audit's emphasis is necessarily placed on the proper functioning of internal controls. These controls are evaluated on the basis of whether functions are segregated in a way to ensure that different people handle various parts of a transaction, thereby acting as checks on one another. Restricted access to assets (cash, supplies, merchandise) or to items used to process transactions (such as checks or purchase orders) is another feature evaluated.

Operational auditing procedures vary in nature, although most are performed on site or within the department or division audited. Two important procedures are observation and inquiry. Observational audits are characterized by observing departmental operations, facilities, and location of assets, as well as how personnel perform individual tasks. The goal is to gain a working knowledge of the actual department functions. Often these observations are augmented by comprehensive pre-audit interviews with department personnel. Inquiry audits use predetermined questionnaires to solicit different types of information, such as employees' training and background and actual job duties and how individuals perform them. In addition to observation and inquiry audits, a sampling of documentation is inspected for proper authorization and correctness of the transaction process.

Financial and regulation audits employ procedures identical to operational audits but are more narrow in scope. Financial audits are concerned with the efficiency and accuracy of the accounting function. Again, operational efficiency is the financial audit's priority: Are personnel properly trained, internal controls in place to ensure proper functioning of the accounting system, and transactions properly authorized? However, the financial audit is necessarily numbers-oriented. Samplings of financial accounts and data are analyzed through various audit procedures, including recomputation of figures and tracing transactions through the accounting system from initial entry to final disposition in accounting records.

Educational background and training. A four-year BS degree in accounting is the most common educational background of internal auditors, although general business degrees are not unusual. Emphasis is on the accounting degree, however, with computer courses or experience an added advantage, as many accounting systems and business operations are computerized.

The junior auditor position is filled generally from two sources: degreed accountants with or without experience and transfers from the general accounting department. Internal auditing work, more than an accounting background, requires a sound knowledge of the company's operations and policies. This is especially true for operational audits. Senior internal auditors are often recruited from public accounting firms. Such recruits possess two to three years' public accounting experience, and in most cases are CPAs.

Attributes of successful internal auditors. There is much similarity between the attributes required for internal auditing and those for auditing in public accounting firms. Here too, highly developed interpersonal skills are a major requirement. The internal auditing function also is often viewed as a "policing" function with defensive and even hostile attitudes often encountered. As an internal auditor, you must develop an attitude and personal style designed to assure those being audited that your role is one of assistance and fraternity. You should also *enjoy* the interaction with fellow employees, as a great deal of time is spent interviewing, observing, and working with others—both the auditors and the audited.

For both financial and operational auditing, technical know-how—specifically, accounting technical know-how—is important. Since internal auditing extends to almost every department within an organization, a general knowledge of how these departments function and interrelate is crucial.

Those persons who find the internal auditor's work interesting typically like detail work and have a spirit for inquiry. Coming up with audit findings and recommendations which may have major effects on company operations requires that you enjoy performing detective work.

The Institute of Internal Auditors conduts a twice-yearly, four-part exam leading to the Certificate in Internal Auditing (CIA). Candidates must satisfy specific experience and education requirements. Holding the CIA license gives the internal auditor both a salary and promotional edge over non-CIAs.

7

Product Management*

Product management is at the center of the marketing process. Its roots lie in the 1920s, when Procter & Gamble initiated the concept by having a "brand manager" for Lava soap. As mass production, standardization, and mass consumption have grown, so has the importance of product management.

The primary function of product management is to place a person or team in control of the activities, growth, and profitability of individual products. By concentrating responsibility in one person, it limits the adverse effects of competing influences within the corporation on product success. Many times the sales, manufacturing, or financial control departments are so caught up in their own activities and responsibilities that they lose sight of what is best for the company's products. It is the responsibility of product management to combine the diverse interests and resources of all corporate departments in such a way that each works toward the continued growth and profitability of all of the company's products. The product manager is a gatherer, a disseminator, and user of information from diverse corporate departments, including sales, market research, manufacturing, legal, advertising, and product research and development.

While product managers work with all functional areas in a corporation, they do not generally have line authority over any of them. Because they act as liaisons, they often do not have authority commensurate with their responsibilities: the functional sections work in support of the corporation in its entirety, not for any one product manager.

*This chapter is based on a paper written by Heidi L. Osroff.

The Product Manager's Job: Functions and Responsibilities

A product manager has general responsibility for all matters related to his or her specified products or brands. In this way product managers champion their brands. Product managers are especially important for small or introductory brands, as they make sure that corporate resources are obtained to facilitate growth. Without the efforts of dedicated product managers vitally interested in their product's success, many new products could be failures before they were given adequate market opportunity to prove themselves.

Product managers are concerned with everything relating to their brand: How it is made, distributed, packaged, promoted, sold. It is the product manager's job to combine and manage all of these factors. He or she must divide attention between planning for the brand's future, implementing present brand activities, and analyzing past brand achievements. Below we discuss these three activities.

PLANNING

Central to the planning process is the development of an overall brand strategy. The prime elements in the product manager's strategic planning, are the "four P's": the *product* itself, *price, places* for distribution, and *promotion*. As a product manager, it would be your task to find the right combination of these elements in order to get the highest consumer acceptance and the greatest profits for the corporation.

You would need frequently to look at the brand with a fresh eye. Is it what consumers want? Does it do what it's supposed to do? Is it the right shape, color, size? How can it be improved? Using consumer and wholesale trade feedback gathered from market reseach and sales data, you would work with the research and development department to see how you can make the brand better. Often, when one sees a brand in a supermarket with a "New and Improved" label on it, one sees the results of this process.

As a product manager, you would have control over the price of your brands. Price can be a large factor in a brand's success. If a brand's price is not competitive with similar products on the market, you run the risk of losing customers to lower-priced brands. But if a brand is priced too low, consumers may feel the product is inferior in quality, and may not purchase it. Studies are often conducted on the price elasticity of brands to determine whether increases or decreases would adversely affect sales, market share, and profits.

Distribution is crucial to a product's success. With a new product, you must develop a distribution system from scratch. Many factors have to be taken into consideration, such as cost, timing, and efficiency. You must ask if existing methods used for other products are adequate, or if new methods should be tested, such as using independent wholesalers, jobbers, or direct mail. Problems with retail shelf space must also be addressed. Will retailers buy and stock the brand? Will its shape or size present problems?

The product manager must also consider whether a new product will meet with the sales force's acceptance. A corporation's sales force is responsible for all of its products, but salespeople tend to concentrate on selling the products that bring them the highest sales results—the ones that virtually sell themselves. Salespeople may feel they are overloaded with products to sell, and as a result you may find that your brand is not being effectively pushed. Product managers often work closely with the sales force to make sure their products are receiving adequate attention and proper distribution.

Promotion is another aspect of product strategy implementation. It is concerned with many areas, from packaging decisions to special sales promotions to retail displays to advertising.

Product managers work with designers—within the corporation, at an advertising agency, or at package-design firms—to design brand logos and packaging that will meet with high consumer acceptance at reasonable cost. Packaging must be effective in design, aesthetically appealing, eye-catching, and in keeping with the image desired for the brand. It must also be convenient in shape and size. Packaging and logo changes are treated with extreme care by product managers, as there is always a danger of consumer confusion and loss of sales if changes are too dramatic or frequent.

Product managers may develop special promotions to support their brands. Many products that are seasonal in nature, such as certain items of sports equipment or food products, can have promotions associated with different times of the year to extend the product's use or even out seasonal sales. Promotions are also used to improve sales in weak markets or to support new products. Promotions can be in a variety of forms, from cents-off coupons to free trials to sweepstakes giveaways. Each promotion is planned by the product manager with help from the company's advertising agency or a separate promotions house.

Advertising is usually the largest part of promotion planning. As a product manager, you would work in tandem with account management representatives from your advertising agency to develop overall advertising strategies for the brand. This involves creative development, media planning, and advertising research analysis. Product managers spend considerable time with their counterparts at advertising agencies, both over the phone and in meetings.

In addition to the strategic planning associated with the product's physical characteristics, price, distribution, and promotion, you would be responsible for overall product financial planning, the profitability of your brands, and related revenues and expenses. Entry-level product management personnel usually prepare annual brand budgets showing expenditures planned for promotions, advertising, product changes, and how they fit in with sales forecasts. Substantial time is spent forecasting revenue figures and developing budgets. Once they are finalized within the product group, they must be approved by top management.

The goal of this financial analysis is the preparation of an annual marketing plan to show the strategic positioning deemed best for the brand in terms of product formulation, distribution, pricing, and promotion. The plan identifies what promotions and advertising are planned—and when—and what product and packaging changes are planned. Expenses and expected revenues are grouped with these activities, and profits are projected. The marketing plan will guide the activities of the product manager throughout the year.

IMPLEMENTATION

Once annual budgets and marketing plans have been approved by upper management, the product manager must implement the planned activities. This involves giving continual attention to many simultaneously occurring projects to ensure that all are running smoothly.

Implementation often involves frequent interaction with the sales force. Product managers go on "store checks" and sales calls with salespeople to learn about the brand's retail position firsthand, to see how promotions are being received, and to get an idea of how the sales force feels about the brand and the promotions behind it. Store checks help in assessing how well the implementation of the plan is going.

As a product manager you would also have formal meetings with the sales force to introduce them to new products, changes in packaging, or new advertising campaigns. These may be elaborate affairs with displays, charts, graphs, and commercials—everything shown to its best advantage to the salespeople. Because they sell brands of other product managers as well, you must compete with those product managers to make sure your brand receives good service from the sales force.

In implementing advertising plans, you would travel to locations with advertising agency personnel to supervise the making of television and radio commercials or print advertisements. You must make sure at the production site that agreed-on strategies are being executed, and that the brand's packaging and logo are being clearly and tastefully communicated.

Plans can change many times throughout the year, and you will find yourself making adjustments and adaptations as necessary. Budgets may be changed in the middle of the year and planned advertising cancelled or rescheduled. Plans which looked good on paper six months earlier may be found difficult or even impossible to implement. Various contingencies must be identified and met as they arise, necessitating careful and continuous scrutiny.

ANALYSIS

Once plans have been implemented, you must analyze the sales, market-share, brand-awareness, and profitability results. The success of all plans—product and packaging changes, promotions, advertising campaigns—is judged on their ability to result in growth and profitability. Plans are analyzed also to see how successful they were in comparison with competitive brands' activities, and to determine *why* they were or were not successful.

Data used in analysis come from a variety of sources. Most large corporations subscribe to consumer- and purchase-tracking services such as A.C. Nielsen and Sales Area Marketing Information (SAMI). These services measure market share, dollar volume, unit volume, advertising and promotion activities, and so forth. Measurements are done by product classification, such as cigarettes, detergents, confections, frozen prepared meals. You will need to follow these surveys carefully, using them to analyze your brand's position relative to competition.

Data also come from actual sales, which were made by region, and are useful in judging the success of products, advertising, and promotion campaigns. If, for instance, you are testing a new product or packaging in a sample market, you can compare sales figures from after the new concept's introduction with figures from before. You could then perform an analysis to see if profits resulting from the changes were greater than expenses associated with them. These analyses are considered in the decision whether to make the changes on a national basis. New advertising campaigns can also be tested on a local basis, and corresponding sales data used to decide whether to make the campaign national.

Product managers analyze consumer attitudes and purchasing behavior as well as sales data. They work in close conjunction with members of the market research department—who are either at the company or the advertising agency—in developing studies to measure such things as brand awareness, quality and price perceptions, and previous and "next-time" purchases. These studies are used extensively in strategy development and provide information about what changes might be made in the product and its packaging and promotion.

Career Progression

An entry-level position in product management is usually subordinate by two or three levels to the product manager. A chart of a typical career ladder is shown in Figure 7.1. The titles associated with these positions vary from organization to organization. For example, an assistant product manager can also be called a marketing assistant or brand assistant. In some companies—such as Revlon—the term marketing manager is used; product management has a different meaning there, referring to those dealing with the actual physical composition of the product—its taste, color, smell, etc.

Whatever it is called, product management is often considered an excellent path to upper management because of the exposure it gives to many facets of business. The amount of formal training involved varies by company. Some combine field trips to meet the sales force with seminars in promotion, time management, presentation skills, and the like. Others put new recruits in a "sink-or-swim" environment where they are assigned to diverse tasks that require on-the-job learning. Those considering product management must determine their own training needs and seek employment accordingly, because a whole

FIGURE 7.1

Product Management Career Ladder

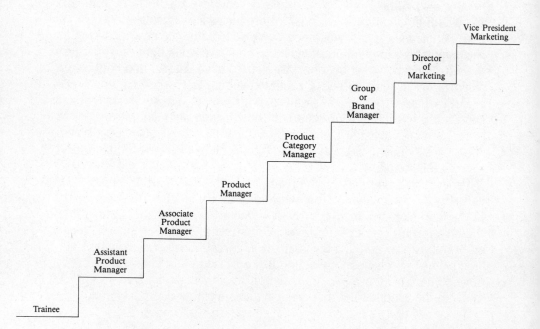

spectrum of training possibilities exists—from sink-or-swim situations to gentle supervision to formal training programs.

The new recruit remains an assistant from one year to eighteen months before moving up to associate product manager. Another year or eighteen months later he or she may become product manager. (These are only general guidelines: Promotion may take two years between levels at one company, eight months somewhere else.) These developmental periods are affected by the number of positions open, how well the firm is doing, and the individual's past work experience and performance.

Many leave product management after several years to become involved in entrepreneurial endeavors, other facets of marketing, upper management, consulting, direct response marketing, service areas (e.g., financial services), or small companies where they can run things instead of getting bogged down in the red tape of a large organization's bureaucracy. While there is certainly upward mobility for effective product managers, bottlenecks do form in the corporate pyramid structure. Therefore some choose to make a lateral or upward move to another company. It is generally considered acceptable to have a resume reflecting several well-planned moves; job-hopping with no clear pattern of career advancement is often questioned.

CAREER MOBILITY AND LIFESTYLE

Great demands are placed on the time, attention, resources, and energy of product managers. If a choice must be made between completing a report on time and keeping a dinner date, the report generally wins. While many product managers have fairly regular hours, there is generally a get-the-work-done ethic as opposed to a 9:00-to-5:00 work one. Still, there is variance: Some managers refuse to take work home at night or on weekends and are quite successful; others stay until 8:00 every night. Much of the work at the office is done in teams, with the product manager assuming the leadership role; work to be done alone gets pushed to before 9:00 AM or after 6:00 PM. Internal atmosphere, pressure, support, and competition vary widely from company to company. Work hours are a function of both personal preference and the particular company and product group.

With few exceptions, product managers and the marketing teams with which they work tend to be young; turnover is high. One product manager has called marketing a function that "worships youth and eats it up quick."

PRODUCT MANAGEMENT OR ADVERTISING?

Many product managers have seriously considered advertising at one time or another in their career. The question whether one should choose product management over advertising account work bears discussion.

One reason for choosing product management is the exposure it gives to the whole business of marketing a product, of which advertising is but one aspect. Product managers can prepare themselves for general management through their normal on-the-job experience, developing an understanding of finance, distribution, promotion, production, packaging, marketing research, and advertising.

Greater involvement and control in decision making is also considered a reason for preferring product management. The account executive at an advertising agency is accountable to both his or her own superior *and* the client, while the product manager need justify decisions only to a more senior product manager.

When you choose between specialization in the advertising field or the broad exposure available in product management, remember that skills from one field are often transferable to another, should your preferences change.

Required Skills and Educational Background

An MBA degree is usually required to enter product management today. While the degree is not essential to perform your job responsibilities, it is generally necessary in order to be hired. Opinions as to the actual value of the education received in getting the degree range from "worthless, irrelevant, totally removed from the real world" to "extremely helpful in teaching the buzzwords and giving experience through case studies, which aid in developing new product strategies." Regardless of this debate, the MBA degree is often used by companies as a screening device to distinguish those with above-average intelligence, discipline, and commitment from those who are average in ability and just seeking a good, prestigious job. Some companies have separate training programs for MBAs, and expect higher performance from them compared to other recruits.

Work experience is also valued; it is not uncommon to find product managers who have transferred from the sales force, bringing practical knowledge to the job, or who have done advertising account work or sales with another company.

Perhaps the most important skill for you to have as product manager is the ability to work with, motivate, and persuade people over whom you have no authority, but upon whom you depend to get work done. You must often persuade managers superior in rank to provide services for your brand. A person with an overly aggressive, domineering, or pushy personality will have a difficult time getting necessary cooperation. Likewise, someone who feels rebuffed by the first refusal of a staff member will not get enough support for his or her brand.

As a product manager you must be able to deal effectively with conflict. Much of the work you will try to get support staff to do will be contrary to their immediate, short-term interests. For instance, a product manager on a new product wants the finance department to support it with a lot of money, while the finance department wants to spend resources only on proven successes. Another example of inherent conflict occurs between product management and production personnel. The product manager wants to time the production of brands around consumer demand cycles, while production people want to produce on a steady, continuous basis to save money. A summary of common organizational conflicts is shown in Table 7.1.

Persuasive skills are another attribute necessary for success in product management. Product managers often act as entrepreneurs, and look at top management as investors in their entrepreneurial endeavors. As a product manager you must be able to sell top management on your ideas in order to get the resources necessary to build your brands. In this process, you are competing against other product managers for limited resources. A competitive spirit will help make you the victor.

Product management is very demanding in terms of hours and energy. You must be aggressive and dedicated, and have enough stamina to stick to it. Ambition is another quality found in successful product managers; there should be desire and ability to contribute to and participate in top-management decision making.

As a product manager, you would be a marketing generalist. Therefore you must have a solid, general knowledge of the subject. You must also come to know the brands you manage inside and out—as well as their consumers. You must not be so theoretically oriented that you are out of touch with the consumer buying the product.

High intelligence is generally considered a prerequisite for success in product management. The field attracts bright, active young people, and you must be able to keep up. Analytical skills are especially important. You will be faced with extensive information on the job, and must be able to identify key factors which can determine results. Much of this work involves quantitative analysis, so being able to work comfortably with numbers is important. You must be able to handle a great amount of detail and must have a fine sense of priorities. During a product promotion, you will be at the center of activities and must direct effectively. You must also be able to react appropriately and effectively when problems arise; overreaction creates more problems than it solves.

TABLE 7.1 _____

Summary of Organizational Conflicts Between Product Management and Other Departments*

Department	Its Emphasis	Product Management's Emphasis
Research and Development	Basic Research	Applied research
	Intrinsic quality	Perceived quality
	Functional features	Sales features
Engineering	Long design lead time	Short design lead time
	Few models	Many models
	Standard components	Custom components
Purchasing	Standard parts	Nonstandard parts
	Price of material	Quality of material
	Economical lot sizes	Large lot sizes to avoid stockouts
	Purchasing at infrequent intervals	Immediate purchasing for customer needs
Manufacturing	Long production lead time	Short production lead time
	Long runs with few models	Short runs with many models
	No model changes	Frequent model changes
	Standard orders	Custom orders
	Ease of fabrication	Aesthetic appearance
	Average quality control	Tight quality control
Inventory	Fast-moving items, narrow product line	Broad product line
	Economical level of stock	High level of stock
Finance	Strict rationales for spending	Intuitive arguments for spending
	Hard-and-fast budgets	Flexible budgets to meet changing needs
Accounting	Standard transactions	Special terms and discounts
	Few reports	Many reports
Credit	Full financial disclosure by customers	Minimum credit examination of customers
	Low credit risks	Medium credit risks
	Tough credit terms	Easy credit terms
	Tough collection procedures	Easy collection procedures

*Adapted from Philip Kotler, *Marketing Management: Analysis, Planning, and Control,* 4th ed. © 1980, p. 593. Reprinted by permission of Prentice-Hall, Inc., Englewood Cliffs, New Jersey.

Product managers need to understand and accept the corporate structure in which they work. You must know who does what, who makes decisions, and what are standard operating procedures. At the same time, however, you will have to be innovative and creative in your job. Sometimes innovation is the best way to get results, and you must be strong enough to back up your opinions with action.

A cooperative spirit is necessary in product management. You work with people all day long—supervisors, subordinates, colleagues, advertising agency personnel, and other suppliers' personnel—so you must be flexible and patient. This work requires a team effort in order to succeed, and all the individuals involved must be willing and able to participate in the effort.

8

Advertising*

Advertising is intended to persuade people of a product's benefits so that it will be preferred to another—whether the product be a detergent, savings bank, candy bar, airline, or automobile. Most advertising is produced by advertising agencies on behalf of their clients—the producers, manufacturers, or distributors of products and services. Agency employees produce what is seen, heard, or read by the public: a print ad, a television commercial, a radio announcement. Behind these finished products are hours of research, market planning, creative development, technical production, and media placement.

Compensation for the agency is usually figured in one of two ways (or a combination of the two). The traditional method is for the agency to retain a commission on all dollars spent on media. The commission is generally 15 percent, although this is open to negotiation, depending on the amount placed (the percentage may go down when media billings are substantial). The other method of payment is a fee to the agency independent of media billings. This is common when extensive research and creative work are done on a product but little media placement is actually done by the agency, as is often the case when a client wishes to introduce a new product into the market.

Departments of an Advertising Agency

The specialization of activities within an advertising agency depends on the size of the company. In smaller agencies one person may handle many diverse activities: An account representative may manage the account as well as purchase media space, write copy, or direct the technical production of a newspaper ad.

In large, full-service agencies, employees specialize in one of the following areas: research, media, business affairs, the creative area, or account management. A summary of each department's primary func-

*This chapter is based on a paper written by Celeste Kennon Rodgers.

116

TABLE 8.1
Full-Service Agency Departmental Functions

Account Management
>Client contact-liaison; supervision; coordination of agency departments

Research
>Researching directional marketing information; testing of communication effectiveness; tracking

Media
>Planning, scheduling, and purchasing appropriate media for display of ads

Business Affairs
>Traffic; talent affairs; legal clearance

Creative
>Inception, conception, production of all advertising

---

tions is shown in Table 8.1. Each provides different career opportunities. Account management is the most common area for people with business degrees. Since the account manager's job is to coordinate activities and information with other departments, we discuss account management last.

RESEARCH

The research department (1) provides information to aid in the creation of advertising, (2) tests advertising's communication effectiveness, and (3) tracks advertising's effect on consumer purchasing behavior.

In order to obtain relevant information, research—both qualitative and quantitative—is designed and carried out. Qualitative research often comprises in-depth consumer interviews, focus groups (groups of consumers brought together to discuss a product), and small-scale pilot studies. This type of research is valuable to a degree in learning what consumers think about products, but cannot be generalized to all consumers because of the small number of respondents. Quantitative research involves larger samples, follows rigorous research and statistical methods, and is intended to allow the application of results to relevant consumer groups. Through the testing and monitoring of large groups, the researcher learns about consumers' attitudes and buying habits.

The first step in advertising research is strategic research. Strategic research investigates what consumers think about a product, what motivates a purchase, what is viewed as negative or positive in a product, etc. With this information, a "creative strategy" can be developed.

The second aspect of advertising research is communication testing or copy testing, which determines how well an advertisement, produced according to a creative strategy, communicates to consumers. A commercial is tested to determine whether it persuades a consumer to purchase the product, or whether it raises any doubts, believability problems, or negative reactions.

The third part of advertising research is advertising awareness tracking. Is an ad or campaign being remembered by consumers over time? Is the ad cutting through media clutter? This can be determined by measuring consumers' ability to recognize key copy points from an advertisement. In a similar way, consumers' attitudes about a product can be traced to see if the advertising is affecting what consumers think.

MEDIA

The media department develops media plans, which indicate when a product is to be advertised and in which medium (i.e., television, radio, magazines, newspapers, billboards, etc.), how much this costs, and what demographic groups are most likely to see or hear the advertisement. The media planner must assure clients that they are getting the most from their media dollars—that the right medium is being used, at the right intervals, at the right time of day, and that the right people are being addressed. Media can be a highly technical field, and a skilled media person has to be knowledgeable about the intricacies of all media and in touch with recent developments.

As a planner, you would develop media plans to fit the specification determined by the client and advertising account management. Generally, the target audience and basic media objectives (what the advertiser hopes to achieve through the advertising media selected) are determined jointly by the client and agency account representatives. With these guidelines you would set a "media strategy." You would investigate what media would best serve the needs of the client within the allotted budget. If the television or radio medium is to be used, you must decide which "daypart" should be utilized to reach the target group most efficiently. You must constantly be aware of the viewing, listening, and reading habits of all demographic groups to effectively determine media time placement.

Once a media plan is developed and then approved by the client, the department must implement it. Media buyers enter the marketplace to buy appropriate media time and space. (Some agencies provide only media planning and contract with outside media-buying companies to do the actual purchasing.) As a buyer, you would negotiate prices for your clients' plan within predetermined cost guidelines. After purchases are made, surveillance is necessary to ensure that proper media mix is executed. The media planner must be prepared to adapt to changes in media budgets on very short notice and to know how to cancel media space already ordered or to plan for and purchase additional media space.

BUSINESS AFFAIRS

The business affairs department has responsibilities in three general areas: (1) traffic, (2) talent and residuals, and (3) legal issues. In small agencies a few people, or even one, may handle all three functions, while a large agency will utilize many people, each with expertise in a facet of business affairs.

The traffic side of the department is responsible for ensuring that advertising materials get to the proper media on time. For instance, the traffic person is responsible for seeing that a video or film copy of a television commercial gets to the proper station on time with instructions for broadcast during the designated program. This procedure can become complicated when the product is currently showing multiple commercials (called a "rotation") on local stations across the nation. When in addition an advertising campaign calls for utilization of many different media types, the traffic person has to coordinate all elements for each medium and deliver them to their destinations on time.

The talent and residuals section of the business affairs department administers payment to the talent: for example, actors in television and radio commercials. Residuals are fees paid to performers in television and radio commercials. Based on information forwarded by the media department—how many times a commercial is run, when it is run, and in how many markets—the talent administrator determines and pays residual fees.

The legal section of business affairs obtains clearance for advertisements. For example, before a television commercial can be shown on any major network, it must be approved and given network clearance. Usually a commercial is shown to the networks at early "storyboard" stages of its development to avoid a situation where the stations refuse to show an already produced commercial.

CREATIVE AREA

The creative department does what advertising agencies are famous for—creating ads. Creative staff is responsible for the content of what is finally seen, read, or heard by the public, from a cola commercial on television to a whiskey ad on a billboard to a coupon in the newspaper. It is the glamorous side of the profession, and provides the image of the free-spirited writer or artist jetting from California where a soft-drink commercial has just been filmed on the beach to a New York photography session for a cosmetic ad with elegant models.

However, while creative people do supervise the filming of commercials and attend photography sessions, this is only one part of the job. The preparation of a finished magazine ad or television commercial is a long, often frustrating process. As a creative professional, you will have to successfully translate the creative strategy—which has been developed by research, account management, and the client based on consumer research and marketing data—into persuasive consumer language. To do this, you must understand how marketers talk and what consumers hear. You must be able to defend your creative opinions, and at the same time be flexible and adaptable. Rarely is a creative idea presented, sold, and produced exactly as first conceptualized. You must accommodate to—or change—both the account representative's and client's opinions.

The basic unit of the creative department is a creative team comprising one or two copywriters, whose main responsibility is to write scripts and printed copy, and one or two art directors, responsible for visual conception and rendering. The copywriters and art directors work together to execute the idea. When the assignment is presented to the creative team, the account representative, copywriter, and art director discuss the creative strategy. A full understanding of the strategy and objectives involved in the project must exist, or there will be a substantial risk that the work will be off strategy, and hence of little value.

Figure 8.1 summarizes how an advertisement is prepared, using as an example the development of a television commercial. After the strategy has been discussed, the team considers some initial ideas. From there the art director develops a visual translation of each conceptual idea, and the copywriter creates a script. The result is a "storyboard," a board with sketches and copy showing the concept as a possible television commercial.

The rough storyboard is shown to the account representatives before presentation to the client. If there is disagreement, it is discussed by the creative team and account representative and resolved to the satisfaction of both. The boards are then colored to make them as attractive as possible, and readied for presentation.

If the client disagrees with the conceptual translation of the strategy, the creative team starts over. If all goes well, the client will probably agree with the concept and have some suggestions for the visual component and the copy.

The presentation-revision-representation process can continue back

FIGURE 8.1 _____

Outline of Creation of Television Commercial

Creative Assignment
|
Discussion within Creative Team
|
Preparation of Preliminary Storyboard Alternatives
|
Presentation to Account Team
|
Revision
|
Re-presentation
|
Presentation to Client
|
Revision
|
Re-presentation/Approval
|
Network Clearance
|
Preproduction Meeting
|
Filming
|
Editing
|
Presentation to Client
|
Final Cut
|
On-Air

and forth between agency and client several times before final approval is obtained. Once approved by the client and cleared by the medium—in this case the television networks—the production phase of the creative process begins.

The production of a television commercial translates creative concepts into the commercial. Large advertising agencies generally have a production staff with experts in the fields of film, radio, and print production. These people possess the technical knowledge to make a storyboard into a commercial. A producer is assigned to a creative project to complete the job once it has been approved by the client.

The producer reviews the storyboard with the creative team and recommends an array of outside film production companies to make the commercial. (Most commercial production is done by an outside production house rather than by the agency itself.) The producer requests bids on the job, with the lowest-priced house generally being awarded the assignment, pending approval by the client.

Once the job is assigned, a preproduction meeting is arranged among the production house, the agency's production and creative teams and account representative, and the client. Casting, set location, costumes, props, camera angles, timing, and music arc discussed and settled. Shortly thereafter, the commercial is filmed. The same group of people who attended the preproduction meeting generally attend the shooting (though a location shooting may limit the group's size because of travel costs). After the commercial has been shot, editing begins—again with agency personnel supervising an outside supplier's work. The edited version is shown to the account representative and then to the client. Upon approval, a final "answer print" is made and production of the commercial is completed. Quantity prints are made, shipped to the television stations, and the commercial is ready for airing.

Account Management

The account management department coordinates and supervises the work done by the agency and maintains the primary contact with the client. All work is generated, approved, and presented by account management personnel, although they do not actually write, render, or produce the advertising; rather, they are the managers of the agency.

Due to the complexity of developing, producing, and distributing ads, the responsibilites of and required skills for account management are diverse. First, as an account manager you would need to understand advertising thoroughly: What it is, how it works, its potential, its weaknesses, and the role it plays in marketing. Second, you must know how advertisements are made. Third, you must know how to get things done. This involves knowing how to organize work and motivate people.

Advertising agencies comprise separate departments working in specialized areas—only when all elements come together is successful advertising produced. Account management acts as liaison among departments. Since no single department can successfully deliver an ad on its own, it is the account manager who must bring it together.

ACCOUNT MANAGEMENT CORPORATE STRUCTURE

A large number of chief executive officers in advertising agencies have backgrounds in account management, as it provides an important perspective on the business as a whole, rather than one specialized area. A standard corporate structure for account management within a large advertising agency is shown in Figure 8.2. The four positions— management supervisor, account supervisor, account executive, and assistant account executive—form the core of account management. They are responsible for day-to-day managing of accounts and meeting clients' advertising needs.

As management supervisor you would oversee all work produced for a client. Like the research, media, or creative directors, the management supervisor often carries the title of senior vice president, especially if he or she handles a large or important client. It would be your responsibility to make a profit for the agency through efficient and skillful handling of each account as well as through growth in account

FIGURE 8.2

Account Staffing Through Management Supervisor

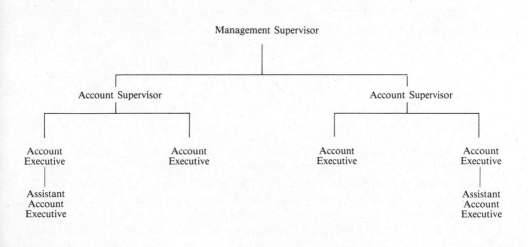

billings. You would not be involved with the everyday execution of account business, but would supervise and approve strategy development. As management supervisor you would also review and approve all research, media, and creative work before it is shown to the client to ensure that it is strategically correct and consistent with agency standards. You would work closely with senior management, including division heads and advertising directors on the client's side.

As an account supervisor (AS), you would generally handle a number of products—the exact number depends on size, complexity, and importance—and report directly to the management supervisor. After working as an AS for two or three years, you might be given the title of vice president. You would be involved in the day-to-day details of account service, supervising the work of the account executives (AEs) and the assistants under the AEs, and reviewing all research and creative media work before it is shown to the management supervisor. You would also provide strategic direction to client staff. Thus, the AS must combine a thorough, detailed knowledge of advertising and the clients' business with marketing expertise. The AS typically deals with product managers, group product managers, and advertising directors on the client side.

The next rank downward is the account executive, the primary action role in account management. As an AE, you would carry out the day-to-day work involved in client service. Anyone who hopes to rise in the advertising corporate structure must master the skills of an AE. Assistant account executive is basically a training position below the account executive; it assists in most of the AE responsibilities.

THE ACCOUNT EXECUTIVE'S JOB

The AE job function can be divided into three roles: client liaison, client contact, and agency manager. These activities together capture the essence of the advertising business—that is, making money by servicing the promotional needs of clients. As an AE, you would interact with the client, ascertain client advertising needs, and work with the various departments of your agency in the development of an advertising program to fulfill these needs. You will be successful if you produce a campaign with which the client is satisfied and on which the agency makes a profit.

Client liaison. It is important for there to be continuity in agency-client relations, therefore one person—the AE—generally deals with the client. The client tells you what is desired and you work with the appropriate agency departments. You act as a focal point of information not only within the agency, but between the client and agency.

A second reason for the AE's liaison role is that an agency must be able to present a unified opinion—i.e., an agency recommendation. If a client talks directly to a research, media, or creative person, personal opinions can become confused with agency recommendations. Although differing personal opinions are to be expected within an agency, a recommendation must be made which the agency as a whole can stand behind. The AE serves as the agency's spokesperson.

A third reason for the importance of your role as liaison is your presumed business background and knowledge. This allows you to envision with the client how a recommended advertising campaign will fit into a marketing plan, and how sales will be affected. Other agency personnel are usually without general business backgrounds and thus less qualified to do so.

Client contact. In addition to your role as a liaison person, you would serve as a contact to whom the client can turn for a variety of needs and services. Here you act as a marketing consultant specializing in advertising.

Knowledge of the client's business is essential to fulfilling this duty. Insufficient knowledge of the product can seem insulting to the client and reflect poorly on the entire agency. Therefore you are expected to be conversant with the product—what it does and how it does it, sales information, pricing. You add to this basic information your marketing knowledge—who buys it and for what purpose, consumer perceptions, advertising background, and so forth. The AE's ultimate achievement is to show the client product manager something new about the product.

Knowledge of the client's business requires knowledge of the competitive environment. No product is ever advertised in a vacuum; advertising must be designed with the competition in mind. This involves tracking and analyzing competitors' sales trends, marketing practices, and advertising. You would present such competitive analyses to the client with recommendations for future action.

Identifying special marketing opportunities for the client is a rewarding part of your job. Often your position in the industry offers exposure to promotional opportunities and media events outside the traditional media mix and unknown to the client. These opportunities are often just the thing to give a product a new push forward in a lagging market. Therefore, your recommendations to the client, if intelligently conceived and carefully put forth, will work to your benefit in several ways, among them these three: first, it shows you understand the product well enough to make suggestions to augment the effect of traditional media in marketing; second, it shows innovation and initiative; third, an accepted recommendation can increase agency billings.

Agency manager. In the role of agency manager, your third function as an AE, you coordinate the actions of other agency departments. You must be a planner as well as a coordinator. Since you are the primary source of client information to the agency, you must pass information on to the departments concerned so they can produce what is required. Careful planning and coordination must be done by you to avoid duplication of effort and time wasted. Since advertising agencies are not generally paid an hourly fee, but rather a commission on media placements or a flat project fee, the most expeditious and efficient approach to the work is likely to be the most profitable for the agency.

As an AE, you are likely to be a scheduler and recordkeeper for the account. You must be aware of key dates and events pertaining to the product, the client, and the advertising planned to support the product. For instance, you have to know when key brand promotions are taking place so that heavy advertising activity can be scheduled, if that accords with the nature of the promotion.

Your role as planner is also important with respect to the production of advertisements. You devise a production timetable when an ad is in the production phase and see that it is followed. Timetables are usually developed backward—from the due date (first air date for a television or radio commercial, material-due date for print) back to the start date—to permit enough time for each stage of production, including time for client and network review and approval at key points. Technical details on time requirements are supplied by production personnel. You must be sensitive to the details that other staff people would not generally know but that could affect meeting schedules. Often these seem to be small details, such as the times when a client will be unavailable to approve work in process; nevertheless, they can delay production. You need to look ahead to see where problems may arise, and have solutions or alternative courses of action at hand.

Your job will involve administrative work as well as planning. Meetings are the most common administrative acts; sometimes your entire work day will be spent in them. An administrative task that stems from these meetings is memo writing. Written records must be kept for documentation and referral. Sometimes it seems that memos are being written for the most trivial matters. The amount of paper which passes across your desk can be astounding, but this control function is a critical one.

Following a meeting with the client, you would write objective or goal statements to accompany the assignments given to the various departments. For instance, before the media planner can develop a plan, he or she needs to know certain key details, such as whom the client is trying to reach, in what regional areas, with what legal restrictions, etc. Your objective statements serve as formal documents to which the media planner, account team, and client can refer.

Another important part of your work as administrator would be account financial control. This involves working on financial matters pertaining to the client and agency. Generally, the advertising budget for the fiscal year is assigned for a product by the client in the final months of the preceding year. In essence, this budget is a lump sum with which the agency is to make a successful advertising campaign. The budget is broken into two parts: media and non-media. Media includes all funds for television, radio, print, or other media. Non-media supports research, creative production, traffic, talent and residuals, and so forth. One rule of thumb used in the industry is that for large package-goods accounts that use television and radio media, at least 5 percent of the total budget should support non-media. Hence, an ad budget of $7 million would have $350,000 for non-media expenses.

When total budget figures are assigned, you must prepare a budget showing where funds are likely to be spent for every month of the year. You would work with the media department to get monthly media cost estimates and with business affairs to get estimates for talent, traffic, shipping, etc. During the course of the year, you would check each month that no area involves overspending; if so, you would arrange

---

TABLE 8.2

Account Executive's Typical Work Day

8:30 A.M.	Arrive and organize work for the day.
9:00	Call client and discuss ongoing work.
9:15	Meeting with account supervisor to discuss meetings for the day.
9:45	Meeting with media department to discuss final revisions in media plan booklets.
11:00	Check with print production manager to see first proof of magazine ad. Discuss modifications to be made by typesetter before exposure to client.
11:30	Talk on phone, write memo to financial department about problem in client invoices.
12:00 M.	Lunch—maybe at desk. And read *Advertising Age*.
1:00 P.M.	Talk to radio station representative about merchandising opportunities for client to go along with upcoming media buy.
1:30	Call client to finalize time for meeting the next day.
1:45	Meeting with research team to work on preparation of rationale for next year's creative strategy.
3:00	Meeting with creative team to review their ideas for a new TV commercial in the present campaign.
4:30	Sit down in office to work on recommendation for use of cable TV.
5:45	Informal meeting with account supervisor and other account executives.
6:15	Arrange papers for tomorrow's client meeting.
6:30	Go home.

FIGURE 8.3

Percent of Time Account Executive Spends with Agency Departments

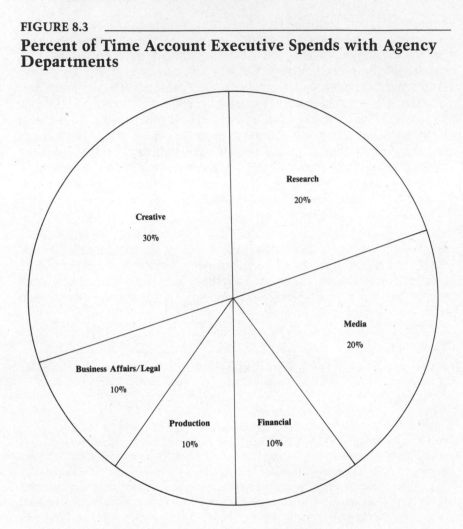

reallocation of funds accordingly. In some agencies staff personnel work specifically on budgets, relieving the AE of this responsibility. However, the AE would still be the one responsible for ensuring that overall spending does not exceed budgeted amounts.

By way of summary, a daily log of typical activities for an AE is shown in Table 8.2. The percentage of an AE's time spent with various departments is shown in Figure 8.3.

Required Skills and Educational Background

The skills required to be effective in advertising vary from department to department. Table 8.3 outlines the educational backgrounds most

TABLE 8.3

Common Educational-Experience Background by Agency Department

Account Management
BA; BS; MBA; previous business experience

Research
BA; BS (psychology); sometimes MA or even Ph.D; previous experience in related field (research supply company)

Media
BA; BS; common entry position into advertising

Business Affairs
No specific background necessary; common entry position into advertising

Creative
BA; BS; Fine Arts, Advertising Art Degree; experience in production for production personnel; "book" of ads produced

---

common to each department: account management, research, media, business affairs, and the creative area. The skills needed in research and creative, suggested by the educational background required, differ substantially from typical business skills. As such, they will not be discussed further here.

Account management and media departments tend to require similar managerial skills but different technical skills. (For more detail on media-sales-related skills, see chapter 10.) Since the AE skills required are the most general, we will focus on this position.

People in account management are generalists within a specialty field; they must be conversant in all areas of both advertising and the client's business. Many skills required of an AE are learned through on-the-job experience. Because of the need for general ability, the educational or professional background of AEs is broad. There is no one professional degree or specific, preparatory type of job experience required. Many advertising professionals feel that the best educational background is one that combines the liberal arts and social sciences with a knowledge of business. While advanced degrees, such as an MBA, are increasingly common, many people do extremely well with a bachelor's degree.

The broad, varied background that is an asset in account management should involve experience in and out of the advertising profession. Many top executives in the field have had experience advertising a number of different products. It is unwise for a new AE to work only on overly specialized accounts or ones that do not teach marketing skills applicable to other accounts. "Packaged goods" accounts (such as soap, personal hygiene products, prepared foods, etc.) make good early job experiences because of their typical use of several media, large ad budgets (especially in larger agencies), and application of general marketing principles. With a background in packaged goods, you will have reasonable job mobility within the industry. Someone who has had experience only in, for instance, retail advertising (such as department store and travel accounts) or non-consumer, technical product advertising may find it difficult to move out of these specialized fields.

Within advertising, people sometimes move from the media or research departments into account management. It is less common for people to move from the creative or business affairs department to account management. These moves can occur to another department within the same agency, to another agency, or from a support company within the profession (such as a media buying-selling company) to an agency. However, such moves are hard to accomplish, and may require a lateral or even lower-level move. For instance, a senior media planner may have to "start over" as an assistant AE. However, he or she may be able to progress more rapidly than others owing to the knowledge provided by the previous specialized experience.

People can also come into account management after working in non-advertising fields. The difficulties here are similar to those mentioned above—in particular, it is hard to get started as an AE coming from a different business background. However, previous experience can be an asset in account work, especially if it relates to the specific account for which the person is hired. This is often true when someone has worked in a sales-related area. Other fields which account management personnel have commonly worked in are communications (television, radio, print), journalism, public relations, and product management. Product management work is a good entree into account management—probably the best type of non-advertising work experience—because of the similarities between the two jobs and the valuable insights provided by experience on the client side. There is frequent movement between these two jobs, and many high-level account managers have worked as product managers. People who move from product management into account work are more likely to move into higher management positions than those entering from other professions.

PERSONAL CHARACTERISTICS

One of the most important characteristics of a successful account manager is the ability to lead others. Leadership is critical in two areas: within the agency and with the client. You must be able to coordinate effectively all of the departments of the agency on your accounts, and be able to influence colleagues so that the best work will be provided for your clients. You cannot take a retiring attitude when disagreements arise among staff departments. You must be willing to take the leadership role required of agency manager.

This quality of leadership extends to dealings with the client. It means being able to persuade the client that the agency is providing the kind of work desired and to stand firmly for your opinions and recommendations. As with the staff departments, disagreements occur between agency and client, and it is your job to influence the client effectively without harming the business relationship.

This often can be a difficult task, so another personal characteristic is needed for success in account management: tolerance. The advertising business is not famous for its calm, peaceful nature, but rather its volatility, fast pace, and, sometimes, chaos. What you as an AE can count on is problems, big and small. Most problems will eventually come to you, and it will be your responsibility to keep the system functioning productively.

There is also a need for practicality. The volatile nature of advertising creates business situations that are far from smooth and orderly. You must be able to make quick, sensible, and effective changes in plans. Advertising requires tremendous cooperation from the parties involved; sometimes they are unwilling to cooperate. Rarely do ideas make it to production without alteration, and you must be the practical intermediary between the client's and the creative person's idea of a solution. You must have a realistic and practical approach to the agency-client relationship; no single idea is so good that it should be pushed to the point where this relationship is endangered.

SKILLS/ABILITIES

In addition to the educational or business background generally required for entrance into and success in account management, there are specific skills which are crucial. One of these is organizational ability. One of your central roles as an AE would be as an organizer of people, data, time, and production elements. The enormous volume of detail involved in advertising management makes organizational ability essential. The AE who is caught in a meeting without needed information is regarded with little favor by both client and agency management.

Skillful use of information is part of this organizational ability. You must be able to organize a large assortment of data into usable, helpful tools. One example would be the preparation of "fact books," summaries of important facts and information relating to a product or industry. These generally include information about the product category and the product's place in it; product formulation; sales history; seasonality, advertising, creative, and spending history; pricing; competitive information; etc. You must be able to gather and organize these various aspects into a coherent, cogent document.

You must also be able to prepare and make oral presentations. AEs are salespeople: you must be able to sell the agency's work effectively to existing and prospective clients. This ability is partly learned through experience. With practice you should soon get a feel for what kind of information is important and what style of presentation works best.

To be a successful account manager you must work well with people. Most of your day is spent in meetings, group preparations for meetings, creative discussions, and work supervision. You must earn the respect of clients, and forge a relationship whereby the client feels comfortable coming to you for help and advice on a daily basis. Depending on the personalities and situations involved, your friendship with the client can be very valuable and rewarding. Entertaining can be a large part of this relationship, and much business can take place over lunch, cocktails, or dinner.

9

Communications and Public Relations*

We are in an age of information proliferation. At no other time has the importance of public relations (PR) and communications been more obvious. Now, with more information and more available means of dissemination, an organization must take care to develop and project its desired image, both in-house and to the public. The public relations, press, and publicity staffs either working within a corporation or serving it as an outside agency, are responsible for disseminating information, building the company image, handling controversy and conflict, and acting as spokespeople for the organization.

As advertising becomes increasingly more expensive, many organizations want to take advantage of available free press coverage. Because competition among companies in various fields for this free press is intense, the art of having an article about an organization, company, project, cultural event, or charity printed at the right time at no cost has become very important.

Various types of organizations, companies, and individuals use the services of a public relations staff: banks, consumer organizations, public utilities, theaters, record companies, hospitals, colleges, labor unions, and artists, to name a few. The location of the PR staff varies: Sometimes it is part of the marketing and advertising departments, sometimes it forms an independent department. In some companies, all the public relations functions are carried out by one person; in others, a separate person carries out each function. Alternatively, an organization can hire an external public relations firm to develop and implement a specific assignment or entire PR program.

*This chapter is based on a paper written by Ellie Schwartz.

FIGURE 9.1

The Public Relations Specialist as a Liaison

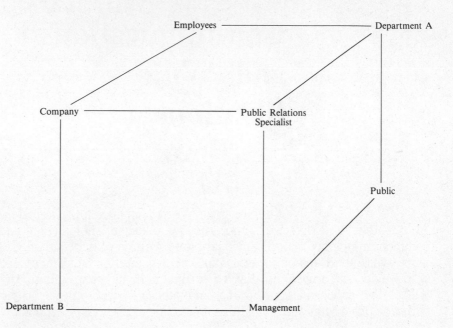

The titles of communications specialists include publicist, press agent, director of communications, account executive, director of press and public relations, promotion manager, director of investor relations, director of media relations, and director of community affairs. A PR professional working within a company acts as a liaison between its different parts and between the public, as shown in Figure 9.1. A PR professional working at a public relations firm or on a freelance basis may handle a single client or a number of separate clients and specialize in specific industries or areas of activity.

The Public Relations Firm: Services Offered

Public relations firms, like advertising agencies, handle accounts from different companies. The account executive in a public relations firm serves as the client's contact with the firm. He or she often handles more than one client—whether it be a company, product, or person—and is generally responsible for performing several PR functions personally. The public relations firm may serve its clients by carrying out research to ascertain existing public attitudes and anticipate potential problems. It then tries to create and mold the organization's image through the dissemination of information in press releases, newspaper articles, press conferences, speeches, and other channels.

Large public relations firms may have specialized departments to handle specific tasks or types of clients. Fields for which a firm might have specialists on staff include fundraising, public utilities, women's organizations, financial public relations, travel. An account executive from an appropriate department would work with a specific company; sometimes several account executives from different departments will work together when a problem requires it.

THE PUBLICIST'S TASKS AND RESPONSIBILITIES

The account executive, commonly referred to as publicist, is at the center of activity in the public relations industry. He or she may work on a corporate staff, for a public relations firm, or on a freelance basis. The freelance public-relations specialist may work as consultant to an organization or person for a contracted period of time, or may help on a special project. We shall concentrate here on specialists who work either for an organization or a public relations firm. It should be borne in mind that many of the tools, skills, and activities we discuss are common to all who work in the public relations and communications field.

The development of a publicity campaign begins with a meeting to decide the campaign goals. For example, if a rock group is releasing its first album, the meeting might examine: What image does the group want? What people does the group want to listen to its music? If a company has developed a product that is poorly manufactured—like the 1972 Pinto, famous for its exploding gas tank—the job of the publicist is to determine how to keep this information from reflecting negatively on the rest of the company's products. These are examples of day-to-day publicity challenges. Some are image building; some fall within the realm of marketing; some involve crisis management.

After diagnosis of the situation, a campaign or problem-solving strategy is formulated. Research may be needed to find out how the public is really responding to a situation. The policy regarding how to respond to a challenge is developed jointly by the publicist and client. The policy recommendation involves deciding what facts to give the public and in what way. In these activities the publicist must use good judgment.

Implementing the agreed-upon policy is next. These questions must be addressed: What tools should be used to bring the information to the public? Who exactly is the public? What media should be used? Should an appeal be made directly to the consumer in a direct-mail campaign? Will paid advertising be effective? Will someone have to make a speech? Sometimes consultation with the client's legal department, sales division, or other departments is essential in formulating and implementing a campaign. Outside organizations and resources may also be used. The publicist will use various combinations of public relations tools in the campaign's implementation. Here are the most important tools used in the industry:

Press release. The press release is a short (usually one-page) summary of a news event, written factually, with as little bias as possible. Usually a date is involved, as in "Stanley Thompson was appointed president of Worldwide Computers, 15 August 1984."

The publicist determines who receives a copy of the press release. If possible, he or she will tap the resource of personal relationships in sending out the release. For instance, if a publicist knows the editor of a certain newspaper, the release may have a greater chance of being printed. Having a general knowledge of the industry and the media interested in the industry, knowing which reporters and editors cover what types of story from what angles is imperative. Often someone who has worked for a trade paper before moving into press relations will benefit from his or her knowledge of relationships in the press and industry.

Ghostwritten article. More extensive than the press release is a full article actually written by the publicist and given to the press. Often, if the editor is a friend or the piece is exceptionally well written, the magazine or newspaper may print it with few changes under the name of one of their own writers. As a publicist, you do not get "byline" credit for what you write. Recognition comes from the company for whom you work, not from the publications that pick up your stories.

Cover letter. Letter writing is a frequent activity of the publicist. Each press release encloses a personal letter to the addressed editor, writer, or station manager that gives background information, explains why the story is important, and lists the name and phone number of a contact for further information. Letters are also written directly to consumers, investors in a company, and city officials. These letters serve the public relations function in that they distribute information selected by the client to the public.

Telephone. Important press releases are followed by a phone call to the writers or editors to whom they were sent. Again, interpersonal skills and strong relationships with members of the media are essential here. The phone call reinforces the press release by bringing it to the editor's attention. Sometimes further information is offered or an interview arranged. The phone is sometimes used to make initial contact and get preliminary information, as in finding out who at a newspaper deals with the issue being addressed. These writing and phoning tasks require follow-up work. People can lose press releases on their desks, not be in when called, or be busy and thinking of something else. Timing is essential; therefore second mailings and repeat phone calls are part of a publicist's daily schedule.

Press kit. The press kit is a folder of materials, including the press release, which gives extensive background information on the subject. The publicist includes biographies ("bios") or fact sheets (three to four pages of interesting and "newsy" information on the subject), as well as clippings of past articles and photographs that the press can use. If the press kit accompanies the release of a new book or record album, a copy may also be included. Press kits typically are distributed to reviewers and interviewers, often before a press conference, to give them background information.

Press conference. The press conference is arranged when a person or event is extremely newsworthy. It usually consists of the client or publicist making a short speech and answering questions on the issue. Arranging the date and place of a press conference requires careful planning. Press kits are compiled for reporters, who are contacted by phone and letter after a release has been distributed. A speech is written for the person holding the conference by the publicist or special speechwriting staff; rarely is it written by the speaker. A copy of the speech is also distributed, once prior to the press conference and again when it is included in the press kit. On the day of the conference, the publicist confirms all arrangements by phone, including attendance by the media. He or she greets the press at the conference, distributes information, and is available for questions.

Interview. The publicist also initiates interviews between the client and reporters. Unlike the press conference, an interview is usually held with only one or two reporters at a time. Arrangements are usually made by phone, and at this point the reporter discusses potential interview questions with the publicist. When the publicist receives a call from a reporter wishing to speak with the client about an issue, he or she makes the necessary arrangements and briefs the client about the topic at hand.

Interviews are not always singly scheduled events. A publicist may plan and schedule a large set of interviews as part of a regional or national tour.

Follow-up. After a campaign has been implemented, the effects are reviewed to determine if it achieved its objectives. Sometimes research is done to determine overall campaign policy effectiveness. An example of a research question is, "What percentage of consumers still feel the new phone company rates are unfair, compared to before the press campaign?" The publicist also reviews newspapers, magazines, and journals daily, and clips out articles about the subject of the press campaign. Copies of articles are sent to the client. The publicist maintains files of these clippings for future reference. Monitoring a press campaign lets publicist and client determine which methods were successful, which need change, and what aspects need emphasis in handling a crisis or building an image.

Public Relations Specializations

IN-HOUSE COMMUNICATIONS

As an in-house communications specialist you would primarily be involved in developing within the corporation a unified image of it and smoothing potential conflict between its different divisions. As a company grows, it becomes more difficult for one division to know the plans, aims, and goals of others. It would be your job as a corporate communications specialist to meet with press and public relations, marketing, and finance professionals from each division to determine their plans and communicate the plans of other departments. Often, the in-house communications staff also provides input at these meetings, attempting to coordinate the company's overall corporate strategy.

For example, a university with many departments may find that its chemistry and sociology departments are planning educational forums for the same week. In-house communications can inform both departments of this conflict and perhaps negotiate alternative dates. If the two events remain scheduled close together, in-house communications personnel can generate press releases and other publicity so that information from one's coverage does not overshadow the other's.

As a corporate communications professional, you must be alert to potential conflict and controversy. For example, an entertainment company with both motion picture and video divisions can experience conflicts as films move from theater distribution to the home video market. You would alert the company's divisions and the board of directors to these activities and possible conflicts.

In general, you will be expected to be a troubleshooter. You must diagnose potential problems and suggest possible solutions from a publicity and press relations viewpoint. This requires the ability to win the confidence of division heads and to participate in and observe activities to gather information. You may report to a vice president, president, or board of directors, informing them of activities in different divisions and developing with them a unified company image and policy for handling controversy and conflict. These activities require well-honed communication skills as well as the ability to get along well with all levels of staff.

You will be responsible for building a company image, possibly through writing and editing a company newsletter that conveys a sense of the organization while making employees feel they are part of it. In this work the communications specialist occasionally has the assistance of writers or editors, but generally does the work alone. In addition to the necessary basic writing and editing ability, previous experience in journalism, including layout and design, is helpful.

The communications specialist generally has a small staff, often only a secretary and assistant. To get help in coordinating programs, you may have to borrow marketing, press, and PR staff from other corporate divisions. Expert interpersonal skills and thorough knowledge of the company—its purposes, goals, different departments, and personnel—are required. You will have to work long, flexible hours and must manage your time carefully as you diagnose problems, use personal initiative to schedule meetings, and strive to create a corporate image.

PROMOTIONS

Promotions serve as a link between publicity and advertising activities. Whereas publicity involves the securing of free media space, and advertising involves directly paying for media space, promotions involve spending money in order to affect people's thoughts on a product but do not primarily describe or dramatize the product. Examples of promotions are ten-cent coupons for spaghetti sauce, free tickets to a baseball game, a free trip to Hawaii, a cosmetics brush given with the purchase of face cream, sweepstakes giveaways, and free factory tours. The organization of a large promotions department is shown in Figure 9.2.

Promotions experts conceive, develop, and execute these and other promotions. This is a highly creative area—the possible types of promotions are endless. A good promotion can often be the critical component that makes advertising, sales, and marketing strategies come together and synergistically provide results.

Promotions experts—who may work with a PR firm, advertising agency, corporation, promotions house, or on a freelance basis—interact with many departments, firms, and people in the development and execution of a promotion. These activities require planning, creativity, financial skills, and interpersonal skills, as well as the willingness to write many memos and make many phone calls to ensure that details are taken care of.

FIGURE 9.2

Example of Promotions Department

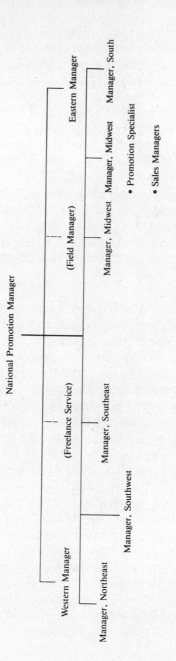

COMMUNITY RELATIONS

As a community relations professional you would make sure that people from the surrounding community know and feel good about the client or company you represent. To achieve this, you would develop programs that might include special events, sponsorships, and so forth. You might arrange for the company to offer audiovisual presentations or forums to educate the community on a topic in which it specializes: for example, a utility company might offer free information to homeowners on energy conservation. You might arrange for your company to donate money to a community event—a bicycle marathon, for example—in the interest of maintaining community goodwill.

You would meet with management and with members of the community to ascertain existing attitudes, available company resources, and the needs of the community. Using this information, you would plan educational forums, sponsorships, or other appropriate activities. After programs are developed, you would work with other PR and advertising people to make sure the community and press are aware of scheduled events. A thorough knowledge of the company, the industry, and the surrounding community is necessary. Planning and control skills regarding finance and budgeting are also helpful.

FUND-RAISING

Some organizations require the services of professional fund-raisers. As a fund-raiser, you would go into the community, to foundations, and to corporations to raise funds for the organization or for specific events. The organizations most in need of fund-raisers are nonprofit organizations, such as dance or theater companies, colleges, churches, and hospitals.

Fund-raisers must be letter writers, brochure writers, and public speakers, among other things. Knowledge of certain areas is essential: the industry the company is part of (such as the performing arts or health professions), law, and what government grants are available. You must also be familiar with financial statements and able to present a positive image of the company and its projects to potential investors.

Fund-raisers may be within the organization—as is an alumni-relations director of a college—or may be part of a firm specializing in fund-raising, usually for a particular industry. Fund-raisers may work on straight salary or commission, and are usually well paid.

A Typical Day

Since personal styles and corporate structures differ—a specialist may handle either a single function or all public relations problems—it is difficult to describe a typical day for any public relations professional.

However, some generalizations can be made. As a public relations specialist you would need to read trade magazines and newspapers for information about your client—whether person, company, or industry. You usually take care of this in the morning, so potential problems from printed misinformation can be dealt with promptly. This activity takes about 10 percent of your time. Approximately equal amounts of time are spent in meetings, at your desk writing, and on the phone, with meetings likely to dominate. About 80 percent of your time is spent on these three activities.

The lifestyle of the public relations person varies, but it is fast-paced with long hours. You may have to attend lunch, cocktail, or dinner meetings. You may also have to travel, particularly in a company with more than one branch office. You can expect to work many twelve-hour days. This is least true for the fund-raisers, who can more easily fit work into the traditional 9:00-to-5:00 day. Typically, speechwriters have the longest day, since traveling is often essential and done on their own time.

Many public relations specialists take work home and can expect to receive on occasion late-night phone calls signaling an upcoming crisis. The communications professional can maintain a family and social life, if family and friends are understanding. Hours and activities vary with the industry. The entertainment-industry professional starts at the office at 10:00 A.M. or noon, but is responsible for attending film screenings, cocktail parties, and speeches which often run into the early hours of the morning.

Meetings are common events for PR specialists. They are held to diagnose a problem, communicate ideas, develop and implement strategy, and evaluate ongoing work. The publicist, in-house communications specialist, and promotions manager spend more time meeting with company personnel than do fund-raisers, speechwriters, and community affairs professionals. Fund-raisers often meet with government committees and foundation representatives; speechwriters meet almost exclusively with the person for whom they write.

Writing is essential in public relations. Speechwriters write speeches; fund-raisers write direct-mail solicitations and grant proposals; other public relations professionals compose press kits and cover letters. Writing may have to be taken home if the workday has been full of meetings and interruptions.

Working on the telephone is crucial to public relations. Interviews are arranged by phone, and press releases are followed up with phone calls. The publicist, community affairs specialist, and promotions manager in particular make frequent phone contact with clients and the public, and are the most likely to receive phone calls from reporters or community members requesting information.

Approximately 5–10 percent of the PR professional's time is spent making presentations. The fund-raiser, spokesperson, and in-house communications specialist will spend the greatest proportion of this time making presentations to company executives and outsiders, and will therefore need more speaking ability and poise than other PR specialists. It should be noted that some industries are casual, some formal, and the public relations specialist dresses to match industry norms.

Required Skills and Educational Background

The skills needed for success in public relations vary from industry to industry, but here are the basics: As a PR specialist you must have strong interpersonal skills and be able to sell an idea or yourself. You must be adaptable: In the music industry, for example, this may mean a morning meeting with the legal staff in a pinstriped suit and then a quick change to blue jeans for lunch with an artist. You must make those you deal with feel comfortable in your presence. As part of the public relations staff in a corporation, it is especially important to treat everyone, at every level, with respect and confidentiality. Here, the ability to listen to opposing sides of a problem is essential.

As mentioned, writing skills are central to PR work. Press releases, memos to top company personnel, and endless letters to the press and public all require this. A good news style is important, as well as the ability to be concise, brief, and clear in statements and letters. Typing skills are also necessary for the quick production of press releases and memos. In this connection, familiarity with a word processor or personal computer is becoming more important in many public relations offices.

Management skills are also essential. You must manage your time carefully, and sometimes your clients' time as well. In addition, you must supervise your staff, which may be small or may be an entire department of publicists, speechwriters, fund-raisers, assistants, and clerical and secretarial personnel. And since this is a time-pressure industry, you must be able to manage both time and people efficiently while maintaining good interpersonal relationships. You must also know your company or client thoroughly and be able to diagnose problems before they happen. Therefore, many successful public relations people have had widely varied work experience and have held other positions in the industry, the press, or the company in which they work. However, someone working in corporate public relations generally chooses and stays with a specific industry because specialized knowledge is so important.

You will probably need research and quantitative skills. For the beginning professional, the ability to do both library and survey research has become essential. For the more advanced professional, being able to understand research and interpret statistical findings is important.

Finally, public relations professionals are finding legal and financial knowledge important. Budgeting a department and anticipating possible crises from a legal or financial viewpoint are important skills.

Job qualifications differ for public relations professionals, depending on where they are hired and what they are hired to do. Minimally, you must have a bachelor's degree. Major-study areas vary, but courses in journalism and writing are expected. Many firms will not hire someone without previous PR experience. Job applicants with graduate degrees in law, journalism, marketing, or business will begin at higher levels than those with only a bachelor's degree.

However, there is no one career path typical for the public relations professional. Those with a bachelor's degree are often advised to begin as a secretary or assistant in the public relations department, in order to learn the business and develop contacts. From there, the trainee will move into a junior role in one of the public relations positions—publicist, speechwriter, in-house communications specialist, etc.—gradually becoming familiar with the duties and skills of each and finally settling permanently into one of these positions or becoming a department supervisor. Since corporate vice presidents are often responsible for communications and public relations, there is upper management potential for the press and public relations specialist.

10

Sales and Buying

Business in capitalistic societies functions on the basis of transactions—the selling of goods and services to purchasers. These goods are either made by the business or bought from the maker. This makes it necessary for business organizations to employ both sellers and buyers to carry on these transactions.

When viewing business in this way, the economic realms of activity can be separated into two spheres: source markets and end markets. A source market is one in which consumers, either business or private, are supplied with goods. It comprises the sellers in the economy. The goods being supplied may be raw materials or semifinished goods such as lumber, steel, flour, cotton, or oil, or they may be finished manufactured products such as houses, automobiles, apparel, machinery, and appliances. End markets are those in which buyers purchase materials, either for consumption, for transformation into other goods, or for resale.

Every transaction involves both a source and an end market, and every business functions in both markets. A good example is a car manufacturer. It is an end market participant as a purchaser of steel, rubber, and glass for use in the manufacturing process, and a source market participant as a seller of automobiles. Another example is a retail outlet which functions in end markets as a purchaser of manufactured goods, and in source markets as a supplier of these goods to consumers.

To survive, a firm must purchase goods and sell goods at prices that will make profits. Retailing again serves as a good example: A store that purchases desirable manufactured goods and sells them at competitive prices stands a good chance of prospering. If it buys products with little consumer demand or offers its merchandise at prices few will pay, its chances for success are reduced.

Businesses tend to concentrate their human, financial, and time resources in the market where competition is most keen and they are needed most. For a manufacturer of detergent products, the materials it purchases in the end market for use in manufacturing are fairly stable in supply, price, and quality; the competition is not dramatic. But the reverse is true in the source market, where its products are competing against many other products similar in price, availability, and quality. As a result, a detergent manufacturer puts more emphasis on its sales employees in terms of their number, status, and compensation than on its purchasing personnel. This is the case with most manufacturers of brand products.

In contrast, a department store faces hard competition as an end market participant, because it must purchase the exact products customers will want to buy later. This requires a great deal of expertise in advance planning and judgment on the part of buying personnel. Consequently, merchandise buyers are recognized as higher in status within the organization than salespeople.

Employment opportunities in selling and purchasing are extensive and varied. The most common career opportunities are described in the sections that follow. It should be remembered that although we have separate sections on selling and purchasing, every transaction involves both a seller and a buyer.

Sales

Selling is the process of persuading a customer to buy something or to act favorably upon an idea that has significance to the selling unit. The emphasis is not on the exchange of money between buyer and seller. Nor does what is being sold have to be a tangible object; it could be an intangible product, such as securities, insurance, or advertising time. Selling can be an impersonal process as well as an interpersonal one; advertising, product displays, and promotional merchandising are impersonal forms of selling.

Selling is today part of the total marketing process, where persuasion is used to convince customers of a product's suitability for satisfying their needs and wants. The selling process starts with a rational analysis of how customers' existing and potential needs can be satisfied through purchase of a product or service. The need might not be perceived by the customer; therefore the selling agent may have to generate interest in the product by persuading potential customers of the benefits which could result from its use. For instance, a manufacturing company might think its production process is fine—until a machinery salesperson shows them how a new machine can improve efficiency and lower costs.

The service orientation of sales is inherent in these activities. Sales professionals, like educators, dispense information potentially helpful to customers. They are a type of consultant, matching solutions with customer needs.

Because of this service orientation, as a salesperson you must be concerned with the benefits that accrue to customers as a result of a sale as well as the benefits to yourself and your company. Therefore, although selling a product to a customer who does not need it, or at a price too high, might result in a quick profit, it would not help in the development of a long-term profitable relationship. You should strive to be seen by customers as a reliable source of quality products or services at fair prices.

To be able to fill the service roles of consultant-educator, you must have extensive knowledge of both the products you represent and the customers. You must know what your product does, how it does it, how it is used, and the benefits it offers. Regarding customers, you must know and understand their needs: what they do and how, what problems they face, and their personal concerns regarding the product and its function. In addition, you must be knowledgeable about competition in the market and your product's relative weak and strong points. This requires a great deal of advance learning on your part before you start selling.

For these reasons, most companies train new salespeople before exposing them to customers. The type of training varies significantly according to company and type of product being sold. Some companies have training programs running one or two years, while some have on-the-job apprenticeships with experienced salespeople.

There is a great deal of opportunity for movement from sales positions into other corporate departments—most commonly into marketing and product management. A schematic representation of career paths in sales and product management for a large consumer manufacturing firm is shown in Figure 10.1. The role of product manager was discussed in chapter 7.

Five areas of sales are discussed below: industrial sales, securities sales, insurance sales, real estate sales, and media sales.

INDUSTRIAL SALES

Industrial sales professionals sell products to organizations rather than to retail consumers. In many firms the industrial sales force is the primary distribution network, especially when the product is specialized or used in other manufacturing processes. Activities in industrial sales can be separated into three main areas: maintenance of present customer relations, solicitation of new customers, and interaction between marketplace and manufacturer.

FIGURE 10.1

Possible Career Paths within and between Sales and Product Management

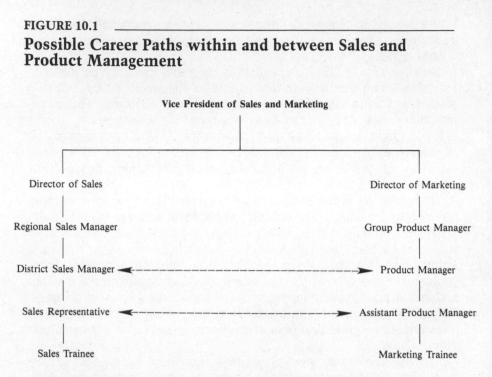

The majority of a manufacturer's sales come from present customers. Therefore, this group of customers cannot be ignored. As a salesperson, you would call upon these accounts on a regular basis to fill orders and arrange details of delivery and payment. At the same time, you would attempt to sell them more of the product and introduce them to new products or new benefits of existing ones. These calls are generally seen as service calls.

In addition to maintaining existing accounts, you would try to open new accounts with promising clients. This involves investigating the marketplace to find out about new businesses that need your products or any businesses that are receiving poor service from competitors. The more successful salespeople also look for opportunities to create demand where seemingly none exists.

After potential customers are identified, you will need to analyze the particular needs of each. Then you must develop a sales presentation tailored to these needs, contact the potential customer, and arrange a sales call. If your presentation is successful, you then service the customer's account.

Since salespeople are the ones in a corporation most in contact with customers, they can provide important information to management.

They are often in the best position to steer product development changes or suggest new products that will find market acceptance. Also, salespeople are often the ones most in touch with the competition and can judge when special opportunities arise.

The sales force can provide data used in the corporation's market analyses. Weekly or monthly sales figures provide information for tracking advertising and promotion effectiveness. Because this data is critical for market development, reporting is an important responsibility of sales representatives.

Since salespeople are the principal representatives of their corporations to most industrial customers, they must be able to maintain and enhance their organization's reputation. They must be knowledgeable about their customers' manufacturing needs and their products' applicability to those needs. To facilitate this, many companies put new industrial salespeople through training programs before sending them into the field.

Experience in sales is not necessarily important in getting an entry-level job, and many companies actually prefer to hire people with no experience, so that they can train them exclusively in their selling methods. Educational requirements vary by company, although a minimum of a bachelor's degree is necessary in many large organizations. Industrial sales of complicated technological products (e.g., conveyor belts, elevators, computers) requires special training; often people with technical bachelor's degrees are hired for these positions. It has become common to see people with MBAs selling high technology or high-priced items, because manufacturers feel that they are better able to analyze a customer's business needs and speak the jargon of business clients.

Positions in industrial sales are often viewed as good training for upper management positions. A large percentage of the presidents of American corporations have sales backgrounds. Salespeople who have the inclination and ability to manage as well as sell have excellent opportunities to move into sales management.

SECURITIES SALES

When investors want to buy or sell securities, they call on securities salespeople, known as stockbrokers or account executives. When stockbrokers receive such an order to buy or sell a security, they relay it through the brokerage firm's order room to the stock exchange where the security is traded. If it is not traded on an exchange, the order is sent to the firm's trading department, which buys or sells it in the over-the-counter market. (A fuller description of department functions in large securities brokerage firms is given in chapter 3.)

In addition to arranging for the execution of buying and selling orders, stockbrokers work as financial counselors for their clients. This can involve advising on the complete financial portfolios or merely supplying the latest price quotations for securities in which the client has an interest. As a broker, you would help clients make financial decisions by furnishing information on the advantages and disadvantages of an investment and the activities and financial position of the corporation represented.

Securities firms make commissions on the trades they execute on behalf of clients. Your income as a broker would be dependent on commissions from trades you arrange. Therefore, you would constantly try to be aware of opportunities that you could recommend to clients, either to expand their existing portfolio with attractive new securities or sell currently held ones and buy better ones. You should maintain a high awareness of the investment market to be able to spot attractive opportunities. For you to do this you will need good working relationships with business people outside the firm and colleagues in your firm (especially colleagues in the research department).

Stockbrokers often specialize in either small, individual clients or large, institutional clients. Individual investors are handled by brokers who specialize in "retail" trade. Institutional investors can be corporations, insurance companies, charity organizations, or other organizations with large amounts of money to invest. Brokers specialize so that they can better serve the needs of their clients. Different clients have different expectations from investments, and you have to be able to recommend securities to match these expectations.

Brokers often specialize also by the type of security sold, such as corporate common stock, corporate bonds, municipal bonds, commodity futures, or stock options, to name a few. By limiting attention to specific categories, a broker can more easily become an expert in a field. Having such expertise makes the information and advice provided to clients more valuable.

As a stock broker you must have highly developed oral communication skills. Most of the work you will do with clients will be over the phone, and you must be able to develop rapport without the benefit of face-to-face interaction. You must also be able to deal with substantial pressure. When there is a great deal of activity on the exchange, the pace quickens, and you act as a funnel for information between the financial markets and your clients.

Regardless of the pressures you face, you must be able to maintain and handle efficiently the details involved in buying and selling securities. You must be well organized to be able to analyze what security fluctuations mean to each of your clients and recommend trades when appropriate. While the buying and selling activity of your job occurs between 10:00 A.M. and 4:00 P.M., successful brokers are alert to opportunities twenty-four hours a day.

Almost all states require that brokers be licensed. In order to obtain a license, you must pass an examination and register as a representative of the firm you work for, according to the regulations of the securities exchanges where your firm does business or of the National Association of Securities Dealers (NASD). The examination, given by the Securities and Exchange Commission (SEC), the NASD, or the exchanges, assesses your knowledge of the securities business. It covers such topics as investment terminology and law, options, bonds, the SEC, and the Federal Reserve System.

Stockbrokers come from a variety of educational backgrounds, but people with business degrees are especially welcomed. MBA's are actively recruited by large security-brokerage firms, especially for work in institutional sales. Most large firms provide training for new brokers through formalized programs. During the training period, new employees are exposed to the securities market as a whole and its specialized segments. They are also trained in subjects needed in order to pass the state brokerage examination. These training programs last anywhere from four months to a year, depending on the firm.

INSURANCE SALES

Insurance salespeople sell various types of insurance policies, including life insurance, property and casualty insurance, health and accident insurance, annuities, and pensions. Customers of insurance policies include individual families and homeowners, corporations, and other large institutions. Because of the different needs of clients, insurance salespeople usually specialize in serving one client group.

Insurance salespeople can be either agents or brokers. An agent works for a single insurance company and sells only policies the company underwrites. A broker is not under exclusive contract with one company; he or she places policies with whatever company best meets client needs.

Insurance sales involve three main areas of activity: identification and solicitation of new clients, client-needs analysis, and client-policy servicing.

Much of an agent's or broker's time is spent trying to find new insurance customers. For salespeople who sell to individuals, this can be done by participating in civic affairs, keeping track of new community arrivals, and monitoring new home purchases. Those involved in institutional sales become aware of new prospects by following business trends in a specific area or industry. For instance, a salesperson would read trade and business journals to find out about new companies that might need group health insurance for an expanding work force or property insurance for new facilities. Once potential clients have been identified, the salesperson approaches them and arranges a sales presentation.

As an insurance salesperson, after having convinced a customer of a general insurance need, you would analyze specific needs. With individual customers this may involve no more than discussing existing financial constraints, future expectations, and finding appropriate pre-packaged policies. With your extensive knowledge of the insurance field, you can often make customers aware of insurance gaps they may not know exist. With institutional clients, however, the process can be complicated, for policies are customized to fit their particular requirements. Insurance policies can be forms of investment as well as expense for clients, so sales personnel often need to give advice on the financial aspects of policies.

When a policy has been sold, your involvement with the client does not stop. You have to be available to answer questions, help in claim settlement, and provide detailed records of policy status on a regular basis. You also should continue to analyze the client's insurance situation to recognize new needs and recommend policy modification or extension. The service aspect of insurance sales is important, because existing customers represent an important source of new business.

Brokers receive commissions from the insurance company that underwrites the policies they sell. Most agents working for a single insurance company are kept on salary for a number of years, after which they receive commission alone. Therefore, as with most sales positions, income for insurance salespeople depends to a large extent on the amount of energy and time put into selling—and its success. The educational backgrounds of brokers and agents vary. Most companies look for mature individuals who are politely persuasive rather than overtly aggressive.

REAL ESTATE SALES

Real estate sales involves working in the buying and selling of real estate property. People in real estate sales are known as agents, and are either brokers or salespeople. A broker is someone who is licensed by the state he or she practices in, having passed proficiency examinations and worked in the field for a minimum period. Brokers are the only people in real estate legally able to close a deal on behalf of a client and receive a commission. A salesperson does the work involved in real estate sales but does not formally close deals. In most states one must work as a salesperson before obtaining a broker's license. Salespeople usually work for or in connection with a broker. As payment for a sale they have arranged, they receive a percentage of the commission received by the broker.

As a broker you would be an intermediary in three-party transactions (the other two parties being the seller and buyer). Brokers are prohibited by law from collecting commissions from both sellers and buyers without full disclosure to both parties. This law exists so that brokers cannot represent conflicting interests in a sale. They work primarily in the interest of one party, and negotiate the best settlement for that party, who pays the commission. It is most common for a broker to work as the agent for the property seller.

Real estate sales can be divided into four main areas of activity: solicitation of sellers, solicitation of buyers, negotiation, and sale closure.

Solicitation of sellers involves the securing of properties for sale, known as listings. As an agent, your ability to get listings will depend upon your reputation for selling properties quickly at advantageous prices; therefore, personal contacts and connections are important. You may also solicit listings through paid advertising and direct solicitation of property owners, known as principals. Once property listings have been acquired, you must secure buyers for them as quickly as possible. Personal contacts and reputation are important here, too, as referrals from other buyers frequently result in sales.

After you find a suitable buyer for a property, terms of sale are negotiated through you. Rarely is a property sold for the exact price a seller asks: usually an interested buyer offers a lower bid. This process is often long and complicated. Here you act as an intermediary between seller and buyer, and as an advisor about terms involved. Terms must be agreed on to the mutual satisfaction of both parties before the sale takes place. Brokers often help buyers develop financing arrangements and secure funds from financial institutions.

After agreement is reached, you assemble the legal documents involved in the transfer of funds and property titles. Working with both seller and buyer, you then explain closing costs and discuss financing arrangements. You function as a collector in the actual payment for the property. For all this you must understand thoroughly the legal aspects of property transfer.

Real estate brokers tend to specialize in selling particular types of property, because of different issues and clientele involved. The largest number of real estate agents sell single-family residential units. Many sell homes on a part-time basis and have other sources of income. Fewer agents are involved in the selling of commercial and investment properties and leases, but the amounts of money involved here are generally much greater. This type of property sale also requires a greater amount of knowledge, not only of real estate but of finance, accounting, law, architecture, and construction. It is rare to find commercial real estate agents working on a part-time basis.

As a commercial real estate broker, you must understand what a property means to the party who owns it and to the party who wants to own it. In other words, you must be knowledgeable about market factors in a particular area: population figures and trends, number of employed individuals, means of employment, per capita income, area business revenues. With this information you can make accurate value appraisals, a crucial skill.

You must also be knowledgeable about your clients, especially about their needs and expectations in buying, selling, or leasing. You must be able to match the right buyer with the right seller, or you will be unable to negotiate the sale. For instance, if you have a listing for fifteen thousand square feet of prime retail space, you must analyze correctly what type of establishment could be suitably located there. You must then convince the appropriate retailer of the advantages the opportunity offers.

The educational backgrounds of successful real estate agents vary. Many feel that there is little correlation between educational level and success in this field. However, in recent years the real estate industry has put increased emphasis on professionalism among salespeople and brokers. There is no doubt that a person with knowledge of the financial, accounting, and legal issues surrounding a real estate investment opportunity will be able to determine and communicate value better than someone without that knowledge. For these reasons, many feel that a business degree, especially an MBA, is useful in real estate sales.

However, an MBA is not a key to success or even a job in real estate. Experience and interest in the field are more important. As already mentioned, in order to obtain a broker's license you must have experience as a salesperson in addition to the ability to pass state examinations. Success comes only to those who have enough interest in and dedication to this work to put in the long hours necessary.

The salary structure of real estate also demands a great deal of dedicated work. As a broker or salesperson you would receive a commission when a sale is actually made and funds are transferred. Often you would work for months or even years on a deal before the sale is consummated, and it is not uncommon for a deal to fall through after months of work. You must be able to live on money you have until you receive the commission. The beginning of your career is the most difficult, as you have not yet established contacts from which to solicit clients. When salespeople go to work for a large realty company, they are often given a beginning salary, drawn against future commissions, to get them going.

In few other career areas is salary so tied to effort as in real estate. If you are not out in the market soliciting sellers, finding buyers, and closing deals, you make no money. On the other hand, in few careers is the earning potential as high. Some agents make an entire year's salary on closing one deal, and a few have established their career in one sale, becoming a millionaire over night.

MEDIA SALES

Media salespeople sell advertising space and time: space in magazines, in newspapers, on billboards, and in other printed media; time on radio and television. Print sales representatives can work for a single magazine or newspaper, or for a group which controls many periodicals. Representatives who sell billboard space work for large companies such as Foster and Kleiser or Outdoor Pacific, which own billboards all over the country. Radio and television time is sold by representatives of local "spot" stations for a particular regional market or by network representatives for national coverage.

As a media sales representative, you will usually have advertising agencies as clients. This is especially true for television network and national magazine sales representatives, who deal directly with advertisers, rather than with the advertising agency, only at special events such as press conferences, advance screenings, or special parties. However, representatives for local television and radio stations and newspapers will solicit advertising directly from local businesses as well as from ad agencies.

Many people describe media sales as a "relationship business" because of the emphasis placed on personal relationships between "reps" (as media salespersons are called) and advertising agency personnel, especially media planners and buyers. As a rep, you must know who is making the decision at an agency about what media to recommend to a client. You must maintain good relationships with these key people so that the station, newspaper, or magazine you represent is considered in all media plans for their clients.

Competition between media is extreme, and you must be able to convince media buyers that your vehicle is best. Sometimes an agency will buy spots on only two of the three national television networks for a particular media schedule; representatives from the three networks must work hard to make sure they are one of the two. Likewise, when planning a print advertising campaign, an agency might decide that its budget can buy space in only one women's magazine; in this situation a rep might have to compete with four or five other similar magazines for the business.

Because of the level of competition in the communications field, there is a great emphasis on service. You must be responsive to the needs of your clients. This can involve allowing advertisers to change media schedules at the last minute, switch time or location spots to take advantage of special opportunities, or cancel media space or time with little penalty. You must also be able to negotiate with clients. The emphasis is on building and maintaining a good relationship not only for the present sale but for future business as well. It is good for sales reps to remember that if they can help their client—the ad agency—look good to the advertiser, they will be in a better position the next time a media buy is made.

Pressure in media sales is high, especially time pressure. Magazines and newspapers must go to print, and television shows must air; therefore space or time must be sold. A network sales representative does not leave the office before selling the time he or she is responsible for on a particular night. It is common for schedules to be changed at the last minute, and the rep has to keep on top of all space or time sold. A rep must also work closely with the advertising agency to make sure that all materials needed for an ad are received before it runs. This is critical in print media, where material is often received as the publication is going to print.

Entertainment is a large part of media sales work. It is not uncommon for reps to have lunch or dinner with clients two or three times a week. To be successful, you must have the willingness, ability, and stamina to socialize.

Extensive knowledge of the communications and media field will be important to you as a sales rep. This includes knowledge of the ratings system, audience tracking techniques, and how media space is priced (CPM—cost per thousand). In this way you can know what your competitors are doing, and how to best sell the benefits of your medium.

Because of the specialized knowledge needed to be a media sales representative, companies often require that new employees have previous experience in some area of communications. Sometimes people move from smaller companies (local radio and television stations or newspapers, which are more likely to hire people without experience) to larger ones. It is also common for people to move from advertising agencies to media sales. In recent years some large communications firms, especially the three national television networks, have become interested in hiring people with advanced business degrees such as the MBA. These network selling jobs are highly regarded and hard to get. Many times people first have to establish their worth in other departments or work in local sales.

Buying

Buying can be categorized into two general areas: industrial buying and retail buying. Industrial buying involves the purchase of supplies, raw materials, and equipment to sustain a business's manufacturing or transformation process. For example, film manufacturers must buy the chemicals necessary to produce film. Retail buying is the purchase of goods for subsequent retail sale where no manufacturing or transformation of the purchased goods takes place (e.g., purchase of clothing for resale by a department store). Industrial buyers are generally referred to as purchasing agents; retail buyers simply as buyers. We shall discuss retail buyers first.

RETAIL BUYERS

Buyers for retail companies are responsible for buying the merchandise sold in retail outlets. Anything one sees in a store is there because a buyer decided to buy it. In a food retail outlet most products for sale are bought on a regular basis; usually the same things are reordered as stocks are depleted. In this respect retail food buyers are similar to purchasing agents. In large department stores, which sell many different types of merchandise, what is sold changes frequently, especially fashion merchandise. Purchasing items for a department store is a complicated, demanding, and exciting job. The career path in retail buying is shown in Figure 10.2.

The primary aim of a buyer is to purchase products that will satisfy customers and make profits for the store. To accomplish this, buyers must stay closely in touch with store customers and what they are buying as well as with the merchandise itself. Buyer activities can be divided into three main areas: analysis, acquisition, and merchandise sales.

As a buyer, you would spend much time analyzing sales reports. Sales reports are compiled from all retail outlets; they show how well merchandise is selling. By studying these reports, you can determine what is selling and what is not, and then look for explanations. Buyers use sales reports and other data to determine buying trends. Demand estimates are also made regarding how much of what items should be bought. Trend analysis and demand estimation are especially important when planning future seasons. Often you will have to buy merchandise

FIGURE 10.2

Retail Buying Career Progression

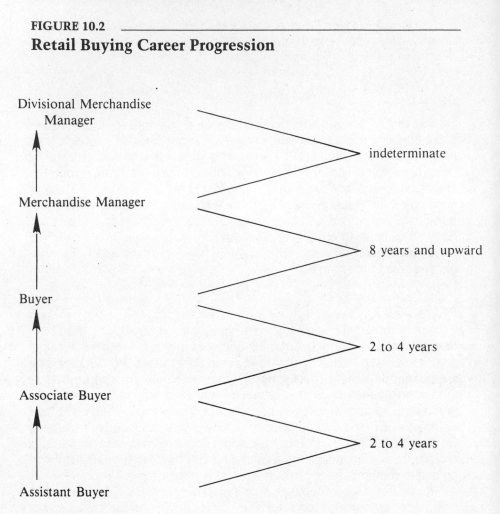

months in advance, and these analyses must be used in the decision-making process.

Buyers also analyze their merchandise in comparison with the competition. This involves checking competitive stores' merchandise on site and studying their advertising and promotion. Buyers who work for department stores that are not fashion leaders often determine what merchandise to purchase based on what the trend-setting stores have in stock at present.

Analysis must be performed of information related to past purchases, present purchases, and projected future purchases. A large part of this information comes in the form of numerical data, with little or no text. You must be able to translate these numbers into ideas useful in decision making. You can also gather information through first-hand experience on the selling floor. By seeing how merchandise is displayed and sold, you can gain insight into its success or failure. In summary, you must look to many sources for information useful in analysis, and not expect it necessarily to be presented in coherent, comprehensible, and usable formats.

Analysis supports your primary function—to buy merchandise for retail sale. To do this, you must be intimately familiar with the merchandise—how much it should cost, how much it can sell for, and what determines quality. You must also know the vendors selling it. It takes time to get to know vendors, and you as an assistant buyer would spend time early in your career with an experienced buyer meeting and establishing contacts with the trade. Good working relationships with vendors can help you get favorable terms in price, payment schedule, and delivery time when you make purchases.

To meet vendors and find out what is available in the marketplace, buyers often attend trade shows related to the products they buy. They also read trade newspapers and magazines on a regular basis. Visiting showrooms is another way of seeing what products a vendor has and assessing quality versus price.

You would usually go to the source of merchandise when buying. This can mean traveling to wherever a manufacturer is located; trips to Europe and the Orient are common for fashion buyers. How often and when you travel depends on what type of merchandise you seek. Products that are seasonal, such as fashion products, demand that you travel to the sources at the time when the merchandise is being made. Summer fashions are usually bought in the fall, fall-winter fashions in the spring. It is harder to predict travel times for buyers of nonseasonal products.

Before merchandise is bought from suppliers, you must decide what prices are appropriate for retail sale. Pricing decisions take into consideration previous sales trends, quality of merchandise, and the competitive situation. You must also follow corporate guidelines in determining prices. When making a pricing decision, you must think of the profit margin at the first selling price and at percentage markdowns if the merchandise does not sell quickly. You must find the price that will balance customer acceptance with desired profits.

Buyers in most retail organizations work with personnel from other departments, such as store operations, inventory control, wholesale trackers, and quality control to make sure merchandise reaches retail outlets properly. It is important for you to know what is happening to merchandise you have bought, so that you can analyze sales results. You need to work with all outlets of a store to make sure that sufficient stock is available where it is needed.

You may be involved in determining display and stock requirements for merchandise you have bought. It is in your interest that the merchandise be attractively displayed so that customer interest will be high. Depending on position and corporate policy, you may also be involved in the recommendation, execution, and approval of advertising and promotions in support of merchandise.

PURCHASING AGENTS

The role of the purchasing agent is to identify the best possible suppliers to provide the products the firm needs. Hence, purchasing agents and industrial salespeople are on opposite sides of a transaction. The activities and responsibilities of purchasing agents are quite similar to those of buyers. However, as a purchasing agent, you would (1) purchase a wider variety of goods, leaving you less opportunity to specialize in a product area; (2) tend to spend more of your time on the phone or alone analyzing product features or literature, and less time traveling or interacting with suppliers; (3) often make repeat orders for the same supplies where product price and quality are comparable among suppliers—which makes delivery, billing, and service more salient purchasing factors; (4) have little seasonality in your purchases unless your firm's product lines are highly seasonal; and (5) make purchases to replace inventory based on economic order quantities rather than estimated market demand. Since purchasing agents are not buying goods for resale, they are buffered from market activity. Their work activities are more predictable than buyers, although not necessarily less complex or less interesting.

Required Skills and Educational Background

SALES

As in most careers, success in sales necessitates in part a high degree of intelligence. We have already spoken of the amount of knowledge you as a salesperson would need to bring to your job: knowledge of your product, your customers' businesses, and market conditions in general. But the intelligence necessary in sales is more intuitive. You must be able to retain information and manipulate it to meet the demands of the moment. This requires creative analytical ability as well as intelligence.

Communication skills are equally important for salespeople, especially verbal skills: Being articulate is considered a prerequisite to a sales career. Persuasiveness and negotiation abilities are crucial.

Sales jobs are not routine in nature; therefore you must be adaptable and flexible. The ability to adapt well in response to situational cues requires that you be sensitive to surroundings, and that you know what type of behavior is called for at what moment. This means having a number of well-thought-out tactics in mind, combined with an equal number of alternative plans if the initial approach fails to get a favorable response.

Basic personal management skills are also important for salespeople, since much work is performed according to your personal time schedule. You must be able to identify what activities should be done when— for instance, how much time should be spent on sales calls versus preparing for them. Time spent traveling must also be allocated, and proper attention given to customers both near and far.

The attribute most often associated with successful salespeople is aggressiveness. Although it is certainly true that you ought not to be shy and retiring, aggressiveness should not be exaggerated. *Perseverance* describes well how successful salespeople channel aggressiveness. Many say that the selling starts when the customer says no; often you will have to stick to it through dozens of rejections before making a sale.

Many people find the rejections salespeople face disheartening and choose not to stick with it despite the financial rewards. Successful salespeople are resilient in the face of rejection and find satisfaction in the challenge of each new sale. Typically, they are motivated by the job itself: they love selling, not just the possibility of high salaries. Their ambitious nature is not just focused on making more money each year, but reflects the thrill of meeting and breaking quotas set by themselves and their companies.

Honesty and integrity are two important attributes for salespeople hoping for success in contemporary corporate life. Sales positions are no longer typified by the traveling salesperson looking for his next naive customer. Today the emphasis is on building a steady, profitable salesperson-customer relationship, and nothing harms this more quickly than unethical practices. A reputable company tries hard to maintain its good reputation—built over years—and does not want to ruin it for the sake of a quick sale.

Salespeople are typically independent by nature and enjoy the freedom sales careers offer. This is seen as a positive attribute by most employers, but successful salespeople have learned that independence does not give them the right to ignore company rules. You must follow standard procedures, especially if you are hoping to advance to a sales management position.

Finally, you must show self-confidence when dealing with customers, so that they will have confidence in you and the products you sell. A summary of attributes and qualities common to successful salespeople is shown in Table 10.1.

TABLE 10.1

Attributes and Qualities Common to Successful Salespeople

Personal Abilities:

Intelligence	Mental alertness
Analytical ability	Imagination
Communication skills	Articulateness
Persuasiveness	Negotiation ability
Adaptability	Flexibility
Time management skill	

Personal Attributes:

Aggressiveness	Perseverance
Intrinsic motivation	Honesty
Integrity	Independence
Cooperativeness	

Personal Style:

Outgoingness	Personableness
Sense of humor	Sincerity
Empathy	Self-confidence
Maturity	Well-groomed appearance

BUYING

To succeed in retail buying you must be willing to work hard. Stamina, both physical and mental, is necessary for the long hours and travel associated with a buying career. You must be self-motivated and willing to stick with projects until completion. This necessitates carefully establishing goals and priorities without close supervision. Working well with people is also required, as you depend on others' cooperation to get the job done. Management skills are necessary in order to move up the buying career ladder, as your responsibilities will expand to include management of a number of assistant or associate buyers.

Computational ability is also crucial. Analysis is performed on data, and you must feel comfortable sifting through it all. Being able to organize a great deal of detail and then act is necessary.

The educational backgrounds of buyers vary. The most important quality retail employers look for in a buyer is an interest in retailing. This can be demonstrated through previous retail experience and education. People with a retailing degree or a marketing or business degree with a concentration in retailing are usually given first consideration. Some large organizations recruit MBAs into training programs, usually with a higher starting salary than recruits with a bachelor's degree.

Buyer training programs tend to be formal in nature, especially in large department stores. The training program can last up to two years, typically consisting of classroom instruction and rotation through the store's departments. You are given exposure to selling-floor operations and become acquainted with store layout, style, and selling philosophy. In the beginning stages of a buyer's career, buying-area exposure is useful. Ideally, as a buyer, you should be able to buy anything a store sells. Moves between departments occur at senior levels, so you should be flexible enough in knowledge, experience, and temperament to be able to accept such new assignments.

11

Human-Resource Management*

Whereas personnel activities used to consist primarily of hiring and firing, the role of today's human-resource management (HRM) department is far more complex. As modern business had grown more sophisticated, it has come to see employees as vital resources, as investments. Accordingly, management of this resource has become an important area of corporate activity. HRM has redefined the personnel function and expanded its role from supplying employees to overall human-resource planning, development, and work-force utilization.

The concept of human-resource management has evolved over the past twenty years. Prior to World War II, personnel was primarily concerned with record keeping and hiring. In the 1950s formal job classifications, pay systems, and administration of fringe benefits were added. In the 1960s, developments in the behavioral sciences led to increased training and development activities. In the 1970s, Equal Employment Opportunity-Affirmative Action (EEO-AA) programs, the Employment Retirement Income Securities Act (ERISA), the Occupational Safety and Health Act (OSHA), and other governmental actions regarding personnel were taken. Proper compliance with these regulations was added to HRM responsibilities. Turbulent economic conditions, new technologies, changing demographics, new lifestyles, and altered worker attitudes in recent years have further contributed to making traditional views of personnel functions inadequate and obsolete.

Today the average company work force is better educated and more diverse in cultural background, interests, aspirations, and expectations

*This chapter is based on a paper written by Pamela Brown.

than previous generations. HRM activities are now designed to improve employee effectiveness within the organization. Human resource managers provide expert advice and assistance to corporate managers regarding the use of the organization's human resources. It is also common for human resource managers to be involved in other corporate activities than personnel, such as acquisition and divestiture, consolidation and diversification, and international expansion.

The current economic environment makes it important for organizations to seek solutions to problems of productivity, turnover, and absenteeism. In the past, unprepared managements paid for poor human-resource practices in financial losses, disrupted operations, employee dissatisfaction, and poor public image. Out of necessity, human-resource management has become professionalized. The prepared, knowledgeable personnel professional orchestrates the organization's efforts to provide meaningful solutions to people problems while laying a foundation for the future.

As a human-resource professional, you would plan and control such areas as:

overall staffing of the company, long- and short-term;
overall organizational effectiveness in terms of worker productivity, employee satisfaction, and competitiveness of incentive and reward systems;
overall effectiveness of the company's compliance with government agencies, regulations, unions, and public interest groups.

Accordingly, corporate development activities are being reoriented and regrouped with new planning and control systems. New HRM activities emerging at the corporate level include

organizational development activities that apply behavioral science techniques to personnel management in general and the planning and control process in particular;
staffing to integrate employment, manpower planning, training, management development, and other programs into an overall planning system;
development of human-resource information systems (HRIS), which apply statistical and mathematical methods to HRM;
government compliance activities (EEO-AA, OSHA) to counsel operating managers and measure and evaluate the company's compliance efforts in regulated areas.

This continuous expansion of HRM's activities and responsibilities has led to greater involvement by top corporate management in planning and control of the personnel function, as well as involvement of other corporate staff units—especially the legal and public affairs departments—to support the personnel roles. The result has been greater general management accountability for personnel management performance, and increased emphasis on HRIS to provide communication and control.

Corporate organizational structure greatly affects the personnel department in how it functions, its sphere of influence, and its location. Usually, personnel units are on the corporate staff. In addition, personnel subunits of varying responsibilities and numbers of employees may report to operating or other staff units.

It is increasingly common for large companies to staff the personnel function at multiple levels. Most companies with under a thousand employees have only corporate-level personnel staff units, while companies with over sixty thousand employees typically have personnel units at several levels. Organizations with many divisions also have multilevel personnel staffs.

Human-Resource Management Activities

The scope of activity in HRM departments depends on corporate size and philosophy. In small companies one or two personnel professionals may work primarily in the areas of compensation and recruiting. In larger firms more extensive HRM systems are needed to administer short- and long-term planning, requiring a staff of specialists. An exemplary organizational chart for a large, specialized HRM department is shown in Figure 11.1.

One problem the HRM field has faced is that personnel functions have often been viewed as a series of separate activities rather than an integrated system. This lack of integration may be due to lack of support from top corporate management and narrow views of specialists, both of which can adversely affect the achievement of overall corporate HRM objectives. Personnel professionals involved in HRM need to consider the activities described below as a system rather than a set of separate activities. The individual areas are building blocks which can collectively achieve overall HRM goals.

We have grouped the range of HRM activities into five categories: human-resource planning; recruitment, selection, and staffing; compensation and benefits; employee and labor relations; and training and development. Many skills and activities are common to all categories; most HRM professionals work to some extent in each area at various points in their careers. We begin with human-resource planning (HRP) which is at the center of HRM and serves to coordinate other HRM

FIGURE 11.1

Typical Large Human-Resource Management Department

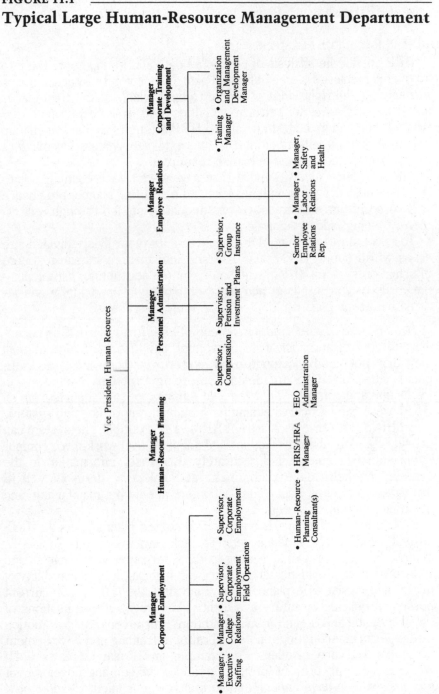

Vice President, Human Resources

**Manager
Corporate Employment**
- Manager, Executive Staffing
- Manager, College Relations
- Supervisor, Corporate Employment
- Supervisor, Corporate Employment Field Operations

**Manager
Human-Resource Planning**
- Human-Resource Planning Consultant(s)
- HRIS/HRA Manager
- EEO Administration Manager

**Manager
Personnel Administration**
- Supervisor, Compensation
- Supervisor, Pension and Investment Plans
- Supervisor, Group Insurance

**Manager
Employee Relations**
- Senior Employee Relations Rep.
- Manager, Labor Relations
- Manager, Safety and Health

**Manager
Corporate Training and Development**
- Training Manager
- Organization and Management Development Manager

functions. A schematic representation of HRM activities and the central role of HRP is shown in Figure 11.2.

HUMAN-RESOURCE PLANNING

HRP entails the analysis of personnel data and its incorporation into an overall human-resource utilization plan. This involves forecasting and planning for the right kinds of people to be available at the right places and the right time to perform activities that will benefit both the organization and its staff. In doing so, HRP attempts to manage change and anticipate the effects of internal and external organizational factors on the supply and demand of human resources.

Effective HRP involves more than a year-end head count. Human-resource planners work with financial and marketing planners to ensure that corporate growth areas will be adequately staffed through recruitment, training, and development.

To assist in this planning, HRP departments typically are divided into areas which supply necessary data and information: human-resource information systems (HRIS); human-resource accounting; career planning; succession planning; and equal-employment-opportunity and affirmative-action planning.

Human resource information systems. Some form of HRIS is necessary to control and coordinate personnel activities. Although a small firm may not need a computerized system, medium and large companies need an HRIS to identify emerging problems and assist in evaluation and control. The amount of information and reports from all HRM areas can be overwhelming for a manual record-keeping system.

An HRIS can serve each area of HRM. For example, the system can provide compensation calculations and analyze EEO work-force composition statistics quickly and accurately. Likewise, information in the system can help make recruitment and selection decisions. HRIS analysts also serve basic administration needs by maintaining and updating personnel records.

HRIS's greatest impact is on human-resource planning. As an HRIS analyst, you would produce reports including information on skills inventories, career paths, career ladders, organizational charts, and availability data. Sophisticated systems can forecast future availability of talent and assist HR planners in analyzing the effects of current personnel policies on future availability. You might run simulations of environmental and organizational conditions, turnover rates, promotion rates, performance ratings, potential ratings, training and development programs, and career ladders. For example, an HR planner may ask, "If we maintain our present promotion and management development policies, will we have enough middle management talent to add a new division in five years?" You would then prepare a forecasting program to

FIGURE 11.2

Human Resource Management: A Conceptual Model

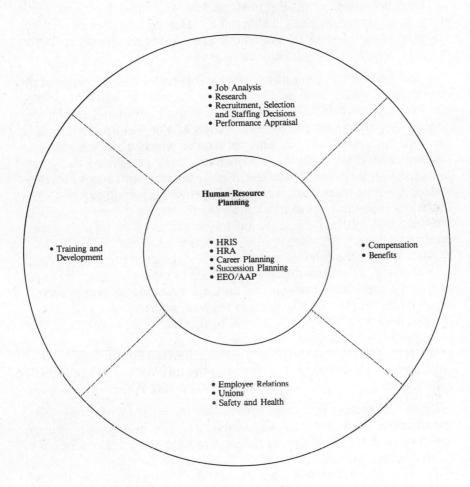

simulate future conditions, using employee career path selections, performance and potential ratings, attrition rates, and current training and promotion policies to derive a five-year prediction of managerial talent availability. From this the HR planner can determine whether a shortage is expected. By altering the model's parameters (i.e., changing a promotion rate or expanding a training program), the planner can study the effects of policy changes on future availability of talent.

Adaptability to changing conditions is crucial for organizations. HRIS helps improve adaptability through the rapid and versatile exchange and manipulation of data, and facilitates planning through the use of forecasting and simulation techniques. Many organizations are now computerizing HRP activities. Over the next decade, the need for appropriate skills in this area is likely to increase. The demand for managers, systems analysts, and programmers specializing in human-resource planning programs should continue to grow.

Human-resource accounting. As a human-resource accountant (HRA), you would analyze the financial aspects of human-resource programs. You would help management analyze personnel and budget actions by performing cost/benefit analyses. For example, you might calculate turnover statistics and determine which variables, such as compensation, sales volume, and unemployment rate, have the greatest impact on turnover. Using these analyses you can suggest ways to reduce costs, reduce turnover, and improve recruiting policies. You might also examine compensation levels to ensure external competitiveness and internal fairness, or to determine if a layoff is cost-effective.

Human-resource cost estimates are often required in capital budgeting decisions, as well as decisions whether to hire experienced people or train inexperienced ones. In addition, HR accountants design reporting systems for HR costs to provide relevant information to shareholders and investors, allocate personnel to projects or operating units, or examine the sources of overhead costs.

In recent years, HRA activities have increased considerably; about 25 percent of the companies surveyed in the mid-70s either had already implemented or were in the process of developing HRA systems.

Career planning. Traditional approaches to HRP focused on skills, and included a job skill analysis, assessment and evaluation of talent, and development of skill inventories. Contemporary approaches also include career planning programs which yield an inventory of available skills and examine the availability of talent for the future through monitoring present employees' career development.

One aspect of career planning is the development of a realistic awareness of career paths. Although there may be few formal paths between positions, the planner identifies possible lines of progression through jobs in an organization or division. The career-planning specialist's definition of work activities involves job content analysis, which provides data for many HRP areas. Job analysis integrates what employees say they do on the job with what managers say should be done. The planner then identifies personal requirements in terms of necessary skills and knowledge, based on the defined work activities.

These requirements are grouped into positions and job families, which are used as a basis for charting career paths and HRP decisions. Because of the multiple uses of job analyses, organizations assign personnel from various areas of HRM to do them, including recruiters, compensation analysts, and human-resource planners.

Once the specialist has developed career paths, career-related information is communicated to employees through pamphlets, newsletters, bulletin boards, and the like. Many companies feel that, although they are responsible for compiling and sharing relevant information, employees are responsible for individual career planning. It is to a corporation's benefit, however, to help generate as many employee career plans within the organization as possible. This is usually accomplished by career counselors who assist employees in identifying career opportunities and training and development activities to prepare them for target jobs. Effective career counseling uses information from all areas of the organization to help employees design a realistic personal-action plan and take charge of their own career.

Career-planning workshops provide another method for communicating career information. Although workshops are usually created by the training and development unit, a human-resource career planner will often assist in the design and implementation stages, and will process the data gathered. This activity involves summarizing employee career plans, reviewing training and development activities, and accounting for time considerations to forecast talent availability. Career planners then incorporate performance ratings, evaluations of potential, and attrition factors to improve the forecast.

Succession planning. A primary concern of human-resource planning is to ensure that the organization has the necessary managerial, technical, and support talent available in the future. The continual presence of a competent management force is critical to the success of an organization. Managers are often highly skilled and require substantial time to develop their expertise. Moreover, they are usually highly paid, and their loss, particularly to competitors, can have a severe impact on an organization. Succession planning has emerged in organizations in order to (1) plan for better training and development of the talent required to meet future business needs, and (2) demonstrate organizational commitment to employee growth, development, and satisfaction. Succession planning is most effective in combination with a career-planning program; the inclusion of employee career aspirations in the succession plan results in a more practical forecast of available talent.

As a succession planner your primary responsibility would be to construct a replacement chart. This chart displays who are the most likely replacements for high-level managerial positions, and the time frame for the replacement. This involves an ongoing process of gathering and coordinating data on employee demographics, skills, abilities, and career plans. Data on employees' performance level, long-range promotability, salary grade, position title, years of service, years to retirement, readiness for promotion, and probability of loss, as well as career goals and aspirations, must be included in the replacement chart.

Once you construct a replacement chart, you can identify organizational areas where shortages and surpluses of promotable people exist, pinpoint promotional blockages, and identify managers who are good (or bad) developers of people. You can also identify individuals who need development and their specific needs. This suggests integration of career succession activities with training and development, as well as with recruiting.

In this work you must have a thorough knowledge of the career paths available to employees, and may assist in the development of career ladders. Interaction with job analysts to facilitate this process is common. You also need to be able to appraise performance and evaluate potential techniques in order to select the most qualified candidates for a position.

Equal-employment-opportunity (EEO) and affirmative-action planning (AAP). EEO-AAP coordinates management efforts to meet the requirements of all government regulations and laws regarding discrimination, equal employment opportunity, and affirmative action.

As an EEO administrator, you would interpret government rules and regulations and recommend appropriate compliance and affirmative action for the company's benefit. You must develop, analyze, interpret and submit EEO statistical reports and other relevant information demonstrating the effectiveness of the company's programs. You might represent the organization in government-conducted compliance reviews—on the federal, state, or local level—and also maintain a liaison role with minority and women's organizations and other community groups. You would process charges and complaints, often working with company lawyers on discrimination charges. Fact-finding is a major responsibility when complaints are filed; in these situations you would develop and present evidence and expert viewpoints. You also would write and review reports for submission to the Equal Employment Opportunity Commission (EEOC) and regularly develop systems to monitor and measure progress.

As an EEO worker you also work with training and development staff to increase minority participation in upward mobility programs, and work with individual managers who are responsible for helping meet AAP goals. You must be aware of current legislation and understand its impact on the organization. You must be able to deal with complaints diplomatically and be investigative. You will also have to write clear, succinct reports.

In summary, the human-resource planner may be involved in any of the five essential areas of activity described above: human-resource information systems, human-resource accounting, career planning, succession planning, and EEO-AAP. In each of these areas the HR planner is at the core of all HRM activities, which include recruitment, selection, and staffing decisions; compensation and benefits; employee and labor relations; and training and development.

RECRUITMENT, SELECTION, AND STAFFING

The attraction and selection of individuals for an organization involve various HRM activities: (1) job analyses to determine the work individuals are to perform, (2) development and application of criteria regarding appropriate skills and abilities in the individuals to be considered, (3) performance appraisals to assess on-the-job performance, and (4) personnel research to ensure the reliability, validity, and relevance of the standards used. These HRM functions constitute a center of activity for entry-level personnel professionals.

Job analysis. Evaluation of positions is the basis for many HRM policies and procedures, and is a typical activity for entry-level employees. As a job analyst, you would produce job descriptions and job specifications by defining positions in terms of tasks and behavior and specifying the relevant personal characteristics (in education, experience, and training) needed for the job.

There are many techniques available—such as factor comparison, Hay's Eight-Point System and the Critical Incident Approach—to assist in preparation of job descriptions and specifications. Since these techniques vary substantially in complexity and applicability, you must be aware of the methods available, as well as the sources of potential error involved, and become thoroughly familiar with the particular method used by the organization. These methods require that you possess the ability to do a detailed analysis and interviewing skills. Typically, you might interview several people about their job responsibilities and skills required (or administer a questionnaire) and then use a computer to analyze the results.

Staff selection and assignment. Here, you would be responsible for the hiring and placement of employees, including recruiting, interviewing, testing, selection, placement, promotion, transfer, and termination. Typical entry-level titles include employment representative, employment specialist, personnel interviewer, and recruiter. Depending on the industry and the size of the firm, the responsibilities of a recruiter range from hiring to career counseling regarding relocation. Since the criteria for staffing decisions are related to job evaluation and performance appraisal, recruiters must often have extensive knowledge of all the job functions within the organization.

As a recruiter, you would meet with managers who have job vacancies to determine the job requirements, and then decide which type of method is best to attract applicants. Usually the choices are college recruiting, newspaper advertisements, employment agencies, and internal job posting, as well as responding to unsolicited resumes and "walk-ins."

College recruiting often involves travel to undergraduate, technical, and graduate schools. It is an important method of finding job candidates because it is relatively inexpensive and allows organizations to review a large number of diverse applicants in a short time. Recruiters often hold ten to fifteen interviews per day when visiting a campus.

Screening resumes is another important responsibility. This can be a time-consuming task, since some organizations receive more than a thousand resumes per week. When a job opening occurs, to select potential job candidates for interviews you review resumes and completed job applications. You may also test relevant skills and abilities, intelligence, or psychological characteristics of applicants, and check references and background information.

After you select the most qualified applicants, you refer them to the managers who placed the "job order." If the manager and other supervisors agree that an individual is qualified, an offer is made, and you confirm that the applicant is aware of the general job duties and responsibilities, pay and benefits, hours and working conditions, company and union policies, promotion opportunities, and other job-related information. In addition, you may maintain files for future reference of records of other applicants, and conduct an exit interview.

Other events that you would process are internal transfers, promotions, and terminations. In some organizations, the responsibilities of a recruiter are extended to include other activities such as career and succession planning; determining which skills, training, and education are needed to fill positions; and finding internal successors and backup replacements. A recruiter may also hold new-employee orientation sessions and develop informational programs to familiarize employees with key human-resource policies and procedures.

Performance appraisal. Performance appraisal is used to assess employees' performance on the job. A reliable, valid, job-relevant, and standardized performance appraisal system is an integral part of HRM and should serve the needs of the entire organization. It provides top management with a means of identifying good and poor performers, and provides criteria by which promotion, training, and firing decisions can be made. It provides managers and personnel with accurate and complete information for decisions on salary increases, transfers, and other career issues; and provides subordinates with information regarding their performance strengths and weaknesses that can be used as a motivation tool. As a performance appraisal specialist, you might provide guidelines for supervisors to follow when conducting appraisals. An example is working with training and development staff to create a workshop to train supervisors in administering the appraisal system and conducting an appraisal interview.

In many organizations the establishment of a performance appraisal system is necessary to facilitate other human-resource planning and development activities. Development of an effective appraisal system is a complex task which must be regularly reviewed, updated, and integrated with areas of HRP, such as career-management and succession planning, compensation, and training and development. Since the performance appraisal system is a core HRM function, many organizations offer entry-level positions in this area as a comprehensive introduction to the organization's HRM philosophy and needs.

Personnel research. Advance warning of changes in human resources is as important to the effectiveness of an organization as is forecasting financial and economic changes. Early identification of potential change allows time to study and understand the problem and then plan and act to mitigate it if it does occur. An effective HRM system should include environmental scanning and personnel research to forecast these developments.

Personnel research and scanning are best done by a team to ensure thoroughness and analysis from a variety of perspectives. Research on the current status of the labor force, on recent legislation regarding EEO and employee rights, on new benefits packages, and on methods of forecasting the supply and demand of human resources can have a significant impact on HRM policies and procedures. Research teams also monitor competitors' actions and evaluate internal programs relative to comparable external programs to determine present and future vulnerability. Journals, seminars, and trade newspapers are common sources of information on recent developments. For example, researchers will often collaborate with other HR managers in developing a new training program or implementing an additional benefits package.

COMPENSATION AND BENEFITS

Compensation and benefits are staff-servicing areas of HRM that can function either together or separately. The compensation analyst is responsible for coordinating the organization's wage and salary program. The benefits analyst administers and provides information about the range of employee benefits available, including health insurance, retirement and pension programs, unemployment compensation, and social security.

Typical titles for entry-level compensation positions are job analyst or compensation analyst. In this area, job analysis is a primary responsibility. As an analyst, you would develop and apply job analysis techniques, sometimes working with analysts from other departments. As a compensation analyst you would gather data through checklists, position-analysis and other questionnaires, observation, and interviews, and then investigate the job's relative position; the technical, managerial and human relations skills required; and the nature of the problems solved. From this information you would write a description of the position. Using the job evaluations, you would grade and price jobs. You may also use survey data to compute wage and salary structures designed for economic feasibility and competitiveness.

Your other duties as compensation analyst would include establishing and maintaining manuals and controls to facilitate wage and salary administration. You would examine company policies regarding payment of minimum wage and overtime agreements with labor unions, and consult with labor relations staff on contract negotiations. In addition, you would review pay policies regularly for compliance with state and federal regulations. You would also conduct wage and salary surveys, and gather data on the competition's wage and salary levels and structures. These activities require that you thoroughly understand the pay system in all its elements, which can include seniority, merit, incentives, and so forth.

Benefits is a service-oriented HRM function. As a benefits analyst, you are primarily concerned with the daily administration of such benefits as group insurance plans and disability insurance. You process medical claims and ensure accurate and prompt payment of claims. You must be aware of local, state, federal, and even foreign laws to ensure that all benefit programs comply with relevant legislation and regulations.

An additional responsibility is explaining benefit options to new employees. You may also have to coordinate other employee services, such as the cafeteria, snack bar, health room, recreational facility, newsletter and other media, and counseling for work-related problems. In addition, you may assist management in decision making on possible benefits and improvements, and participate in establishing objectives by informing management of current trends and developments in employee benefits.

EMPLOYEE AND LABOR RELATIONS

Employee relations involves both labor relations and employee health and safety activities. Labor relations positions have principal responsibility for collective bargaining, preparations for contract negotiations and administration, grievance settlements, and arbitration. Safety and health positions have the responsibility of preventing injuries and impairments to employees and coping with the results of accidents that do occur.

Labor relations. Titles include labor relations specialist and labor relations advisor; these positions frequently require a master's degree in industrial or labor relations. As a labor relations specialist, your primary responsibilities would be grievance handling, arbitration, contract negotiation and administration, legislative analysis, and strike preparation. In order to carry out these responsibilities, you will need to analyze (or develop) the organization's labor relations program. This involves analyzing the text of collective bargaining agreements and developing interpretations of the intent, spirit, and terms of contracts. Another important responsibility is to counsel management in the development and application of labor relations policies and practices. Labor specialists may help establish bargaining agreements, in which case initial proposals for wages and benefits must be developed, limits for the bargain set, and issues defined regarding which the company can expect a strike.

You would also represent management in investigating, answering, and settling grievances. You would arrange grievance meetings among workers, supervisory and managerial personnel, and representatives of the labor union. The grievance procedure is central to employee-management relations, and thus grievance settlement is an important part of the labor relations specialist's work.

Your other labor relations activities include preparation of statistical reports on the types and frequency of action taken concerning grievances, arbitration, mediation, and related labor relations matters in order to identify problem areas. You must verify adherence to terms of a labor contract by monitoring day-to-day implementation of policies concerning wages, hours, working conditions, and productivity. You often represent management in periodic labor-contract negotiations and serve as an information resource on such matters as the provisions of a current contract and the significance of proposed changes. You furnish reference documents and statistical data concerning labor legislation, labor market conditions, prevailing union and management practices, wage and salary surveys, and employee benefits programs.

You will need in this work an extensive knowledge of economics, labor law, and collective bargaining. Familiarity with the text and implications of the Wagner Act, Taft-Hartley Act, and Tandrum-Griffin Act is required. You must understand union tactics, such as strikes, boycotts, pickets, and lockouts. A law degree is not required for entry-level positions, but those responsible for contract negotiations are often lawyers. A combination of a law degree and labor or industrial relations degree is becoming increasingly desirable. A growing number of people enter the field directly with a master's degree but many also transfer from other areas of HRM. Labor relations specialists tend to be the most highly paid specialists in HRM.

Safety and health. Since the passage of worker's compensation laws and the Occupational Safety and Health Act (OSHA), every employer has a legal obligation to provide work in a workplace that is free from recognized hazards to the physical and mental health of its employees. Employers must comply with all safety standards developed under the act and are subject to penalties for noncompliance.

The primary responsibility of a safety coordinator, safety manager, or plant inspector is to prevent accidents or injuries and investigate the causes of those that occur. This involves checking for (1) unsafe work behavior, such as performing operations without supervisory approval, removing safety devices, operating vehicles at unsafe speeds, horse-play, using improper equipment, and failure to use safety attire and devices; (2) unsafe physical conditions, such as inadequate mechanical guarding, defective equipment, unsafe design or construction, hazard-ous processes, and unsuitable lighting and ventilation; and (3) unsafe environmental conditions such as excessive noise, heat, vibration, and radiation; chemical contamination by fumes, gases, and toxic materials; biological threats due to bacteria, fungi, and insects; and conditions leading to unnecessary physical and psychological stress.

After accident investigations, safety managers must recommend corrective measures, and develop and coordinate an accident preven-tion program. This includes establishing safety rules, regulations, and standards, and communicating them to employees by way of a safety education program and safety manuals. Records of all accidents must be kept and on-site treatment of injuries given.

As a safety manager you must have thorough knowledge of OSHA and other safety regulations, and often must be a member of a recognized safety organization. Safety instruction and knowledge of first aid are required.

TRAINING AND DEVELOPMENT

Training and development (T&D), a central tool of human-resource management, is a principal vehicle for developing the skills and abilities of employees other than through job assignments. It also provides a means of influencing employees' values, attitudes, and practices. It is a powerful communications medium controlled by the company.

Positions in T&D usually require a minimum of two or three years' experience in teaching or some professional training experience. As a training specialist, your first responsibility might be to identify the T&D needs of employees through analysis of data collected through questionnaires, interviews, and job analysis. Achievement tests, aptitude tests, and discussion are used to provide data. From the results of a needs analysis, you would define training programs and materials. This involves establishing behavioral or learning objectives for programs; determining program content; evaluating alternative instructional methods, such as books, films, videotapes, role-playing, and demonstrations; preparing scripts for films and videotapes; and determining what training materials are needed—for example, workbooks, special exercises, or business cases.

You would then decide whether to use an existing program, purchase an external program, or create a new one. Existing programs often need to be revised. Choosing an external program involves evaluation and cost/benefit analysis. Creating a new program is more complex, since it involves the development of criteria for selecting program participants, exercises, materials, and self-assessment tools. Appropriate sequencing of courses and programs (e.g. prerequisites, curricula, etc.) is also required. Once you develop the training programs, you must implement them. Behavioral modeling techniques, role-playing, simulations, lectures, discussion, and audio-visual equipment are frequently employed.

In addition to developing, analyzing, and implementing formal training programs, you would counsel individuals on career development, skill development, and other T&D matters. You may also assist managers in implementing on-the-job training.

To coordinate and manage an effective T&D program, you must be able to evaluate instructors, program-resource people, and proposals from outside consultants. Administration, record keeping, and updating duties are fairly heavy in this work. They include preparation of budgets and plans for T&D programs; maintenance of cost/benefit information; program logistics, such as facilities, lodging, and meals; recording of training participation; and tuition reimbursement.

T&D departments are generally responsible for marketing their programs within the organization. This requires having good working relationships with managers as clients, and making formal presentations of T&D programs to management personnel. It includes, among other things, the preparation of reports, manuals, proposals, and speeches about T&D programs. Frequently you would write articles for periodicals and internal publications, as well as memos and announcements.

Advanced research in the training field, such as experimenting with new T&D techniques, is common, and you must keep abreast of this and T&D in other organizations. Often you will attend seminars and conferences.

Planning a career in T&D is a complex and individualized process. Many combinations of degree specializations, roles, program areas, and work settings can lead to success in this field. Formal education is important; advanced degrees are held by as many as 50 percent of those in T&D. Participation in continuing education, workshops, seminars, and noncredit courses are the primary source for updating skills and developing new ones. T&D professionals are gaining both in status and importance in their organizations as successful firms turn to developing management talent internally rather than recruiting it from outside.

Entry-Level Opportunities

Human-resource management offers extensive opportunities. The Bureau of Labor Statistics predicts that HRM will grow 168 percent faster than other professional fields in the next several years. The need for experts to oversee compliance with government regulations will continue to increase. And the growth of employee services will continue, particularly in career planning and developmental programs, pension and other benefit plans, and personnel research. Employers are recognizing the impact of human-resources management practices on the "bottom line," and coming to depend on the services of trained individuals to make the most of the organization's human resources.

Traditionally, people have entered the HRM field from other departments within the organization, or have had a specialized background such as education in labor and industrial relations. Today several universities offer master's degrees in HRM. People entering the field commonly have an undergraduate major in business, or a master's or doctorate in business, labor relations, public administration, or industrial psychology. Some companies offer a general training program for entry-level people, with rotation through various areas for exposure to all functional areas of HRM.

Entry-level opportunities in HRM are usually in technical areas such as job analysis or performance appraisal. These positions offer new employees a chance to learn about the company and the types of people who work there. A job analyst investigates positions by reading position descriptions and interviewing managers and job incumbents to determine actual job qualifications. By doing this a new HRM employee learns what jobs are performed in the organization and what skills, attributes, and abilities are necessary to perform them. Similarly, an employee who works on the development and use of a performance appraisal system investigates positions and determines performance criteria. Through these activities, they learn the organization's selection standards. College recruiting is another typical entry position; this work helps the HRM employee learn about the organization's public image.

Once an HR manager has developed technical expertise, he or she is considered a specialist. Specialists often supervise several clerical and technical support employees. In some organizations, specialists remain within one area throughout their career. Indeed, many satisfied training specialists, EEO representatives, recruiters, etc., decide either to remain in their present position or to seek a managerial position within their specialty. Others, however, wish to gain expertise in other personnel areas, either to become a specialist in a different area or to become a generalist or middle-level HR manager. Figure 11.3 suggests some of the possible career opportunities for those preferring to work at a variety of HRM activities.

At the middle-management level in HRM, which requires several years of HRM experience, duties encompass a broad range of activity: You may direct the overall personnel program and coordinate subordinate programs, such as the training or benefits program. Or, you may contribute to planning the future direction of the organization. You may also advise other managers in the management of their personnel. At this level, titles and job responsibilities vary greatly.

At the executive level there are vice presidents of human resources and directors of personnel. These managers are involved in long-range, strategic planning with other high-level corporate managers. HRM executives influence company policies and recommend personnel-policy changes. Responsibilities are great and the position is vital to the successful operation of the organization. Top personnel executives spend considerable time with people outside the HRM office and the organization.

Required Skills and Educational Background

As an HRM worker, you must have more than a liking for people. As an HR manager you must have empathy for them and understand what motivates and leads them. You must be able to deal tactfully and patiently with people of varying intelligence, education, and ability— from line managers to clerical staff, from incumbent top management to entry-level job candidates.

You must be able to communicate effectively, both orally and in writing. You should be detail-oriented, since there is substantial administrative work. Analytical ability may be necessary, depending on your

FIGURE 11.3

Options for a Career in HRM

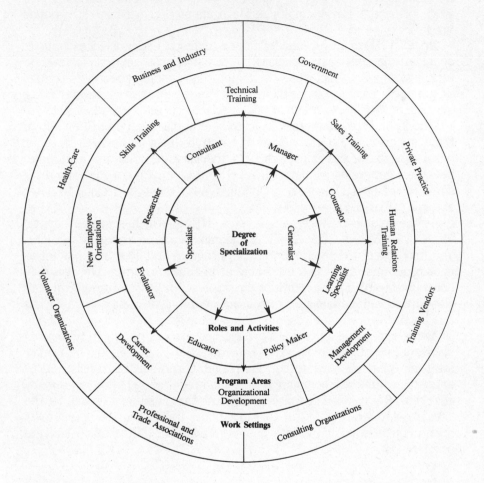

specialty. HR work often involves the collection and manipulation of numbers to arrive at useful statistical summaries, so you should not be afraid of digging into numbers.

Flexibility and adaptability in unexpected situations are important personal characteristics. Since HRM is involved in making the most of the work force as a resource in the organization, you must be adaptable to the various circumstances presented by employees. The service aspect of HRM work should be recognized, and you must be willing and able to fill legitimate employee needs as they arise.

12

Systems Analysis*

The purpose of a systems analyst's job is to determine the information needs of computer users, to review whether the user's current information system satisfies his or her needs, and to propose improvements over the current system. As a systems analyst, you would determine users' needs by considering the timing, quantity, quality, and cost of information they require in the performance of their jobs. Next, you would examine whether the current method of collecting, tabulating, and reporting information is accomplished in an efficient, reliable, and timely manner. Then you would consider a range of alternatives and suggest the one offering the greatest potential benefit for the lowest cost.

The systems analyst generally works on a project-by-project basis and recommends one of several alternatives for each project:

1. maintain current information systems
2. collect or process the same information more efficiently
3. capture additional information valuable to users
4. restructure the basic ways the current system collects, processes, records, or reports the data

Sometimes analysts discover that existing systems, whether automated or manual, are the most reliable and cost-efficient means of processing data. This is especially true of low-volume information systems in stable markets. For example, an executive secretary who has been asked to get some information on a prospective client for a sales presentation can get this information directly from the firm's library. Unless the library is extensively used, there is no justification for setting up a computerized information system in its place. If, however, such information retrieval becomes an important part of everyday corporate activity, an analyst might suggest modifications to enhance the efficiency of the current information system. For example, if retrieval of current stock prices is important for decision making, an

*This chapter is based on a paper written by William G. Greenbaum.

analyst would first study the established procedure for capturing stock prices in order to determine if it offers timely access to the data, and then investigate the most efficient, cost-effective way to report them.

Analysts usually are forced to make tradeoffs between efficiency, cost, and reliability. Capturing stock prices directly from quotation machines when the market is active would be efficient but costly and subject to loss of important data if a brief computer outage occurred. Subscribing to Dun & Bradstreet's financial database or copying day-old stock prices from computer tapes onto computer disc storage would be less costly and less variable, but the information would be less up-to-date.

After analyzing who uses the data and for what purpose, the systems analyst might suggest collecting more information than the current system collects. For example, the analyst might conclude that users need summaries of stock prices on a daily and weekly basis, rather than monthly. The analyst can then suggest subscribing to a system that provides this information plus average stock price, grouping by size or industry, or whatever variables are appropriate. Finally a systems analyst may sometimes recommend restructuring the flow of information if he or she sees that it is present in the corporation but not getting to the right people in the right order.

More and more often, systems analysts are recommending that organizations switch to use of computers, expand present computer capability, or upgrade systems to incorporate new technologies, especially in cases where activities involve systematic data capture, manipulation or retrieval. People use computers for three basic purposes: daily operations, strategic decision making, and office automation. Some systems provide a combination of these uses; others are specialized.

Systems that run daily operations are often referred to as transaction systems. They record decisions to buy or sell, receivables and payables, cash receipts and payments, and changes in physical inventory, or they run production processes. Accounting procedures are commonly handled by transactional systems, as are the retail arms of many organizations. The last time you reserved a theater seat through Ticketron or an airline seat with a commercial carrier, you benefited from such a system.

Decision support systems provide managers with critical information at a level of detail appropriate to their decision making. For example, managers might prepare pro forma financial statements with financial spread-sheet software on a personal computer. Or a marketing department may collect data on computer records to compare sales revenues, sales-force activities, and product sales performance across several sales territories for a given period. After collecting and entering relevant data on computer-readable records, marketing experts can manipulate the data and print tables of relevant figures.

Office automation covers such things as word processing, electronic filing and information-retrieval systems, and electronic mail. Such automation adds to greater office efficiency, especially in corporations where creation and storage of paper work is a large part of the workday activity of management and support personnel. Electronic mail is especially useful for firms that depend on timely interoffice communication. Users can send letters or memos to other users via time-sharing terminals. This reduces mail costs and delays dramatically.

As a systems analyst, you may also suggest that your firm discontinue use of a computer or remove an application from a computer system if it is not saving work. Sometimes a computer operation is simply too troublesome for the firm's personnel to manage. Or, in declining markets, the volume and frequency of transactions may be low enough to warrant reversion to a manual system.

In all of these situations, the systems analyst's job is to serve the information needs of other people. An irony here is that usually the users of the information system lack the technical know-how to assess the quality of your work in process. Only afterward can users see whether your solutions solve more problems than they create.

The Systems Analysis Field

Virtually all firms whose existence depends upon their ability to use computers to manage extensive information employ systems analysts. These organizations fall into several broad categories:

1. manufacturers of computer hardware or software
2. users of computers and computer services
3. computer consulting firms

The manufacturers listed above produce computers, ancillary devices (e.g., storage disks, tapes, input-output devices), hardware components (mainframes, circuit boards), or software components (programs and programming languages). Manufacturers have the most extensive computer-education programs for both their own systems analysts and their customers. To develop innovative, competitive products, they allocate large budgets for research, development, and marketing. Systems analysts are involved in all these areas.

Systems analysts working for computer companies tend to assist sales personnel in the sale and service of computers. Because computers are expensive pieces of capital equipment, a systems analyst is often involved in analyzing a potential customer's needs in order to recommend the most relevant type of computer equipment for purchase or lease. In effect, the systems analyst acts as a consultant to the purchasing firm, while employed full-time by the computer manufacturer.

Computer-using organizations can buy or lease computers or rent the right to use a computer via remote terminals through time sharing. The largest American user of computers and computer services is the federal government, followed by large financial institutions such as commercial banks, securities brokerage firms, and insurance companies. But users exist in every conceivable field: profit and nonprofit, manufacturing, service, agricultural. Once a computer is purchased or leased, systems analysts work with the client's existing system to solve organizational and managerial problems.

Computer consulting firms are in the business of placing experienced computer science professionals with computer users on a project basis. Often their consultants are independent subcontractors. They perform programming, analysis, user training, and management consulting for their clients. Consultants' fees are usually substantial, because clients have hired them for time-critical work on projects that demand the attention of an expert. Consultants are self-managing, skilled professionals. Some consultants manage the work of staff programmers, in addition to doing their own analysis and programming. (A further discussion of consulting roles is provided in chapter 13, and in the MAS section of chapter 6.)

Systems Analyst's Position Within the Corporate Structure

Within corporations, systems analysis is most commonly included as one of the data processing department's responsibilities. Much systems analysis work involves managing projects and performing analysis on projects that also involve computer programming. As a systems analyst you would typically report to a systems manager in the data processing department, and have programmer-analysts reporting to you on projects you share. Alternatively, you might work in user departments and report to the project manager in the user department. Figure 12.1 summarizes the basic role and the relationships of a systems analyst and points to some of the career moves possible.

Because many systems analysts once were programmers and now work closely with them, it is worthwhile comparing the primary functions of these two positions. A programmer's job is essentially to translate a procedure from a set of human-language instructions into a machine-readable language. Programmers are usually given the instructions they need to accomplish the translation from the systems man-

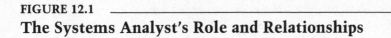

FIGURE 12.1

The Systems Analyst's Role and Relationships

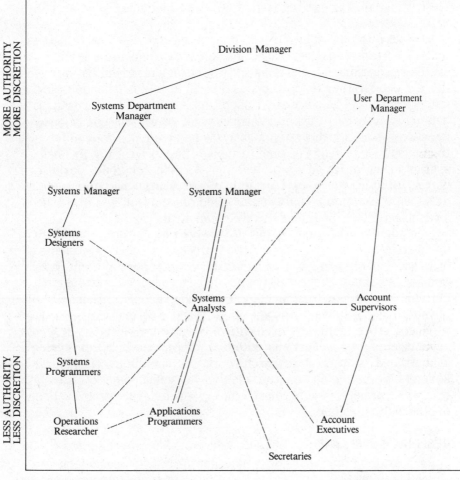

Information sources for systems analyst
Typical lines of authority

ager, the systems analyst, or the end user for whom the work is being performed.

In contrast to programmers, systems analysts attempt to perceive a rational organization in the flow of information, describe it, and propose specific measures that programmers, users, and managers can take to improve it. System analysts investigate and solve problems creatively. They are frequently responsible for project design, budgeting, and feasibility studies on problems that are less well-defined than programming assignments.

Another position within the data processing–systems analysis area is that of systems designer. Systems designers develop software for systems programmers. Systems software is any program that manages the computer rather than produces directly useful information for the user's business. The software is used to store, retrieve, or manipulate data so as to provide useful information for users. Designers answer questions about which systems analysts know enough to ask but lack the technical knowledge or time to answer themselves. For example, a systems analyst would know whether a computer could perform a certain task or run a certain kind of program, while the systems designer would know exactly *how* it would run and would be in charge of assembling and testing the software components.

One other specialization in this area is operations research, which is involved in the analysis of production processes. While systems analysts suggest ways to make information systems more efficient, operations researchers suggest ways to make production systems more efficient. Operations researchers study how people, machines, and physical objects move, consume energy and raw materials, produce products, stock them, and make them available for selling at the most advantageous price. There is potential for overlap between systems analysis and operations research work, as operations often include several information systems in addition to production processes. An operations project may therefore employ several systems analysts and operations researchers.

RESPONSIBILITIES AND ACTIVITIES

As a systems analyst, you would usually work simultaneously on several projects that are likely to be at different stages. (A flow chart of the activities involved in a project is suggested in Figure 12.2.) Meetings, analysis, interviews, and writing occur as part of your daily work. Many systems analysts work 9:00-to-5:00, although some start early and some go home late. All have periods of exceptional challenge and stress throughout the year—particularly with respect to implementing on-line operating systems.

FIGURE 12.2
Project Design for a Systems Analysis

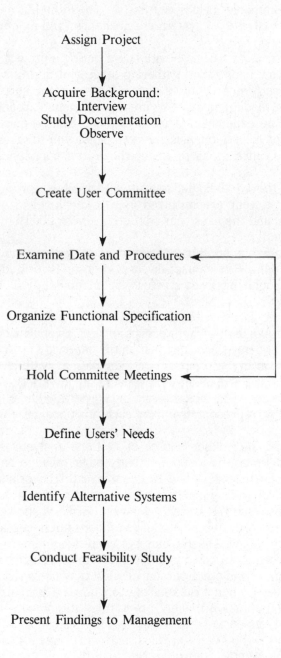

Because you may be involved in several projects at one time, your attention may well be pulled in many directions. You may find telephone messages from users or managers when you arrive at the office. Mornings commonly include setting up appointments and interviews with users, analyzing of system specifications, and meeting with managers or users.

You will spend a lot of time with users during a project, especially in the preliminary information-gathering stage and during system implementation. Early interaction is especially important here. If incorrect decisions are made, and systems are then designed around them, later revision can be expensive. When users' questions require an involved explanation or discussion, it is a good idea for you to meet face-to-face in the user's office so as to foster the user's confidence in you and promote his or her involvement in the project. The user must believe that you are there to help find a solution that is best for the user's area, not to impose your preconceived ideas. The level of understanding between you and the user bears directly on your ability to enhance the user's productivity.

To determine a potential user's needs, you will need to collect background data. Often a user discussion group is formed; data is then collected through interviews, study of documentation, and personal observation.

Interviewing is often the forum in which analysts and users first meet. It is important for both groups of professionals to communicate their needs openly, especially in initial interviews. Analysts often interview a variety of users. For example, a systems analyst in a brokerage house would interview users in a variety of roles: line manager, broker, securities analyst, and corporate officer. A user group might include a representative from each functional area which will use the system.

The second information source of systems analysts is documentation. Documentation is a common body of knowledge and terms that employees and managers use to communicate the principles of their business and their daily tasks. However, documentation has one weakness as a resource for systems analysis: While it shows most of the rules that users are supposed to follow, it does not necessarily show the rules they do follow. Discrepancy between documented and accepted operating procedures could indicate poor communication between upper management and other personnel. Or it may show that experienced employees know when it is expedient to ignore rules in order to get the job done. Sometimes managers break rules to compete for the firm's resources or expedite their projects. The analyst is in a position to discover many who bend the rules, and while investigating should be aware of the potentially sensitive nature of the investigation.

The systems analyst must consider company regulations in light of the actual environment in which people work. Many people resist following rules; some managers resist enforcing them. Many people have constructive ideas that managers have yet to hear or adopt. All of these conditions contribute to the inconclusiveness of systems documentation.

Observation is one way to collect information that has not yet been documented. Using direct observation, you can see the impact of individual differences on the way people work. For example, some people work slowly because they are new and are being careful. Others work quickly because they are competent enough to do so. Others are careless, working quickly but making errors, and requiring double-checking by another person or machine. Such differences and idiosyncrasies have to be kept in mind when designing systems for users.

Observation is also a reasonable way to verify the information you receive through interviews, meetings, and documentation. You should always verify information from an independent source before you use it. Verification is important because individuals can be misinformed, misinterpret things, or be biased. An enthusiastic worker may exaggerate requirements, informational needs, and so forth. An insecure or bored worker may omit information. A dissatisfied worker may even subvert the process of systems analysis by withholding or distorting data.

When analysts finally have the background they deem important, they typically recommend that the user committee clearly define the needs of the user population. A committee of three or four users tends to be large enough to provide a representative variety of opinions, and small enough to facilitate productive discussions. Because the user group will be influential in the design of the system, it is important that its members approach these discussions with the whole firm's best interests in mind, not only their own department's interests.

As a systems analyst you may use your free time to conduct business on a more informal level. For example, you may use lunch time to meet with users, perhaps to determine the next step of a project. You can use this time to seek out inside information that will help you make the project schedule more realistic, or to learn which documentation to study and which to ignore. Spending lunch with other analysts facilitates comparing ideas on projects, discussing new projects, and exchanging referrals to help users and managers. Of course, job notes are also compared: Who is hiring, who is looking for work, what other projects are up coming.

You would typically devote the afternoon to further data collection, informal user training and consultation, and following up a morning discussion of user requirements for a new system. For example, a morning in which a meeting resulted in revision of user requirements would typically be followed by an afternoon in further consultation with other users, fellow analysts, or your manager.

You must consider the feasibility of any new system model along technical, economic, and personnel lines. Technical questions include: What does a particular system do? What tasks would be done well by machine, what by people? Can a computer reliably perform the work involved? What configuration would make an operation practical, what optimal? In what ways should users gain access to the system? What future applications are likely to grow from this system and others of equal importance to the company? Your training will suggest answers to many of these questions; others will require consultation with other analysts and programmers.

An economic analysis must answer these basic questions: What is the break-even point, where the return equals the cost of designing and implementing the proposed system? What is the net present value of this project? How much time will it take for the system to pay for itself?

You must also assess whether the organization has enough personnel to staff the new system and benefit from it, or whether the new system will allow management to reduce staff and reorganize its operations. The latter possibility is attractive to upper managers, but often threatening to employees and middle managers. For example, a new information system might allow a company to reduce its personnel costs by 40 percent and raise productivity by 200 percent.

Finally, you must consider what retraining of personnel will be needed in order to be able to use a new system, whether upper management will adequately support training needs, and how long it will take before personnel will be productive with the system. You may be able to answer these questions by finding out about other firms that have installed similar systems. Since other firms may keep this information from public view, you may have to become somewhat of a detective as well as analyst and project leader.

A feasibility study is the final product of your analysis. This study proposes alternatives to the current system to meet users' needs. It evaluates the technical, economic, and organizational costs and benefits of each alternative, and then proposes the best one to management.

Table 12.1 summarizes the proportion of time a systems analyst typically spends on several tasks, including administrative-clerical, analytical-technical, managerial, and marketing tasks. Note that routine administrative-clerical tasks take up more time than analytical-technical tasks. Management activities take about as much time as analytical-technical activities, and marketing activities are a major activity. In a service business, nearly every contact with a supplier, customer, or user involves marketing and selling yourself and your service.

TABLE 12.1

Time Spent on Different Tasks by Systems Analyst

Percentage of Time	Task	Description
20–30%	Administrative-Clerical	Do paperwork and confirm standards.
20%	Analytical-Technical	Determine user requirements; conceptualize system objective; model and compare alternative systems.
20%	Managerial	Chair meetings with users; supervise programmers; write proposals; train programmers and analysts.
30–40%	Marketing	Promote services; present system or proposal to management and users; explain alternatives to users; train users.

PERFORMANCE EVALUATION

Schedules and formats of performance evaluations vary by organization. A brief, weekly discussion of goals and a semiannual or annual written report on performance are typical. Monthly progress meetings or reports share useful information, such as new developments that may affect a project, staff changes in personnel, and unexpected delays.

Systems analysts are evaluated in several areas of performance, including

1. quality, timeliness, and ease of maintenance of deliverables. (A deliverable item is anything that you agree to produce and turn over to the systems manager. Two examples are a description of user requirements and a feasibility study of a new information system. The systems manager judges how useful this work is to users.)
2. project management skills.
3. success in communicating with and motivating users' programmers and technicians.
4. willingness to comply with company standards and to suggest improvements.

Consistent quality in an analyst's work is critical. Analysts work in an environment which demands reliability as new development projects arise. An analyst's ideas used on one project often influence the types of system proposed later. Timeliness is equally important; most delays in analysts' work ripple outward to other parts of the project. Deliverables must also be easy to maintain. For example, a design that accommodates modifications with few adjustments to system documentation saves staff time and ensures that old documentation remains useful for reference or training.

As an analyst, your project management skills will be essential in turning in deliverables on schedule and within budget. This involves planning, organizing, and conducting business effectively.

Systems managers look for evidence that systems analysts can motivate users to participate in systems development. If users are aware of the potential of a new system to make their job easier, they are more likely to be enthusiastic about planning it with the analyst. Therefore you must be able to communicate technical concepts to non-technicians. Analysts need to get users to see that the analysis phase is an opportunity to shape the future of the firm.

As already mentioned, an important part of your work as a systems analyst is in the documentation, accounting, and control of systems. You must describe the information flow of a system in a format and vocabulary that is both understandable and conformable to management's standards. You must communicate in clear, technical writing, and be able to recognize and dispel others' confusion regarding systems on which they work and that you are trying to improve.

A systems analyst's objective in assembling programmers and other technicians is to foster team spirit. During a project assignment, the group members will learn more quickly and produce better work if they discuss each other's work. Like the systems analyst, no programmer can be expected to know or remember everything about a data processing system or item of hardware or software. Pooling the talent makes the best use of that talent for the broadest group of programmers. Cooperation among programmers will ultimately put proposals into action. Your ability to manage their work is one of the most important skills in delivering a system.

Finally, the willingness to accept and at the same time suggest improvements in company standards is important to systems managers. A systems manager in charge of five analysts does not have time to constantly check each one's activity. The manager needs people who can be trusted to follow instructions and use methods that management approves. At the same time the firm needs the flexibility to change systems and processes when necessary, as when faced with new technology and economic trends. The analyst who works within company standards while being able to suggest constructive improvements takes on a partnership with the manager. Managers consider such an analyst a resource worth nurturing, particularly if he or she proposes changes of standards with creativity, objectivity, and neutrality.

Required Skills and Educational Background

Traditionally many people have moved from being a computer programmer to systems analyst. A possible career progression is programmer trainee to programmer to programmer-analyst to systems analyst. Programmer-analysts who hope to become systems analysts typically develop expertise in applications programming that permits flexibility later in their career. Then they can either concentrate in more technical areas of systems programming and design, or apply their technical background to practical business and management problems and become a systems analyst, operations manager, or operations researcher.

In recent years, systems analysts have been actively recruited from business schools—out of both undergraduate and graduate programs—in such fields as computer applications and information systems (CAIS), operations research, statistics, and computer science. Although people with these backgrounds do not necessarily have computer programming experience, they can bring a more "macro" view to the systems analyst position. For those with no programming background, training is initially in programming and then in systems analysis. Training programs usually emphasize the computer language COBOL. COBOL is an efficient language for high-volume transaction processing, and can be used to manipulate information in many ways that other computer languages do not allow. Because most corporations have made many applications in COBOL, it would be very complicated for them to switch to another language. Hence, COBOL training is likely to continue to provide a marketable background for someone interested in systems analysis.

Once programming basics are mastered (either through job experience or formal instruction), systems analysis training commences. Systems analysts are sometimes trained via an apprentice program. Junior analysts will often perform clerical or programming work for senior analysts. The senior will give the junior analyst simple modules of a larger system to analyze and document. As proficiency develops, the senior analyst will then delegate more difficult programs. The apprentice also observes meetings the senior analyst has with users, technicians, and managers. Through example and experience, the junior analyst learns the subtleties of project management.

To some extent classroom preparation in computer applications and information systems has replaced apprenticeship for systems analyst trainees. However, classrooms have the disadvantage of ignoring the interpersonal, social, and interactive nature of the systems analyst's job. Many feel that corporate training environments using only classroom training will produce mediocre systems analysts, because of this lack of practical experience. Somehow the training program must teach the systems analyst's basic skills—logical reasoning, creative thinking, clear writing, researching, leadership, personal presentation, listening, public speaking, and interviewing. Many of these cannot be taught in classroom settings alone.

Sometimes programmers who become systems analysts find themselves frustrated in that they cannot apply the skills and techniques that made them successful programmers to systems analysis. Systems analysis work is much more socially oriented than programming, and those who do switch must be able and willing to make the necessary personal adjustments. Businesses currently have a shortage of qualified systems analysts; many whom they train are either not as competent as desired or not sufficiently motivated to do the work. Hence, there is great opportunity in this field for people who can combine computer facility and good analytical skills with enjoyment of analysis of business problems and interaction with others on the job. Conversations with managers, analysts, and users suggest the following as the most essential skills for systems analysts: *listening*—to be able to articulate proposals, reports, and memos correctly as well as interview and observe; *speaking*—to interview and to conduct meetings; *reading*—to use existing documentation and keep up with innovations reported in trade journals. Other essential qualities include an understanding of and desire to solve business problems; a strong liking for extensive social contact at work; and the desire to continue learning throughout one's career.

Employers tend to look for people who are skilled in communication, analysis, and project management. Good writing skills enable you to write clear reports, memos, and proposals. Listening and speaking skills are useful in group meetings, where you must resolve conflicts among users and technical specialists, or in presentations. You will also need to be effective at interviewing users and establishing rapport with them in order to obtain useful information efficiently.

To be a good analyst you must solve business problems. The first step is to define a problem. This often involves reinterpreting others' definitions, and discarding personal biases in an attempt to articulate some sort of truth about systems.

Project management skills enable you to delegate assignments and coordinate everyone's actions toward a final report. Managers value an analyst's ability to form an effective team, schedule realistically, motivate and teach users and technicians, produce deliverables of consistent quality, and cooperate with management, keeping them informed of project progress.

Employers desire analysts who are interested in understanding how various parts of an operation fit together, in seeing the "macro" rather than the "micro" picture. Some employers are also interested in hiring analysts with active social and intellectual interests outside of work. This attribute helps to keep fresh ideas and a sense of spirit in the workplace. Most of all, employers need people who want to solve users' problems and enhance the quality of information available to them.

13

Business Consulting*

The field of business consulting has been increasing in size and stature in recent years. This growth has meant career opportunities for college and business school graduates and business professionals changing careers. Opportunities have been especially good for MBAs. This has resulted in business consulting being referred to as a "glamour industry." For the past several years the best-rated schools have had more business school graduates go into consulting than any other field.

Consulting is not a well-defined field. Definitions of a consultant range from "anyone who is out of work and owns a briefcase" to "a specially trained and experienced person who makes an organized effort to help management solve problems or improve operations through the application of judgment based on knowledge, skill, and systematic analysis of facts."

Consultants are found in many areas of business. The services they provide can be classified into three general categories: technical expertise, project assistance, and appraisal of operations. The earliest efforts in consulting (and still the most frequent) were in providing technical knowledge and skills. Organizations often hire a consultant who has expertise and specialized knowledge and can apply it to the client's situation. Government regulations (e.g., EEOC regulations in personnel and EPA regulations in environmental planning), electronic data processing (EDP), management science, and economics are some technical areas in which consulting is common.

Client firms may also hire consultants for help during fluctuations in work load or when undertaking a project for which they are not appropriately staffed. In this case, the consultant provides a service—

*This chapter is based on a paper written by Maura C. Lockhart.

rather than gives advice and information—through assisting on or independently completing a project: for instance, the design and implementation of a management information system.

The third type of consulting occurs when an organization needs an independent and objective appraisal of its operations. Appraisal areas include identifying organizational strengths and weaknesses for strategic planning, assessment of company financial performance, analysis of markets, and cost reduction.

These three categories of consulting represent broad generalizations. The consulting field is wide-ranging and diverse. While a full treatment of it in all its breadth and diversity is beyond the scope of this chapter, we will describe the major types of firms that make up the field, the activities and functions common to most areas of consulting, and the entry-level opportunities that exist.

The Consulting Industry

The size and structure of the consulting industry is difficult to estimate because the definition and scope of business consulting are so vague. Some recent statistics suggest, however, that its size is considerable. It is a $35 billion industry with over 20,000 firms and 36,000–56,000 full-time consultants. The number of part-time consultants is thought to be double this number. Approximately 2,500 new consultants enter the field each year, and the outlook for the field is positive.

SIZE AND STRUCTURE OF FIRMS

Consultants work in a wide range of organizations, from companies of one or two partners to firms with thousands of employees. Consulting divisions exist in many large companies with another primary business, especially large public accounting firms (as noted in chapter 6). Consultants are also found in universities and nonprofit research organizations. The majority of consulting firms fall into four major categories:

1. Large consulting firms. These are firms whose only business is consulting. They typically employ more than fifty consultants; a few of the largest employ more than a thousand consultants. Large firms may either be a "generalist" firm or have many divisions each with its own specialty. Some examples are the well-known management consulting organizations Arthur D. Little; Booz, Allen & Hamilton; McKinsey & Company; and the Boston Consulting Group.

2. Small and medium consulting firms. This type of firm employs from two to fifty consultants. It is estimated that 20–30 percent of all consultants work in firms of this size. These are often specialty firms, offering a small range of services or catering to a special type of client.

3. Management-advisory-services (MAS) divisions of CPA accounting firms. These are divisions within organizations that also offer accounting, auditing, tax, and other financial services. These divisions are typically quite large and operate internationally. The services offered by MAS divisions usually involve information systems, electronic data processing (EDP), financial management, and strategic planning. Although these "firms" are really divisions of larger organizations, *Business Week* reported that in 1978 six of the Big Eight CPA firms were listed among the top ten management consulting firms in terms of dollars billed. (For a discussion of CPA firms in other respects than MAS see chapter 6.)

4. Individual consultants. This group includes individuals who are sole owners of businesses, professionals (e.g., CPAs and engineers) who work as consultants outside their full-time employment, and university-affiliated academics (typically in business schools) who consult part-time. Individual consultants are almost exclusively specialists who provide limited services to a narrow group of clients. Academicians and professionals with expertise in such specialty areas as transportation, productivity, and the behavioral sciences have begun to compete effectively with the larger consulting organizations.

The structure of consulting organizations varies as widely as the size of firms. Figure 13.1 shows the corporate structure of a typical large consulting firm with many specialties. The divisions can be classified according to geographic lines, service specialty, or the sector of the industry they serve. The structure of specialty divisions within such a firm is shown in Figure 13.2. Each division, led by a director, consists of approximately thirty to forty consultants at various levels. Typically, these levels are supervising-managing consultants, operating-senior consultants, and junior consultants.

Medium-sized specialty and MAS consulting firms have fairly similar organizational structures. These firms usually have four pyramid-like levels with operating consulting teams made up of members from each level. Such a firm is seldom divided into divisions. Partners and managers may have specialty areas, but working groups are formed for each engagement.

SPECIALIZATIONS

Aside from organizational size and structure, consulting firms are classified along dimensions such as scope, area of concern, approach, and range of services offered. The most important of these classifications is area of concern. A general distinction can be made between firms that are generalists and those that are specialists. The generalist

FIGURE 13.1

Typical Structure of a Large Consulting Firm

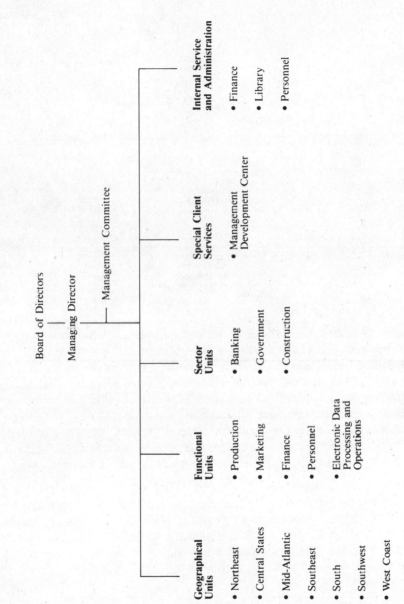

FIGURE 13.2

Typical Structure of Consulting Division

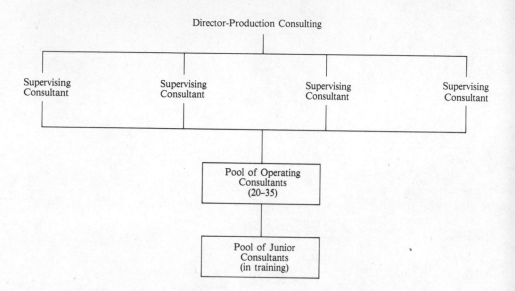

firm can provide a wide range of services and is available to solve any client problem. An example of this type of firm is the Arthur D. Little organization, whose motto is, "Almost nothing is none of our business." Recently, however, there has been a move toward more specialization, with some firms limiting service to one area and others dividing into divisions with different specialties. Specialization can be by management function, the client's industry, size of project, or other criteria. The most common dimension of specialization is management function. The major specialty areas in business consulting are as follows:

1. General management consulting. This type of consultant frequently works directly with the client's top management team on matters of general concern. Projects in general management might include studying strategic issues (such as allocation of resources or long-term strategies) and advising management on them, evaluating management decision making, and revising organizational structure or management style.

2. Financial management. A financial consultant advises management on issues of financial planning. Projects in financial consulting might include study of and recommendations on capital expenditures, enterprise development, and the design and implementation of an accounting system.

3. Marketing management. Consulting in marketing can take place at three levels. The highest is marketing strategy formulation. The next is marketing activities and operations. Projects at this level include evaluation of sales and advertising, assistance with distribution, and product development. The third level is marketing research. Here the consultant collects data and may advise the client about decisions to make on the basis of the data.

4. Production management. Consulting in production management can focus on the product itself (design, quality, etc.), the methods and organization of production, or the people involved in production. In the second area, a project might involve redesigning the work-flow layout to improve productivity, or assisting in inventory control. A project involving the "people side" of production might be concerned with compliance with government safety rules or development of a program to improve job satisfaction.

5. Information systems and data processing. Consulting in information systems is a primary interest of systems analysts and MAS consulting divisions. These consultants deal with issues regarding the kind of information, how much, and in what form it is needed for management decision making and control. They also assist in system development, improvement, and integration. A possible project could include development and implementation of an EDP system for a client, or a feasibility study of computerizing financial control systems. (Systems analysis careers are discussed in chapter 12.)

6. Personnel management. Traditionally, consulting in this area focused on personnel administration, job evaluation, and the development and evaluation of compensation systems. Recently this area has expanded to include more behavioral-science research methods and intervention strategies. Projects range from job analyses and employment-test validity studies to designing and implementing career-planning and organizational development programs. A related area in which consultants practice is labor-management relations. A consultant might work as an advocate for one side or a mediator between union and management.

7. Government-related consulting. Government-related consulting firms specialize in keeping up with current legislation in specific areas in order to advise clients on compliance with government regulations. A firm might advise clients on regulation of packaging and advertising, deregulation of transportation and financial services, and how the client will be affected by and if possible take advantage of changing regulations.

8. *Strategic planning.* This is one of the fastest-growing areas for management consulting firms. Consultants help management develop and evaluate long-term strategic plans, and advise them on major decisions such as acquisitions and mergers.

Table 13.1 identifies some of the specialty areas of the largest consulting firms in the United States. In addition to differing in area of specialization, consulting organizations differ in approach and range of services provided. Regarding approach, some firms are problem solvers: they advise management on particular problems as they occur. They provide expert information and often recommend a program of corrective action. These firms are usually referred to as resource consultants. Process consultants, in contrast, play a more developmental role: They attempt to teach management team techniques for problem solving.

The service provided by a consulting firm can be full service or limited. Full service includes studying a problem, making recommendations for change, and implementing and evaluating the change. A limited-service firm might provide only one of these services. For example, a marketing-research consulting firm might collect data and make recommendations, but the client would decide what actions to take.

The Consulting Process

Most consulting engagements proceed through similar steps. It must be kept in mind, however, that although the process described herein is

TABLE 13.1

Specializations of Selected Firms

Arthur Anderson & Co.	Management information systems, accounting
Arthur D. Little	Product development, management services
A.T. Kearney	Operations improvements and corporate strategy
Booz, Allen & Hamilton	Large-scale industrial and development projects
Boston Consulting Group	Strategic planning
Hay Associates	Human-resource management
Lester Knight	Productivity, management, and engineering systems
McKinsey & Co.	Top-level counseling and corporate planning
Price Waterhouse	Accounting, financial planning

similar for all the consulting areas, the context of each study is determined by the area of the consultant's expertise. The major activities involved in a consulting project take place in five stages: problem identification, fact finding and data gathering, data analysis, proposals and recommendations, and implementation.

1. Problem identification. The first major activity in a consulting project is definition of the problem to be addressed. Often the client will have identified the problem before the consultant arrives, but sometimes consultants are expected to work with the client in problem definition.

2. Data collection. In the data gathering stage, information pertaining to various aspects of the problem is collected. This process can be similar to a scientific research process. As a consultant, you would collect information through various means, which can include any of the following: literature search, company document review, interviewing, administering questionnaires, direct observation, and research experiments. The methods used in data collection vary according to the type and amount of information needed. For example, a production study of a particular industry might include information on the nature and location of markets, types and sources of raw materials, production processes and equipment, business practices unique to that industry, history and growth of the industry, and information on how the present economic climate might affect the industry.

Many consultants feel that data collection is the most important part of the engagement. Certainly the success of a project rests on the quality of data used to diagnose problems and propose changes. Thus, you must develop knowledge of the appropriate types and amount of data to be collected: too much or too little or the wrong type can have negative effects on the usefulness and profitability of a consulting project.

3. Data analysis and synthesis. When you are confident that the necessary information is at hand, you then analyze and condense it and come to some conclusions. Methods of analysis used depend on the nature of the data and the techniques you favor. Typically, numerical data are subject to statistical analysis. More qualitative data can be content-analyzed—for instance, noting the kinds of issues that are repeated in employee interviews. Much of the analysis involves in-depth discussion among consulting team members about the importance of information, conclusions drawn, and implications for the future. In the synthesis process massive amounts of data are combined into a meaningful whole, relationships among different aspects of the project are identified, and the results of the analysis are evaluated. The results of the analyses and synthesis provide the basis for recommendations to the client. Thus, they must be thorough and concise. Analytic skills and creativity play an important role in this stage of a consulting project.

4. Proposals and recommendations. Once the data have been synthesized, the consulting team must use the information to generate solutions. In some cases this takes place with client participation; in other situations the consultants work alone. Alternative solutions are then evaluated (again either with or without the client) and recommendations developed. When a proposal has been developed, the consulting team presents it to the client. This presentation may take place in a small meeting with a few managers, or, more commonly, in a formal presentation to the client's management team. In the presentation, sales skills are important in gaining client acceptance of the recommendations.

5. Report and implementation. The final step of the consulting engagement is delivering the final product. This may consist of a final report containing information and recommendations, or a program of sources designed to carry out recommendations. Traditionally, firms first deliver a report, and then offer a change program as an additional service. In preparing and presenting the final report, communication skills are paramount. It must be well written and complete, yet concise to be of use to the client. The presentation must be professional, hence public-speaking skills are essential. If major changes are to be implemented, knowledge of organizational change and development techniques are also necessary.

In addition to these five stages, consultants spend time with prospective clients before the actual project is defined and contracted. Securing engagements entails marketing, sales, and public relations work. Except for the largest and most well-known firms, consulting firms must market their services to survive.

Not all consulting firms perform these activities. While all firms must generate business and develop clients, a particular assignment may consist of any combination of the above steps.

The above activities suggest three major work roles: (1) data processor—collecting and analyzing data and making recommendations, which involves substantial intellectual activity; (2) project manager—running projects, planning and budgeting, controlling the process, supervising, and motivating the consulting staff; and (3) entrepreneur—marketing the consulting firm's services and generating business. A successful consultant must be able to perform each role equally well.

Making a Business Consulting Career

ENTRY-LEVEL POSITIONS

Your activities as an entry-level consultant (often called staff consultant, assistant consultant, or junior consultant) are designed to build on the technical and interpersonal skills that you bring to the job while developing the specific consulting skills of data processor, project manager, and entrepreneur. In large firms, assignments may also be made to develop skills in data collection and analysis, communication, and technical knowledge. In firms with many specialty divisions or a generalist outlook, staff assistants are often given a broad range of assignments in their early years to expand their exposure to different areas before they choose a specialty. Staff consultants become involved in the data-collection, analysis, and report-writing stages of consulting engagements, while managers and partners usually solicit business and make presentations. An entry-level consultant might also work on program implementation once a program has been approved.

The types of assignment you might have include gathering and analysis of data for a marketing study, developing computer systems and programs for inventory and production management, interviewing middle-level managers about management practices and synthesizing the interview results, or drafting a preliminary report on a project.

At the entry level you rarely work alone, and are generally a member of a two-to-five-person consulting team that includes colleagues from several levels of the firm. Consulting teams are often led by a manager or partner who plans, assigns, and evaluates the work. A number of senior and staff-level consultants actually carry out most of the work. Consulting teams may be permanent or temporary. In most MAS divisions, new consulting teams are formed for each engagement, with a manager choosing senior and staff consultants based on qualifications and experience—and experience needed. In some firms teams are permanent, based on specialization.

Depending upon the size and scope of the consulting engagements, you might work on just one large project or a number of smaller projects in the first few years. Since you are likely to be heavily involved in the data-collection and implementation stages, much of your time will be spent interacting with employees at the client's place of business.

CAREER ADVANCEMENT

Career levels and a typical career progression are shown in Table 13.2. In most consulting firms there are three or four levels: entry-level consultants, operating or supervising consultants, managers, and principals or partners. The number of levels and amount of time spent

TABLE 13.2

Career Progression in Consulting

Years	Titles	Main Functions
0–3	Trainee Junior consultant	Foundation skills Learning the consulting business
3–5	Operating consultant Senior consultant	Technical and supervisory skills Executive consulting assignments in specialty area
5–11	Supervising consultant Managing consultant	Managerial skills Supervise operating consultants
12 +	Director Partner Principal	Professional entrepreneurial skills Manage a consulting organization (or division) Negotiate new assignments

at each level depend upon the size and type of firm. In fast-growing smaller firms an MBA might reach partner status in as few as five years. However, the norm is closer to ten or twelve years.

At the second level operating consultants develop their technical skills and expand their knowledge in specific areas. Operating consultants are expected to be able to work independently, and may have an individual project or supervise a number of junior consultants. At this level, the consultant becomes involved in representing the firm to the client, attending meetings, and making presentations. Examples of the types of activity that an operating consultant might engage in are designing a management information system and determining requirements, then supervising staff consultants in implementation of the system; devising a long-range strategic plan for a small business client; and preparing a preliminary report on companies that are potential takeover or merger candidates. The most important skills at this level are supervisory skills, communication skills (written and oral), and expertise in a technical area.

At the senior or management level a consultant's role focuses more on project management. The managing consultant is responsible for the administrative duties of planning, budgeting, and selecting staff for each engagement. He or she is also responsible for billing and fee collection as the engagement progresses. The managing consultant has a great deal of contact with the client's top management, and is primarily responsible for assessing client needs, preparing engagement proposals, and making formal presentations of results and recommendations. The managing consultant is also responsible for leading a number of consulting teams and assisting in the development of young professionals. At this level there is a shift away from technical skills and a focus on administration, personnel development, financial management, and organization development.

To reach the highest level in a large consulting firm (usually partner or principal), a consultant must show exemplary consulting skills and specialized knowledge. He or she must be a leader in an area of expertise. At the partner level, entrepreneurial skills become paramount. Partners are responsible for running the business of the firm, marketing its services, and generating consulting projects. As leaders in their fields, partners are also expected to be involved in professional associations and activities.

As in most organizations, the number of consultants at each level declines as one moves up the hierarchy. In a large firm there may be five to ten times as many junior consultants as partners. Some consultants spend their whole career at the operating level, but the majority either move up the hierarchy or out of the firm. The next section will discuss briefly those who leave.

LIFE AFTER CONSULTING

Only a moderate proportion of those who start their career in professional consulting will make it their lifelong work. Many consultants leave before attaining the managerial or partner level to return to business or teaching, move into higher-level line positions in their specialty industry, or start their own consulting practice. The relatively high salaries in consulting sometimes lead consultants to demand salaries that are higher than can be offered in line jobs. This, coupled with the level of skill and experience attained in relatively few years, makes the operating level a popular one at which to move out of consulting. The latter factor is also one of the reasons many people start their careers in consulting. The field offers diverse projects and a chance to develop technical and managerial skills in less time than it would take in most other industries or career areas. Management experts believe that the entrepreneurial world of consulting helps develop the psychological skills that senior line managers need, and the group project work teaches the selling of ideas and encourages risk taking. Consultants tend to take on the problems of huge corporations and test their ability to solve them under the supervision and coaching of senior professionals. Thus, consulting is considered a good entry-level position for many industries.

Required Skills and Educational Background

The profile of the management consultant is often discussed in the consulting literature—the conclusion being that there is no one ideal person or style. Nevertheless, we can identify characteristics common to successful management consultants which differentiate them from professionals in other industries.

PERSONAL CHARACTERISTICS OF CONSULTANTS

As a consultant, you must be forceful and self-confident. Management teams from the largest organizations in the country are very demanding in the services they require. To obtain projects, which are usually granted after competitive bidding, you must feel certain that you offer the best services and be able to so convince the client. Due to the competitiveness of the field, you must be able to deal with rejection and failure without loss of self-esteem or confidence. Because you tend to work on a larger number of projects than professionals in other industries, and because your projects typically begin with a problem situation, the risk of failure is higher in consulting. You must enjoy risk taking and have no fear of failure.

Successful consultants tend to be self-motivated self-starters. Most consulting people are entrepreneurs motivated by achievement and recognition rather than company loyalty and job security. Consulting projects usually entail severe time-limits requiring initiative and a high energy level from all members of the consulting firm.

Consultants typically enjoy problem solving and are curious. Often finding the solution to a problem requires the ability to see beyond the facts available and generate novel responses. The diversity of your work and its problem-centered nature require that you have a high tolerance for ambiguity. The course of a project may change many times in response to new data and results at different stages; you need to be flexible enough to change, but level-headed and stable enough to perform consistently while the project is in flux.

SKILLS AND ABILITIES

The most important requirement in the consulting business is expertise through technical knowledge in a particular industry, function, or technique. While consultants are hired because they are experts, there are other skills essential to successful consulting.

The Association of Consulting Management Engineers has developed a list of key skills, shown in Table 13.3. Most listings of these skills—to be found in various publications and the recruiting materials of most consulting firms—generally put them into five categories: (1) expertise

TABLE 13.3

Characteristics of Management Consultants

1. good physical and mental health
2. professional etiquette and courtesy
3. stability of behavior and action
4. self-confidence
5. personal effectiveness (drive)
6. integrity (the quality that engenders trust)
7. independence (To be a successful consultant, you must be self-reliant, not subordinate to the opinions of others. You must be able to form your own judgments in the areas of your competence and experience, at the same time recognizing the limitations of your competence, experience, and judgment.)
8. strong analytical or problem-solving ability (the ability to analyze, assemble, sort, balance, and evaluate the basic factors in problem situations of different degrees of complexity)
9. creative imagination
10. skills relating to interpersonal relationships
    a. orientation toward the human-relations aspect of problems
    b. receptivity to new information or points of view expressed by others
    c. ability to enlist client participation in the solution of problems
    d. ability to effect a transfer of knowledge to client personnel
11. ability to communicate and persuade with above-average facility

in the field (as described above), (2) technical skills, (3) communication skills, (4) interpersonal skills, and (5) administrative skills.

The most important technical skills required of a business consultant are uncovering problems and solving them efficiently. These are distinct abilities which require analytic thought and ingenuity. Another important technical skill is research skill. A great deal of work as a consultant involves thorough research—the collection and synthesis of information and in-depth analysis of diverse data.

Communication skills are important to consultants, as they often spend more than half of their time communicating. You must be adept at public speaking and able to express yourself clearly, concisely, and precisely in both oral and written forms. Since you may make formal presentations, visual communications skills are also helpful. You must be adept at listening and observing; much of the data in a consulting project is collected by observation or interview. An aware and perceptive consultant should be able to gather data from both what is said and what is not said.

Interpersonal skills are required, as you must be able to work effectively with a variety of clients and with staff at all hierarchical levels in both the client's firm and yours. You must be able to engender trust and openness in clients. This is important in collecting information and in creating acceptance of organizational change during implementation of programs or policy changes. You must also show strong leadership. A senior or managing consultant must be able to motivate and lead others as well as work with them in developing their skills.

Administrative skills are required mostly at the top levels in the consulting hierarchy. Consulting managers must be able to manage people, projects, and data. They must be knowledgeable and skilled in business, marketing, fee collection, and new business development. Entrepreneurial skills are necessary at the manager-partner level in consulting firms. They are especially important for independent consultants.

EDUCATION AND BACKGROUND

Most consulting firms require at least an MBA or other advanced degree, although a few MAS firms will hire qualified applicants with a bachelor's degree. The MBA or advanced-degree major required depends on the type of consulting involved. The most popular degrees in large consulting firms and MAS divisions are accounting, general business, computer science, engineering, finance, information systems, and marketing. An MBA degree is often preferred because the case-analysis research method taught in many business schools is similar to that used by entry-level consultants.

Many consulting firms require work experience in industry; some will consider experience a substitute for an MBA. Someone with experience and in-depth knowledge of a particular industry or function is particularly well suited for a consulting position. Although there are no age requirements for consulting positions, the typical entry-level age range is twenty-six to thirty, reflecting educational and prior work experience requirements. There is also an informal upper age limit, ranging broadly from thirty-six to fifty, for entry-level positions in many firms. This is because the work patterns required in the early years of a consulting career (long hours and extensive travel) are thought to require young, healthy individuals with a high energy level, willing to make sacrifices in other areas of life to move ahead. In some firms it may also reflect the desire to maintain an image of young, aggressive, fast-paced consultants trained in the latest techniques and technologies.

TRAINING AND CERTIFICATION

There are few formal entry-level training programs in consulting firms. Rather, initial training occurs on-the-job under the supervision of an operating consultant or managing consultant. However, the ever-changing business environment and the explosion of new business technology make ongoing training essential in the business consulting field. In order to stay on the leading edge of an area of expertise, consultants participate in both internal and external training and development programs.

As a consultant progresses through the hierarchy, internal, firm-sponsored training programs usually emphasize the development of appropriate consulting skills. In order to update technical skills and learn about new theories and techniques, you need to stay abreast of current literature in the field. Because of the fast pace of the business day, this reading is not usually done at work. It is also important to attend regularly seminars and meetings of professional associations; university-sponsored courses are attended occasionally.

The training function is becoming more important now that the certification of consultants has become an issue. Business consultants as such are not regulated by law. A number of professional associations do award certificates to consultants who meet some minimum requirements, but these are not licenses and few consultants actually have them. At present, anyone can be a consultant and solicit business. While some specialists have to meet licensing requirements (e.g., CPAs, engineers, psychologists), until the field of business consulting is better defined attempts at certification and licensing will probably fail.

THE CONSULTANT'S LIFESTYLE

A management consulting career is often envisioned as being glamorous. Consultants are thought to whip around the world, meet with Fortune 500 presidents, and collect high fees. The average consultant's life, however, is far from this image. As an entry-level consultant you would be expected to work long hours (fifty to seventy per week), including weekends. You may spend many weeks each year at clients' out-of-town locations (which are rarely in Paris or London); this means that you may have to sacrifice social and family concerns while building your career. Many consulting firms have strict standards regarding their employees' behavior. Some consultants are known to consider client confidentiality so important that they will even refuse to tell their families or friends where they are traveling.

If you are willing to make a commitment to a consulting career, there is good compensation for your sacrifices. You typically have autonomy in your work, high earnings, and a great deal of status and respect in the business community. You also have tremendous career opportunities both within and without consulting. If you are willing to make some sacrifices and work long and hard hours, a consulting career can be highly rewarding.

14

Getting the Job and Making It Work for You

Chapter 1 provided a framework for you to establish your career management plan. Chapters 2 through 13 analyzed several relevant career areas. Now that you have a better idea of what is right for you, here is some advice on how to land the job that will be the start of your career.

Your Job Search: Initial Approach

A job search is very demanding, both emotionally and physically, as anyone who has sought a professional-level position in business knows. Because looking for a job is so difficult, there are hundreds of books to assist you in obtaining your preferred position. Four of the best are:

> *What Color Is Your Parachute?* by Richard Bolles (Ten Speed Press, 1982)
> *Who's Hiring Who?* by Richard Lathrop (Ten Speed Press, 1977)
> *Go Hire Yourself an Employer* by Richard Irish (Doubleday & Co., Inc., 1973)
> *Put Your Degree to Work* by Marcia Fox (W.W. Norton & Co., 1979).

One other—targeted to those with an MBA degree—is also recommended:

> *The MBA Career: Moving on the Fast Track to Success* by Eugene Bronstein and Robert Hisrich (Barron's Educational Series, Inc., 1983).

NARROWING THE SEARCH

Nearly all job-search books emphasize the importance of self-assessment and establishing career preferences and objectives. Without realistic and meaningful career goals, your job hunt will generally be disappointing and unproductive. If you have not established your career preferences, the opportunities you find will seldom lead to job and career satisfaction.

If you are floundering among too many possibilities and too few clear preferences—stop. Go back and refine your self-assessment and career objectives. Eliminate those career areas that do not directly satisfy your objectives *and* fit your skills, interests, values, and preferred lifestyle. Once you have narrowed your search down to one or two *(not* three) of the career areas discussed in chapters 2 through 13, continue your job search.

You must focus on no more than two types of positions in business for several reasons. First, employers are not interested in hiring someone who is shopping around for a career. The surest way to receive a rejection letter from a prospective employer is to indicate your willingness to do anything. Companies do not hire business professionals to do anything—they hire them for their particular skills, to accomplish specific tasks.

Second, no matter how much time and energy you think you have to devote to the process, it will not be enough to explore more than two areas. Your time and energies will be drained before you can effectively explore your second career preference. You say, "Not me!" Chances are you are wrong; but even if you are not, it means many hours each week of unsuccessful, dissatisfying experiences.

Third, a job search is emotionally demanding. The ups and downs—and usually there are many more downs—play havoc with your emotions. The ambiguous and uncertain outcome of many efforts often makes it difficult for you to relax. Many people experience high levels of stress, sullenness, and even depression and anger while looking for a job. Do you really need to lengthen the process by looking everywhere, refusing to focus your efforts and ignoring your preferences for fear of missing an opportunity that probably will not satisfy you anyway?

SELECTING THE INDUSTRIES AND COMPANIES YOU PREFER

Once you have focused on one or two career areas, you must select the specific industries and companies to approach. Informational interviews; "networking" with friends, relatives, alumni, and other professionals; and extensive library research on the industries and companies of interest will help you make your selection. Many of the above-mentioned job search books include resource sections on how to learn more about specifics of an industry and company. Another book that is useful in this regard is *Self-Assessment and Career Development* by John Kotter, Victor Faux, and Charles McArthur (Prentice-Hall, 1978), particularly the bibliographies to chapters 2–13 and the appendix sections. Some useful resources include trade or professional associations for the industries of interest (e.g., the American Bankers Association), trade publications *(American Banker)*, related publications *(The Wall Street Journal)*, and corporate annual reports.

Your pre-job-interview's explorative process may overlap with the actual job interview process. As you learn more about specific industry and company characteristics, you frequently generate job leads which can turn into job interviews. Informational interviews, networking with friends and associates, and library research should be continued even after job interviews have started; this will reduce the likelihood of the job search process coming to an unexpected halt should job interviews not turn into job offers.

What about employment agencies, newspaper ads, executive search firms, and so forth as a source of job leads? Certainly all sources of job leads are potentially valuable. Several of the job search books mentioned earlier discuss various sources of job leads in detail. We find that employment agencies and newspaper ads are of limited use in securing professional business employment. While you may certainly use such sources to augment your job search activities, they should never replace informational interviewing, networking with friends and acquaintances, and library research as a way to learn about prospective employers.

Your Job Search Tools

The tools of a job campaign are the resume and cover letter and your job interview skills. Examples to assist you in writing and designing your resume and cover letters can be found in the recommended job search books. These books also provide advice on handling interviews.

RESUME

A resume is simply a brief, descriptive summary of your career-related life experiences, skills, and accomplishments. It provides a prospective employer with a fairly standardized yet individual statement of who you are—your educational background, past employment, work experiences, accomplishments, and interests. Most individuals seeking entry-level positions construct a one-to-two page (preferably one-page) resume that summarizes their life chronologically—with most recent employment or education first—or functionally—with most relevant skills and accomplishments first. Chronological resumes are most effective when past work experiences are similar to the current career preference. For a functional resume you analyze past experiences in terms of relevant functions or skills; the resume is designed to convince the prospective employer that you possess those skills that will be useful in the career you are applying for. The functional resume is the best choice for people changing career areas, since past work experiences may be viewed by prospective employers as irrelevant unless the transferable skills are clearly identified. A mix of the chronological and functional styles can be used when you move from one career area to another, closely related area (e.g., from product management to advertising, or from securities analysis to corporate finance).

What should be on a resume? Your name, address, phone, educational background, work experiences (including employers' names and addresses), accomplishments, special skills (computer languages, foreign languages, etc.), and particular personal characteristics (hobbies, accreditations, skills, etc.) that indicate your suitability for the position you are seeking. Including a clear, concise, and specific statement of your career objective for the next five years is optional, but something we recommend highly. You may also include information about your personal interests and awards you have received.

What should *not* be on a resume? Any overt statement of age, race, sex, marital status, family situation, or religion should be omitted, as well as anything that cannot be substantiated. It is risky to list more than one objective, or to display prominently more than one career area among the accomplishments and personal characteristics. It is *unnecessary* to state, "References are available on request," or, "Willing to relocate," and so forth. Of course references, further data, and the issue of relocation will be discussed before a job offer is made—but cluttering up your resume with such obvious statements communicates nothing to the prospective employer and wastes space.

COVER LETTER

A cover letter introduces you to a prospective employer via the mail. If you can meet the prospective employer directly, without having to write (for example, through a college placement interview), you are one step ahead. However, more often than not, some form of direct-mail campaign will be necessary to reach some of the organizations you are interested in. Therefore, you need a *very* effective cover letter. If your cover letter is poor, the reader may not even look at the enclosed resume.

A good cover letter is more personalized than the resume. Cover letters should always address a specific person within the prospective company. You must find out who the relevant person is, and address him or her in the letter by name and title. Cover letters should be targeted to that employer's current employment needs, if at all possible. It is best to write a letter expressing interest in and capability for a specific position that is vacant at the time of writing.

A good cover letter provides the opportunity for you to show some of your business-related skills. It should—

- reflect some of your knowledge of the employer and industry,
- reveal your goals in approaching this specific company,
- suggest how you will be able to apply your skills in the position you seek,
- provide a more informal and realistic picture of your personal style,
- demonstrate your ability to think and reason,
- illustrate your written communication skills,
- clarify any ambiguous points on your resume (a gap in employment, a major career change, etc.).

A letter that accomplishes these points will require several hours of effort. Like a resume, a cover letter is not a quick and simple tool for obtaining job offers.

RECRUITING INTERVIEWS

Recruiting interviews, unlike job interviews, are generally prearranged by a college placement office, employment agency, or personnel office of the employer. They allow the employer to screen dozens of potential candidates for several possible openings. Recruiting interviews are often done by a professional recruiting interviewer over the course of a few concentrated days or weeks. Each interview is scheduled for a fixed amount of time (generally thirty minutes), and is usually sandwiched between other recruiting interviews. Primarily, recruiting interviews allow an employer to see many job applicants— with the intent of rejecting 50 to 80 percent outright. If you get past the recruiting interview, you are asked back for a job interview. However, if you are able to obtain a job interview without going through a recruiting interview, by all means do so. This will help you avoid possible recruiting-interview rejection. For example, a good cover letter sent directly to the manager with a position vacancy may lead to a job interview.

As you participate in a recruiting interview, keep in mind its purpose: The recruiting interviewer is primarily looking for reasons to exclude each applicant from a subsequent job interview. Reasons typically mentioned for rejecting applicants are that the interviewee—

- knew little or nothing about the company,
- was interpersonally ineffective (e.g., arrogant, poor listener, obnoxious, too aggressive, too withdrawn),

- was unenthusiastic or seemed to lack interest,
- lacked clear career preferences and goals,
- was shopping around,
- was unqualified in terms of education or work experience.

The first two reasons are the ones most often mentioned by recruiters, the last two least often.

Recruiting interviews do offer certain benefits to you. First, they are usually arranged by someone else—taking the burden of coordinating the interview off you. Second, since the recruiting interview is less focused on a specific position than a job interview, you need not be as knowledgeable. Recruiting interviews provide an opportunity to learn more about a firm and the positions available in it, while allowing you to display what you have already learned through other sources (informational interviews, library research, networking, etc.). Finally, recruiting interviews tend to occur intensively for a four-to-six-week period. Many individuals get keyed up for this period, and then go back to other activities until actual job interviews and offers begin to materialize. The concentration of effort into a relatively short period of time is particularly helpful to the less experienced job seeker.

JOB INTERVIEWS

All the advice to job seekers about job interviews can be summarized in a single sentence: Be prepared and be natural. Be prepared by knowing as much as possible about yourself (self-assessment), your resume (the readiness to answer any question about what you have included on or omitted from the resume), your preferences, the employing organization, the target position, and the interviewer. Be natural by treating the actual interview as a *discussion* between two people with similar goals but, perhaps, different perceptions of the information being shared. Both of you have the goal of achieving an effective job-person match. Here are some useful interview tips:

- Don't try to control the interviewer; control your responses.
- Don't try to please; try to discuss and share information.
- Don't take notes during the interview; be attentive and enthusiastic.
- Don't do all the talking; interviews should be interactive.
- Maintain normal eye contact.
- Respond to nonverbal as well as verbal stimuli.
- Use your responses to emphasize your strengths and self-assessment themes.
- Be honest and open.
- Send a follow-up note.

Is the Salary a Fair Offer?

Among all the attributes of a particular job in business, the salary offered is probably the most frequently discussed among job seekers. Interestingly, nearly 50 percent of all people seeking professional careers in business who receive multiple job offers end up choosing a position that is *not* the highest salary offer. This is because salary should *not* be the prime reason for selecting a position. On the other hand, the salary offered is an implicit statement of worth and is one of the important factors leading you to choose one opportunity over another.

Relative salary information by career area is provided in Table 14.1. These figures allow you to compare your job offer to the offers others may be receiving in the same and different career areas. The salary ranges shown are 1984 projections for individuals with a BA or BS degree. However, many factors can affect an offer, including a graduate degree, years of work experience, the nature of the work experience, the geographic location of employment, the current supply and demand for personnel in the career area, and the particular industry.

As a simplified rule, an MBA degree is worth from $3,000 to $8,000 per year more to an employer than a BA or BS degree. Each year of

TABLE 14.1

Projected Salary Range by Career Area for Entry-Level Positions (BS or BA Degree, 1984)

Career Area	1983 Salary Range
Accounting, private	$13,400–20,400
Accounting, public	15,100–21,500
Advertising account executive	13,700–22,100
Banking	13,800–20,000
Business consulting	16,900–28,100
Buying	12,500–19,700
Communications and public relations	12,300–18,400
Corporate finance	14,700–22,100
Human-resource management	12,700–19,600
Investment banking	18,400–31,700
Product management	15,800–24,800
Sales	11,000–27,500
Securities analysis	13,100–18,800
Systems analysis	16,700–29,100

NOTE: The salary range encompasses the middle 80% of the salary offers; the top and bottom 10% are excluded.

full-time business work experience up to about five years is worth $700 per year more in an initial salary offer for an entry-level position. Up to three years of work experience that is directly related to a position is worth approximately $1,200 per year of experience toward an entry-level position salary. For more than three years of experience, higher-level positions with higher-level salaries are typical.

The cost of living and desirability of living in different geographic areas also affects salary offers. Employment offers in large cities in the Northeast and on the West Coast are usually 10–20 percent higher than comparable employment offers in other locations, such as smaller cities and rural areas. You can refer to a general salary guide, such as the *American Almanac of Jobs and Salaries* by John W. Wright (Avon Books, 1984), to estimate the appropriate salary for particular locations.

While the supply and demand for professionals in a particular career area affects salary, the specific dollar value of the supply-demand effect in a particular career area and year is difficult to estimate. Reasonable projections are contained in the *Almanac of Jobs and Salaries*.

Salary offers also vary by industry—even for the same professional position. Table 14.2 projects 1984 salaries by industry for professional employment for typical MBA entry-level positions.

Making Your Choice

The key to evaluating a job offer and selecting a position in business is knowing what you want and whether or not a particular employer is likely to provide it. Your self-assessment and career goals together with the information you have been able to gather about the particular position and company should provide the base on which you can make your decision.

First, find out as much as you can about the job being offered—what tasks are to be performed, with whom, under whose supervision or control, and in what organizational environment. If possible, have several interviews with your future boss and other individuals with whom you will work before you accept a job offer. These meetings will allow you to systematically explore whether or not a particular job is right for you.

Then, consider the likely flow of career positions, salary increments, and job responsibilities over time. If a high initial starting salary is to be followed by very small salary increments, the attractiveness of the offer is reduced. Conversely, a highly prestigious position may have little or no career-progression possibilities, making it a deadend job. Or, much-sought-after work in a specialty area or specific market or on a

TABLE 14.2

Projected MBA Average Starting Salaries by Industry for Professional Employment (1984)

Industry	Average Salary
Accounting	$25,800
Advertising	28,600
Aerospace	27,800
Automotive	26,100
Banking (commercial)	27,700
Chemicals	29,400
Communications (non-utility)	30,100
Construction and real estate development	27,900
Consulting	38,400
Consumer products	30,500
Electric and electronic	29,100
Energy	30,800
Food and beverages	29,100
Government and nonprofit	25,500
Instruments	30,700
Insurance	25,100
Investment banks	37,200
Machinery and tools	28,300
Metals and mining	29,600
Packaging and glass	30,100
Paper and forest products	29,000
Pharmaceuticals	30,900
Public relations	26,100
Retailing	26,100
Service: hospital/health	26,700
Service: travel/hotel	27,100
Service: other	27,300
Textiles	29,100
Transportation	28,300
Utilities (telephone, gas, electric)	28,200
Widely diversified manufacturing	30,100
Self-employed	35,500

particular new product may change rapidly if the product-market area experiences unfavorable sales or profits.

The process of evaluation and choice is filled with emotional ups and downs. Therefore, you may find it helpful to evaluate each position through use of a self-administered questionnaire after each job interview. This will help you avoid overreacting. The questionnaire should be designed to reflect your chief concerns about career choice. Systematic use of such questionnaires allows you to track how you perceive various employers throughout the job search.

Choosing one job over others involves saying no to one or more companies. Rejecting an organization is more difficult than it sounds. Some people suffer through weeks of painful deliberation—just to avoid making a choice. And after they have made the decision, they often feel down about the opportunities they passed up. Remember that such post-decision depression is common; try not to let it prevent you from making the right decision.

Making a career choice is just one choice among dozens that you make over the years. If it does not end up being as rewarding a choice as you first thought, you must simply explore other options—with your current employer and superiors as well as with other firms. Choosing a position in business is just one step in the process of managing your career.

Career Mobility

A final factor to consider in selecting a career area and choosing a position within it is the relation of that career area to other areas. Chapters 2 through 13 have discussed career paths within specific areas and have identified many of the pathways and linkages to other career areas. A comprehensive map across all the career areas discussed is provided in Figure 14.1. It is a diagram of the most likely connections among the twelve career areas. Shorter lines between career areas signify a closer linkage between those areas. The absence of a line between two areas does not mean that people never move between them, but rather that movement is relatively infrequent, and often requires additional training or a return to entry-level work.

The linkages among the finance-related careers (commercial banking, securities analysis, investment banking, corporate finance, private accounting, and public accounting) are fairly strong. The linkages among marketing-related careers (product management, advertising account management, communications and public relations, and sales and buying) are moderately strong, but less common than among finance-related careers. The human resource management and systems analysis areas have few linkages to other areas. These are fairly specialized,

FIGURE 14.1

Most Prevalent Linkages Among Career Areas
(Shorter distances imply stronger linkages)

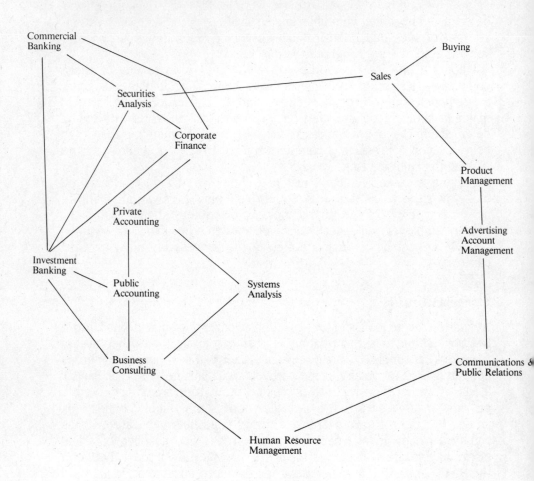

technical career areas that offer limited career mobility to other functionally based career areas. However, mobility *within* these areas is substantial. The business consulting area links well to four career areas—investment banking, public accounting, systems analysis, and human resource management—and weakly with all other areas (not shown in Figure 14.1). Because of the nature of business consulting activities, individuals with particular expertise and strong communications skills can enter business consulting, and business consultants can often leave consulting for other career areas.

BIBLIOGRAPHY

CHAPTER 1
Laying the Groundwork for Your Career

Campbell, D.P. *Manual for the SVIB-SCII*. Stanford, Calif.: Stanford University Press, 1977.

Holland, John, L. *Making Vocational Choices: A Theory of Careers*. Englewood Cliffs, N.J.: Prentice-Hall, Inc., 1973.

Kotter, J.P., Faux, V.A., & McArthur, C.C. *Self-Assessment and Career Development*. Englewood Cliffs, N.J.: Prentice-Hall, Inc., 1978.

Storey, Walter, D. *Career Dimensions II*. Croton-on-Hudson, N.Y.: General Electric Company, 1976.

RESOURCES

Strong-Campbell Interest Inventory—available through NCS Interpretive Scoring Systems, Inc., P.O. Box 1416, Minneapolis, Minnesota 55440.

Study of Values—available through Houghton-Mifflin, Hopewell, New Jersey 08525.

CHAPTER 2
Commercial Banking

BOOKS

Boynton, Ralph E. *Your Future in Banking*. New York: Richards Rosen Press, Inc., 1976.

Davis, Mary Lee. *Careers in a Bank*. Minneapolis: Lerner Publications, 1973.

Hartburger, Neil. *Your Career in Banking*. New York: Arco Publishing, Inc., 1980.

Mainstream Access, Inc. *The Banking Job Finder*. Englewood Cliffs, N.J.: Prentice-Hall, Inc., 1981. (Includes an overview of banking, interviews with bankers and an extensive bibliography.)

Paradis, Adnan, A. *Opportunities in Banking*. Skokee, Ill. VGM Career Horizons, 1980.

Sextant Systems, Inc. *Banking*. Milwaukee: 1970.

Whatley, Jo Ann. *Banking and Finance Careers*. New York: Franklin Watts, Inc., 1978.

Wright, Don. *Banking: A Dynamic Business*. Dallas: Don Wright Associates, 1980. (Discusses the structure and organization of the banking industry and includes a chapter on "Careers in Banking.")

PERIODICALS

ABA Banking Journal
Journal of Commercial Bank Lending
National Banking Review

PROFESSIONAL ASSOCIATIONS

American Banking Association
American Finance Association
National Bankers Association

CHAPTER 3
Securities Analysis

BOOKS

Bolten, Steven, E. *Security Analysis and Portfolio Management.* New York: Holt, Rinehart & Winston, 1972.

Brooks, John. *The Go-Go Years.* New York: Weybright and Talley, 1973. (A lively, highly readable account of the ebullient stock market of the late 1960s and the forces that led to its demise. Good background reading.)

Fischer, Donald, E. *Security Analysis and Portfolio Management.* Englewood Cliffs, N.J.: Prentice-Hall, Inc., 1983.

Garbade, Kenneth, D. *Securities Markets.* New York: McGraw-Hill, Inc., 1982. (A comprehensive overview of the securities market; one of the most current.)

Goodman, George, J.W. (alias "Adam Smith"). *The Money Game.* New York: Vintage Books, 1976. (Widely acclaimed as a modern classic; an irreverent, entertaining, inside view of the stock market.)

Graham, Benjamin, and Good, David L. *Security Analysis: Principles and Technique.* New York: McGraw-Hill, Inc., 1962. (Still the bible of securities analysis. An authoritative, thorough textbook.)

Henle, Faye. *Careers for the 70's: Securities.* New York: Crowell-Collier Press, 1972.

Latane, Henry A. *Security Analysis and Portfolio Management.* New York: Ronald Press, 1975. (Basic text on finance and investments; covers the range of investments from analysis of individual securities to the final combination of securities into a portfolio.)

Malkiel, Burton G. *A Random Walk Down Wall Street.* New York: W.W. Norton & Co., Inc., 1973. (A highly readable account of analysis in action—mod-psychology stock-picking theories and the author's investment advice.)

Miller, Eugene. *Your Future in Securities.* New York: Richards Rosen Press, Inc., 1974.

The New York Society of Security Analysts. *Career Day: November 23, 1981.* N.Y.S.S.A. and Rainbow Enterprising, 1981. (Transcript of a seminar sponsored by N.Y.S.S.A. including remarks by several practicing analysts about their careers.)

Shepard, Lawrence. *The Securities Brokerage Industry.* Lexington, Mass.: DC Health and Co., 1975. (The first two chapters detail the structure and organization of the securities industry.)

U.S. Securities and Exchange Commission. *Report of Special Study of Securities Markets of the Securities and Exchange Commission.* Washington: U.S. Government Printing Office, 1963. (Despite its publication date, an empirical goldmine containing information on every aspect of the securities markets. For selective reading.)

PERIODICALS
Financial Analysts Journal HG
Financial World
Institutional Investor
Investment Dealers Digest
Magazine of Wall Street

PROFESSIONAL ASSOCIATIONS
The Financial Analysts Federation
    1633 Broadway
    New York, NY
New York Society of Security Analysts
    71 Broadway
    New York, NY
Securities Industry Association
    20 Broad Street
    New York, NY
National Association of Securities Dealers

CHAPTER 4
Investment Banking

BOOKS

Altman, Edward I., and McKinney, Mary J. *Financial Handbook, 5th Ed.* New York: John Wiley & Sons, Inc., 1981. (Includes description of financial services provided by investment banks.)

Carosso, Vincent P. *Investment Banking in America: A History.* Cambridge: Harvard University Press, 1970. (Report of a study analyzing the changing role of the investment banker in the American economy.)

Carosso, Vincent P. *More Than a Century of Investment Banking: The Kidder, Peabody and Co. Story.* New York: McGraw-Hill, Inc., 1979. (Describes the growth and development, adjustments and readjustments, of one of today's top Wall Street investment banking houses.)

Jensen, Michael D. *The Financiers—The World of the Great Wall Street Investment Banking Houses.* Weybright & Talley.

Phalon, Richard. *The Takeover Barons of Wall Street: Inside the Billion Dollar Merger Game.* New York: G.P. Putnam's Sons, 1981. (Chronology of an acquisition, detailing the investment banker's role.)

Shepard, Lawrence. *The Securities Brokerage Industry.* Lexington, Mass: Lexington Books, D.C. Health Co., 1975. (The first two chapters detail the structure and organization of the securities industry.)

PERIODICALS
Journal of Portfolio Management
Financial World
Institutional Investor
Investment Dealers Digest
Magazine of Wall Street

PROFESSIONAL ASSOCIATIONS
Association of Investment Brokers
Financial Analysts Federation

CHAPTER 5
Corporate Finance

BOOKS

Brealy, Richard, and Steward Myers. *Principles of Corporate Finance,* 1st ed. New York: McGraw-Hill, Inc., 1981. (Textbook which clearly describes many of the corporate finance functions in detail; also provides an exposure to present analytical techniques.)

Brigham, Eugene. *Financial Management: Theory and Practice,* 3rd ed. New York: The Dryden Press, 1982. (Textbook describing both the theory and the functions that exist in finance today.)

Harvard Business School Finance Club. *Careers in Finance,* 1st ed. (A collection of articles presenting typical careers and career paths of MBAs in finance.)

Smith, Dan G. *Women in Finance.* Skokie, Ill.: VGM Career Horizons, 1981.

Whattey, Jo Ann. *Banking and Finance Careers.* New York: Franklin Watts, Inc., 1978.

PERIODICALS
Journal of Finance
Financial Management
Financial Review

PROFESSIONAL ASSOCIATIONS
American Finance Association
Financial Management Association

CHAPTER 6
Accounting

BOOKS

Abraham, Stanley Charles. *The Public Accounting Profession*. Lexington, Mass: Lexington Books, 1978.

American Institute of Certified Public Accountants. Task force on the Report Committee on Education and Experience Requirements for CPAs. *Academic Preparation for Professional Accounting Careers*. New York: ALCPA, 1978.

Buckley, John W. *The Accounting Profession*. Los Angeles: Melville Publishing, 1974.

Carey, John L. *Getting Acquainted with Accounting*. Boston: Houghton Mifflin Co., 1977.

Higgins, John Joseph. *Interviewing for a Career in Public Accounting*. Hampton Press, 1981.

Hopkins, Leon. *Accountancy and Law*. London: Haymarket, 1976.

Locklear, Edmond. *Your Future in Accounting*. New York: Arco Publishing, Inc., 1971.

Lodge, Arthur. *Opportunities in Accounting*. Louisville, Ky: VGM Career Horizons, 1977.

Montagna, Paul D. *Certified Public Accounting: A Sociological View of a Profession in Change*. Houston: Scholars Book Co., 1974. (Based on a two-year study of public accountants; includes a discussion of the public accounting Big 8 Firms, the "public accountants world of work" and career patterns.

Plevyak, Paul P. *Exploring Accounting Careers*. Cincinnati: South-Western Publishing Co., 1976.

PERIODICALS
Accountants Digest
Accounting Review
Internal Auditor
Journal of Accountancy
Journal of Accounting Research
New York Certified Public Accountant

PROFESSIONAL ASSOCIATIONS
American Accounting Association
American Institute of Certified Public Accountants
American Association of Women Accountants
Institute of Internal Auditors

CHAPTER 7
Product Management

BOOKS

Association of National Advertisers. *Management of the New Product Function: A Guidebook*. 1980.

Beaumont, John Appleton. *Your Career in Marketing*. New York: Gregg Division, McGraw-Hill, Inc., 1976.

Bikkie, James A. *Careers in Marketing*. New York: Gregg Division, McGraw-Hill, Inc., 1978.

Britt, Stuart Henderson, ed. *Marketing Managers' Handbook*. Dartnell Corp., 1973. (Includes a chapter on careers in marketing, managerial perspective, staffing marketing function, etc.)

Cleary, David Powers. *Great American Brands: The Success Formulas That Made Them Famous*. New York: Fairchild Publications, 1981. (Follows the passage of several famous brands from inception to marketing insight to success.)

Cravens, David W., Hills, Gerald E., and Woodruff, Robert B. *Marketing Decision Making: Concepts and Strategy*. Homewood, Ill.: Richard D. Irwin, Inc., 1976. (General background in marketing; includes a description of the product manager's responsibilities and position with the organization.)

Dunne, Patrick N., and Obenhouse, Susan. *Product Management: A Reader*. Chicago American Marketing Association, 1980. (Includes addresses, essays and lectures on product management.)

Haas, Kenneth Brooks. *Opportunities in Sales and Marketing*. Skokie, Ill.: VGM Career Horizons,

1980. (Geared more toward undergraduate college students and includes chapters on structure of the industry, retail sales, and industrial sales.)

Hise, Richard T. *Product Service Strategy.* New York: Petrocelli/Charter, 1977. (Introduction to marketing concepts and strategies, the development and implementation of product and service objectives.)

Holbert, Neil. *Careers in Marketing.* Chicago American Marketing Association, 1976.

Kotler, Phillip. *Principles of Marketing.* Englewood Cliffs, N.J.: Prentice-Hall, Inc., 1980. (General marketing background, textbook including a discussion of the position of product manager.)

Kreif, Bernard. *Marketing Effectiveness Through Organization and Structure.* New York: John Wiley & Sons, Inc., 1975. (Includes job descriptions.)

Maresca, Carmela. *Careers in Marketing.* Englewood Cliffs, N.J.: Prentice-Hall, Inc., 1983.

The New Role of Marketing Professional. American Marketing Association, 1977. (Proceedings of 60th International Marketing Conference in Chicago.)

Payne, Richard A. *The Men Who Manage the Brands You Buy: A Candid Report on the Product Management System, Its Functions, Its Frustrations.* Chicago: Crain Communications, 1971. (Personal reflections on a career as a product manager; interesting and informative.)

Pessemier, Edgar A. *Product Management: Strategy and Organization.* New York: John Wiley & Sons, Inc., 1982. (Text divided into process, strategy formulation, analysis and management, and organization and control functions of managers.)

Smith, Gary R. *Exploring Marketing Occupations.* New York: Gregg Division, McGraw-Hill, Inc., 1976.

Solomon, Marc. *Marketing and Advertising Careers.* New York: Franklin Watts, Inc., 1977.

Wind, Yoram. *Product Policy: Concepts, Methods and Strategy.* Reading, Mass: Addison-Wesley Publishing Co., Inc., 1982. (Discusses the effects of tools, theories, strategies and the market environment on product decisions.)

PERIODICALS
Academy of Marketing Science Journal
Advertising Age
Industrial Marketing
Journal of Advertising
Journal of Marketing
Marketing News
Marketing Times
Product Marketing

PROFESSIONAL ASSOCIATIONS
American Marketing Association
250 S. Wacker Dr.
Chicago, IL 60606
(312) 648-0536
National Council on Physical Distribution
2803 Butterfield Road
Oak Brook, IL 60521
(312) 655-0985

CHAPTER 8
Advertising

BOOKS

Caples, John. *Tested Advertising Methods.* Englewood Cliffs, N.J.: Prentice-Hall, Inc., 1981. (A copy writer's compendium of tried-and-true techniques for creating advertisements with maximum sales effectiveness.)

Gardner, Herbert S., Jr. *The Advertising Agency Business.* Chicago: Crain Books, 1980. (Concentrates on the management of advertising agencies; emphasis on financial analysis, personnel management, agency organization, etc.)

Groome, Harry Connelly. *Opportunities in Advertising Careers.* Louisville, Ky.: Vocational Guidance Manuals, 1976.

Kirkpatrick, Frank. *How to Get the Right Job in Advertising.* Chicago: Contemporary Books, 1982. (Description of various positions and departments within advertising; discusses top agencies, training programs, and provides salary information.)

Ogilvy, David. *Confessions of an Advertising Man.* New York: Antheneum Publishers, 1981. (The opinions, prejudices, and theories of one of the most famous advertising executives; very readable with anecdotes about famous campaigns.)

O'Toole, John. *The Trouble with Advertising.* New York: Chelsea House Publishing, 1981. (A contemporary appraisal of the advertising business by the Chairman of the Board of Foote, Cone & Belding Communications.)

Paetro, Maxine. *How to Put Your Book Together and Get a Job in Advertising.* New York: Hawthorn Books, 1980. (An entertaining "how-to" book about putting a book together, plus some job-search strategies strictly for advertising.)

Reeves, Rosser. *Reality in Advertising.* New York: Alfred A. Knopf, 1981. (A classic work. Formulates certain theories about advertising based on twenty years of intensive research.)

Roman, Kenneth, and Maas, June. *How to Advertise.* New York: St. Martin's Press, 1976. (Written for the advertiser; explains how to use television, radio, print, outdoor and direct mail effectively.)

Seiden, Hank. *Advertising Pure and Simple.* New York: Amacom, 1978. (An opinionated, interesting book meant to help in the creative development of successful advertising.)

Valnoff, Stanley M. *Advertising in America: An Introduction to Persuasive Communication.* New York: Hastings House, Publishers, Inc., 1979. (A basic text in advertising; history, departmental functions, various media types, social commentary. Useful bibliography and index.)

Winters, Karen Cole. *Your Career in Advertising.* New York: Arco Publishing, Inc., 1980.

PERIODICALS
Advertising Age
Journal of Advertising
Journal of Advertising Research
Marketing Times

PROFESSIONAL ASSOCIATIONS
American Association of Advertising Agencies
666 Third Avenue
New York, NY
(212) 682-2500

(The 4 As publishes dozens of pamphlets relating to the industry and associated skills. They are not given to the general public, but are often available through member agencies. The pamphlets were written by advertising professionals and provide much useful information. As an introduction to the industry they publish "Advertising Agencies—What They Are, What They Do, and How They Do It" (1976). A particularly helpful series is entitled: "What Every Young Account Representative Should Know about . . ." with the following subjects: "Account Management" (1978); "Creative Research" (1978); "The Creative Function" (1979); "Print Production" (1978); "Writing Plans and Recommendations" (1977); "Cost Control and Profit Responsibility" (1979); "Direct Mail Advertising" (1978).)

Advertising Council

CHAPTER 9
Careers in Communications and Public Relations

BOOKS

Berneys, Edward L. *Your Future in a Public Relations Career.* New York: Richards Rosen Press, Inc., 1979.

Fins, Alice. *Women in Communications.* Skokie, Ill.: VGM Career Horizons, 1979.

Harrenstein, A. Dean. *Introduction to Communications Careers.* Bloomington, Ill.: McKnight Publishing Co., 1975.

Herman, Margaret (ed). *Careers for Writers: Working with Words.* New York: Barnes and Noble Books, 1977. (Includes discussions of writing careers in news media, magazines, advertising, technical writing, radio and television, and book publishing.)

Henkin, Shepard. *Opportunities in Public Relations.* Skokie, Ill.: VGM Career Horizon, 1977. (Geared more toward college students, the book includes discussions of, "What is public relations?" preparations for a career in P.R., and P.R. work in other fields.)

Mainstream Access. *The Public Relations Job Finder.* Englewood Cliffs, N.J.: Prentice-Hall, 1981. (Includes an overview of the field, interviews with P.R. specialists, and an extensive bibliography.)

Miller, Rex. *Communications—Industry and Careers.* Englewood Cliffs, N.J.: Prentice Hall, 1976.

Monaghan, Patrick C. *Public Relations Careers in Business and the Community.* New York: Fairchild Publications, 1972.

Polking, Kirk. *Jobs for Writers.* Cincinnati, Ohio: Writer's Digest Books, 1980. (A guide to freelance writing opportunities in forty-three different areas.)

Stein, Meyer L. *Your Career in Journalism.* New York: Julian Messner, 1978.

Wakin, Edward. *Jobs in Communications.* New York: Lothrop, Lee & Shepard Books, 1974.

Weinstein, Bob. *Your Career in Public Relations.* New York: Arco Publishing, Inc., 1983.

Williams, Gurney. *Writing Careers.* New York: Franklin Watts, Inc., 1976.

Zimmerman, Caroline A. *How to Break into the Media Professions.* Garden City, N.Y.: Doubleday & Co., Inc., 1981.

PERIODICALS
Billboard
Contacts
Public Relations Journal
The Publicist
Variety

PROFESSIONAL ASSOCIATIONS
Public Relations Society of America
845 Third Avenue
New York, NY 10022
International Association of Business Communicators
870 Market St. Suite 940
San Francisco, CA 94102
Society for Professional Journalists
S. Wacker Dr.
Chicago, IL 60606
Radio and Television News Directors Association
Radio and Television Correspondents Association
Society for Technical Communication
International Communications Association
Women in Communications

CHAPTER 10
Sales and Buying

BOOKS

Bodle, Yuanne Galugos. *Retail Selling.* New York: McGraw-Hill, Inc., 1977.

Buskirk, Richard Hobart. *Retail Selling.* San Francisco: Canfield Press, 1975. (Intended for people interested in careers in retailing. Gives "a real taste for what retailing is" and how to do it. Includes exercises.)

Coner, James M. (ed.) *Sales Management: Roles and Methods.* Santa Monica: Goodyear, 1977. Discusses strategic sales management and the major responsibilities of sales managers.

Haas, Kenneth Brooks. *Opportunities in Sales and Marketing.* Skokie, Ill.: VGM Career Horizons, 1980. (Geared toward college students and includes chapters on the selling industry, retail sales, and industrial sales.)

Haas, Kenneth B., and Earnest, John W. *Creative Salesmanship: Understanding Essentials,* 2nd ed. Riverside, N.J.: Glencoe Publishing Co., Inc., 1974. Includes chapters on, "Opportunities in Selling" and "Selling As a Career."

Harvey, Reed A. *Managerial Need Satisfaction in the Retailing Environment.* New York: National Retail Merchants Association, 1971. (Discusses the retail trade as a profession and includes an annotated bibliography.)

Mainstream Access, Inc. *The Insurance Job Finder.* Englewood Cliffs, N.J.: Prentice-Hall, Inc., 1982. (Includes an overview of the insurance industry, interviews, and an extensive bibliography.)

Mainstream Access, Inc. *The Real Estate Job Finder.* Englewood Cliffs, N.J.: Prentice-Hall, Inc., 1981. (Includes an overview of the field, interviews with real estate agents, and an extensive bibliography.)

Pederson, C.A., and Wright, M.D. *Selling: Principles and Methods.* Homewood, Ill.: RDI Irwin, 1976. (A basic text in sales. Includes a chapter on the duties and responsibilities plus what qualifications are needed for sales.)

Rachman, David J. *Retail Strategy and Structure: A Management Approach,* 2nd ed. Englewood Cliffs, N.J.: Prentice-Hall, Inc., 1975.

Segal, M.E. *From Rags to Riches: Success in Apparel Retailing.* New York: John Wiley & Sons, Inc., 1982. (Part of the Wiley small business series—contains everything the successful small retailer needs to know.)

PERIODICALS

The American Salesman
Appraisal Journal
The Insurance Salesman
Journal of Retailing
Marketing Times
Mass Retailing Merchandiser
Modern Retailer
Women's Wear Daily

PROFESSIONAL ASSOCIATIONS

National Retail Merchants Associations
100 West 31 Street
New York, NY 10001

Sales and Marketing Executives International
380 Lexington Avenue
New York, NY 10017

National Association of Retailers
430 N Michigan Avenue
Chicago, IL. 60611

American Association of Life Insurance
1850 K St., N.W.
Washington, D.C. 20006

Insurance Information Institute
110 William Street
New York, NY 10038

National Association of Insurance Agents
85 John Street
New York, NY 10038

Manufacturer's Agents National Association
P.O. Box 16878
Irvine, CA 92713

CHAPTER 11
Human-Resource Management

BOOKS

Armstrong, Michael. *A Handbook of Personnel Management Practice.* Englewood Cliffs, N.J.: Prentice-Halll, Inc., 1982.

Brandis, John. *Manpower Personnel Management.* Reading, Mass.: Educational Explorers, 1972.

Cayer, Joseph N. *Managing Human Resources: An Introduction to Public Personnel Administration.* New York: St. Martin's Press, Inc., 1980.

Mach, David. *Opportunities in Personnel Management Careers.* New York: Vocational Guidance Manuals, 1970.

Meltzer, H., and Nord, Walter R. (eds). *Making Organizations Humane and Productive: A Handbook for Practitioners.* New York: John Wiley & Sons, Inc., 1981.

Pond, John H. *Your Future in Personnel Work.* New York: Richards Rosen Press, Inc., 1978.

Stockard, James G. *Career Development and Job Training: A Manager's Handbook.* New York: Imacom, 1977.

Traynor, William J. *Opportunities in Personnel Management.* Skokie, Ill.: VGM Career Horizons, 1978.

PERIODICALS
Personnel Journal
Personnel Administrator
Human Resource Planning
Human Resource Management
Occupational Outlook Handbook (U.S. Dept. of Labor)
Conference Board Research Publications
Human Resource Planning Newsletter (Available from Advanced Personnel Systems, 756 Lois Avenue, Sunnyvale, CA 94087.)

PROFESSIONAL ASSOCIATIONS
American Society for Personnel Administrators (ASPA)
30 Park Drive
Berea, OH 44017

American Society for Training Development (ASTD)
PO Box 5307
Madison, WI 53705

International Association for Personnel Women (IAPW)
150 West 52nd Street
New York, NY 10019

International Personnel Management Association (IPMA)
1313 East 60th Street
Chicago, IL 60637

American Management Association (AMA)
135 West 50th Street
New York, NY 10020

Human Resources Association (HRA)
Dr. William Pyle, Director
Industrial Relations Center, 5th Fl.
Business Administration Building
University of Minnesota
Minneapolis, MN 55455

Organizational Development Network
1011 Park Avenue
Plainfield, NJ 07060

CHAPTER 12
Systems Analysis

BOOKS
French, Jack. *Up the EDP Pyramid.* New York: John Wiley & Sons, Inc., 1981.

Greene, Laura. *Careers in the Computer Industry.* New York: Franklin Watts, Inc., 1983.

Mainstream Access, Inc. *The Data Processing/Information Technology Job Finder.* Englewood

Cliffs, N.J.: Prentice-Hall, Inc., 1981. (Includes an overview of the field, profiles of professionals, and an extensive bibliography.)

McDaniel, Herman. *Careers in Computing and Data Processing*. New York: Petrocelli, 1978. (Includes a chapter on careers in systems analysis.)

Muller, Peter. *The Fast Track to the Top Jobs in Computer Careers*. New York: G. P. Putnam's Sons, 1983.

Weintraub, Joseph. *Exploring Careers in the Computer Industry*. New York: Richards Rosen Press, Inc., 1983.

PERIODICALS

Computer Decisions
Computer World
Data Processing Digest
Datamation
Journal of Systems Management

PROFESSIONAL ASSOCIATIONS

American Society for Information Science
Association for Systems Management
Society for Information Management

CHAPTER 13
Careers in Business Consulting

BOOKS

Altman, M.A. and Well, R. *Managing Your Accounting and Consulting Practice*. New York: Matthew Bender & Co., 1978.

Association of Consulting Management Engineers. *Selected References on Management Consulting*. New York: ACME, 1975. (A bibliography of more than 400 books, papers, articles, and speeches dealing with the profession of management consulting.)

Bermont, Hubert. *How to Become a Successful Consultant in Your Own Field*. Washington, D.C.: Burmont Books, 1978. (Written by a business consultant; an easy-to-read personal account of a career in consulting.)

De Com, A. *The Internal Consultant*. American Management Association, 1967.

Fuchs, J.H. *Management Consultants in Action*. New York: Hawthorn Books, 1975. (An anecdotal account of a career in independent consulting; amusing and easy to read.)

Gallessich, June. *The Profession and Practice of Consultation: A Handbook for Consultants, Trainers of Consultants and Consumers of Consultation Services*. San Francisco: Jossey-Bass, Inc., 1982. (Examines the roles and purposes of consultation, its "body of knowledge," and the development of consulting as a new profession.)

Hollander, Stanley C. *Management Consultants and Clients*. East Lansing, Mich.: MSU Business Studies, Michigan State University, 1972. (This volume provides an annotated guide to more than 1,200 selected books, monographs, articles, dissertations, and reports on various aspects of consulting.)

Holtz, Herman. *How to Succeed as an Independent Consultant*. New York: John Wiley & Sons, Inc., 1983. (A "how-to" book that ranges from founding an independent practice to fee collection. Includes a chapter on skills needed and how to develop them.)

Hurt, Alfred. *The Management Consultant*. New York: Ronald Press, 1977. (Includes discussion of consulting as a profession and the types of firms and clients.)

Hyman, Stanley. *Associations and Consultants: External Aid to Management*. London: George Allen Irwin, 1970. (The report of a three-year study of forty organizations investigating what they do to aid management, how many there should be, and how their performance can be assessed.)

Kelly, Robert E. *Consulting—The Complete Guide to a Profitable Career*. New York: Charles Scribner's Sons, 1981. (Provides a general outline of the consulting field, including the process

of consulting. Contains self-assessment exercises: "Is a consulting career right for me?" and a
number of chapters on starting an independent consulting practice.)

Kubr, M. *Management Consulting: A Guide to the Profession.* Geneva, Switzerland: International
Organization, 1976. (A comprehensive acccount of consulting as a business and as a career.
Includes chapters on consulting in seven specific areas as well as three chapters on career
issues.)

Lippitt, Gordon, and Lippitt, Ronald. *The Consulting Process in Action.* La Jolla, Calif.: University
Associates, 1978. (Discusses consultation, phases of consulting, and the multiple roles of
consultants. Written by two management consultants, it contains much personal experience.)

Wolf, William B. *Management and Consulting: An Introduction to James B. McKinsey.* Ithaca,
N.Y.: Cornell University, KR Publications, 1978. (Discusses the management consulting
philosophy of James McKinsey—founder of one of the largest and best-known consulting
firms.)

PERIODICALS
Harvard Business Review
Sloan Management Review
Organizational Dynamics
Strategic Management Journal
Journal of Business Strategy

PROFESSIONAL ASSOCIATIONS
Association for Internal Management Consultants
Association of Management Consultants
Association of Consulting Management Engineers
Institute of Management Consultants

Chapter 14
Getting the Job and Making It Work for You

BOOKS
Bolles, Richard, N. *What Color Is Your Parachute?* Berkeley, Calif.: Ten Speed Press, 1983.
Bronstein, Eugene, and Hisrich, Robert D. *The MBA Career: Moving on the Fast Track to Success.*
Woodbury, N.Y.: Barron's Educational Series, Inc., 1983.
Fox, Marcia, R. *Put Your Degree to Work.* New York: W.W. Norton & Co., Inc., 1979.
Irish, Richard, K. *Go Hire Yourself an Employer.* New York: Anchor Press, 1973.
Lathrop, Richard. *Who's Hiring Who?* Berkeley, Calif.: Ten Speed Press, 1977.
London, Manuel, and Stumpf, Stephen, A. *Managing Careers.* Reading, Mass.: Addison-Wesley
Publishing Co., Inc., 1982.
Wright, John W. *The American Almanac of Jobs and Salaries.* New York: Avon Books, 1982.

INDEX